THE GOSPEL OF ATHEISM AND FREETHOUGHT

ACCORDING TO SHERLOCK

THE GOSPEL OF ATHEISM AND FREETHOUGHT

ACCORDING TO SHERLOCK

MICHAEL
SHERLOCK

First Published in Great Britain 2014
by Dangerous Little Books

© Michael Sherlock

TABLE OF CONTENTS

PREFACE

The title of this book may upset both atheists and theists, to varying degrees, so I thought I would use this preface to briefly explain why I selected the title and at the same time, explain how this book is structured. The Gospel of Atheism and Freethought – According to Sherlock is a parody title, so before theists get too excited and accuse atheism of being a religion complete with its own Gospel, I must disabuse them of this fallacious notion. Atheism is not, and cannot be, a belief system, for two fundamental reasons. Firstly, atheism is not a system and secondly, it has no beliefs and is therefore not a belief system, but an unsystematic absence of god-belief. For this reason, I do not call myself an atheist, and as shocking as it may be to some, nor do I call myself a non-figure skater. In my humble opinion, the correct title for a person who does not believe in the supernatural should be 'sane.'

The word *gospel* stems from the Greek, *evangelion,* meaning *good news* and once again, in my opinion, given the tragic nature and history of god-belief, the growing number of non-believers and the proliferation of their godless literature is good news. Women are being afforded more rights, same-sex couples are suffering less persecution and science has been granted an increased freedom to express its more rational methodological naturalistic philosophy, to the benefit of our species as a whole.

This gospel is set out in three parts, which I call books and in the first two parts, the Book of Atheism and the Book of Freethought, the reader will find a diverse range of anti-theistic memes, quotes and musings, written in both personal and impersonal speech. I chose to write these sayings in both personal and impersonal speech to mimic and mock the Gnostic Gospel of Thomas, which is also a book of sayings. The final part of this book, the Book of Heresy, is a series of atheistic articles, essays and pieces, written in a more narrative style to parody, albeit abstractly, the four official gospels of the New Testament.

FOREWORD

Michael Sherlock is new on the scene but has a lot to say. But perhaps most importantly, his studies in social anthropology and comparative mythology make his an interesting and much-needed perspective to religious criticism.

Sherlock's *The Gospel of Atheism and Freethought* is a well-sourced work that accomplishes what many books in the marketplace of secular non-fiction have failed to do: it presents a coherent and thorough analysis of the major flaws, inaccuracies, and moral dilemmas present within the Abrahamic faiths, while putting forth a strong case for abstinence from faith all together.

The Gospel of Atheism is wide-ranging, tackling some of the biggest problems with the major world religions while at the same time analyzing their histories from an academic perspective. Sherlock even tackles common arguments put forth by Christian apologists like C.S. Lewis, who argued that at the heart of Christianity is a "myth which is also a fact." The book's extensive coverage of seemingly semi-related topics is a breath of fresh air in what is often a monotonous genre.

Sherlock also goes out of his way to educate and inform readers, while keeping it interesting as a means to drive home his arguments. Sherlock's *7 Parenting Tips for God*, for instance, include such seemingly obvious gems as, "Don't kill your children," and, "Don't allow your children to suffer for your shortcomings." Keeping the reader's interest and hammering home point after point, *The Gospel of Atheism* puts the final nails in the coffin of a wide variety of widely held, but false, religious beliefs.

Sherlock pulls no punches in extolling the virtues of skepticism and critical thinking, refusing to treat any religion or denomination as a sacred cow beyond reproach. His approach is to bombard the reader with facts and reasonable conclusions, and I think he's accomplished that. Filled with questions and sourced facts that would make any believer think twice, his newest book presents some of the most comprehensive arguments against the great faiths and in favor of non-belief.

DAVID G. MCAFEE

David G. McAfee is a journalist and author of *Mom, Dad, I'm an Atheist: The Guide to Coming Out as a Non-believer* and *Disproving Christianity and other Secular Writings*. He is also a frequent contributor to American Atheist Magazine. McAfee attended University of California, Santa Barbara, and graduated with dual-degrees in English and Religious Studies, with an emphasis on Christianity and Mediterranean religions. www.DavidGMcAfee.com | www.facebook.com/AuthorDavidGMcAfee

THE BOOK OF ATHEISM

SEVEN PARENTING TIPS FOR GOD

TIP 1

Don't Kill Your Children – This may seem obvious, but having thoroughly read the *Bible*, it is something I think God could work on. The idea is to raise your children, so killing them for disobeying or irritating you, is not advisable.

TIP 2

Consistency – Rules must be consistent. If you make rules, like don't eat pork, relax on Saturday, whatever, and then you turn around and say, "well, don't worry about all that," it is going to undermine your child's perception of you as an authority figure and leave them confused, particularly if you have gone against the first tip and killed some of them for breaking these flimsy rules.

TIP 3

Punishment – Related to tip 1. If you are going to use timeout as a means of disciplining your children, it should be for a specified period of time, not an eternity. Timeout is useful for allowing the child to think about what they have done wrong and how they can improve in the future, so setting them on fire for an eternity, contravenes this, and the first tip and is counterproductive to the development of the child.

TIP 4

Be fair – Don't bestow rewards on some of your children and punishments on others, for no apparent reason. For example, if you have a girl and a boy and you don't allow the girl to share the same rights and privileges as the boy, she may eventually suffer from low self-esteem and this is only going to undermine your desired outcome. Needless to

1

say, it is also going to create unwarranted tension between the two. Further, try not to favour one child over another, for example, don't constantly say to one, "You are my favourite," as it is not only going to lead them into decadence, but it will cause the others to resent both you and your favourites.

TIP5

Respect – Respect is a two way street, so if you want your child to respect you, you must be deserving of that respect and also return it. Demanding respect simply because you created them, is not fair, as they had no choice in their manifestation and also, it is going to make you appear tyrannical, which will eventually cause your children to lose faith in you.

TIP 6

Don't allow your children to suffer for your shortcomings – An example might be; you have made a mess at work and everything appears to be going wrong, so you hatch an idea to kill your child to fix it all. This is a definite no no.

TIP 7

Supervision – Children require constant supervision, particularly younger ones. Leaving them unsupervised in a snake infested garden is just bad parenting, so take care to always look after them. After all, as a parent your responsibilities should always outweigh your rights.

As a father myself, I know it can get tough sometimes, but keep these tips in mind and remember, when scolding your children, don't use fire.

♦

Christianity is a very pretentious religion. It is built on pretend biographies, written by pretended authors, who describe a pretend son of a pretended god, who they pretend could perform miracles. But the pretentiousness doesn't stop there, for they also pretend to describe a pretended resurrection in a bid to sell to pretentious fools, a pretend salvation that will take the saved to a pretend heaven, whilst avoiding a pretend hell and all of this pretence, they pretend, is historical, logical and scientific.

◆

What fascinates me about many religious people is that these same believers will scrupulously investigate a financial investment before making a commitment, but when it comes to their mind, their very essence, they give not a single glance; they spend not one moment in investigating the source of their lifelong beliefs. Subsequently, these poor duped individuals become victims of one of the most crooked scams known to man and woman alike, a scam that has been designed to rape not only your mind but your money too. What's worse is that in many, if not most cases, these duped individuals, if we may use the term "individual," pass this scam onto their loved ones.

◆

A small and reasonable dose of faith is a necessary element of life, without which, it would be nearly impossible to live a happy and healthy life. Religion, however, takes this necessary element, increases the dosage ten fold and turns faith into a harmful addiction.

◆

Gone are the days when the chronically religious burnt us in their fires; long past is an age when the Catholic and Protestant Churches sent bloodthirsty warriors to snuff out the lives of infidels, non-believers and heretics. Today, there is no excuse not to speak up, no reason why we should not study, embrace and voice our heresies, for this is the age of the freethinker, the age of the infidel and the true lover of liberty. These are our days now and it is up to us to use every intellectual resource at our disposal to once and for all dispose of this plague we have called, "religion".

◆

God is not a tyrant. He is not oppressive, unjust, unforgiving and cruel. Nor is he unkind, hostile, vicious and misogynistic. I would also say that he is not a psychopath, a rapist, a murderer, a narcissist nor even an ignorant xenophobe. No, God is merely the collective projection of the fallacious fantasies of his deranged male authors.

◆

Santa doesn't like poor kids. How else would you explain the disparity between his generosity to the rich and his stinginess toward the poor? I think the same can also be said of God and Jesus, and for the same reason. None of the above characters actually exist.

♦

The *Bible* tells us that "man" is charged with ruling over the beasts of the earth and the birds of the sky. What a silly decision that was! We are led to believe that this "perfect creator" has created a species, which is the only one on earth that kills for an idea, murders out of jealousy and destroys its own environment. Nature is not dependant on this so-called ruler, "man," we are dependent upon it. Looking at our species from a distance, we would be forgiven, I think, for seeing ourselves as being little more than self-destructive narcissists. Where is the intelligence in this design?

♦

When you think about it, the central symbols of the Christian religion are really quite horrific. Christians worship an executed man, tortured and nailed to a piece of wood, and on top of this arcane insanity, they practice eating his flesh and drinking his blood. They pray, so that they may one day be raised from their graves like zombies and look down on a pit full of tortured and burning humans. What's most disturbing is that somehow this behaviour is still, to this day, deemed virtuous and acceptable for both adults and children to enjoy.

♦

So, of all of the thousands of gods that exist and have existed in the minds of human beings, your god is the one true God? What are the odds?

I do have one question.

If you wouldn't bet your life savings on a horse with the same odds, then why bet your entire earthly existence, your mind, your psychological sovereignty, on a fictitious concept that, unlike the lame horse, probably doesn't exist? For this reason I say, God is worse than a lame horse.

♦

Notwithstanding the fact that the tradition of Mosaic authorship has been completely debunked, many Christians and Jews not only believe that Moses wrote the first five books of the *Bible* and in so doing, wrote about events that occurred after his own death, but that he also referred to himself in the third person as the "humblest man on earth" (Numbers 12:3), which, if you think about it, is a rather ironic statement for a humble man to make.

◆

Here is a question I love to ask Christians:

How much of your religion can you actually locate in your *Bible*?

I know for a fact you can't find:

Sunday Mass, Sunday as holy day, The modern church Service, the sermon, rosary beads, nuns, praying before statues & other graven images of Christ, Christmas, the Easter celebration, the Eucharist, as it is practiced today, priests, calling priests, "father," etc…

The funny thing is; the religion you practice today is an offence not only to reason and common sense, but to the *Bible* as well.

◆

If Jesus was an historical person and his words are accurately relayed in the Gospels, we must admit that he was a very poor judge of character, for in one instance he pledges his entire earthly kingdom to Peter and then moments later calls him a Satan.

And I say also unto thee, That thou art Peter, and upon this rock I will build my church…

~Matthew 16:18

But he turned, and said unto Peter, Get thee behind me, Satan: thou art an offence unto me.

~Matthew 16:23

I guess, if the story were true, it would go a long way to explaining the vile nature of the Church's history.

◆

There is only one place in the entire *New Testament* which expressly justifies the Christian Trinity (1 John 5:7–8). Here is the thing. It wasn't a part of the original Greek manuscripts of the *New Testament*, but became part of the later spurious textual tradition incorporated into the "Textus Receptus," and entered into the error ridden King James Version of the *Bible*.

◆

There is an immeasurable group of hidden atheists out there, atheists who cannot be seen or heard. These are the undercover atheists, those who wear a religious label for the sake of family, tradition and even peer pressure, but who do not truly believe. I suspect that this group is as old as god-belief itself and we even witness their presence in the book of Revelation (3: 15–16), in which, the author rails against them. I predict that with the current and steady increase in non-belief, more and more of these undercover atheists will come out of the gloomy halls of theism and into the light of reason.

♦

Duplicity is, in my opinion, the central nervous system of all religion. Religion is idiocy in the guise of intelligence, hubris masquerading as humility; it is belief dressed as knowledge, hate disguised as love and fiction parading as fact. Had it not been for its ability to shield its true nature from an otherwise intelligent species, I dare say its flames would have been extinguished by now.

♦

You are God, the creator of the entire universe and you have one chance to communicate with your creation. You ponder over whether to include in this divine manifesto, details of quantum physics, cures for diseases that will rear their ugly heads in the future, or even write extended disclaimers that prevent your words being used for violence and oppression…Then it hits you! Don't waste time on all that nonsense; tell them about that guy who had drunken sex with his daughters, that's far more entertaining!

♦

In my opinion, the success of atheism doesn't rest solely on the advancement of science or on refutations of the *Bible* and the *Qur'an*, but in demonstrating the psychological and neurological processes by which a believer defends their irrational beliefs.

♦

If you want me to take Intelligent Design "Theory" seriously, show me something peer reviewed by an actual scientific organization/institution. Now, I'm not talking about some ad hoc, quasi, pseudo-scientific institution, established for the exclusive purpose of propagating the now debunked ancient science of a theological worldview, but an actual scientific organization. Go ahead, I'm waiting...

◆

You don't have to study religion to know that it is nonsense; you just need a brain that is not overwhelmed by dopamine.

◆

As time and science advance, the majority of intelligent Christians are being forced to acknowledge that many of the stories in the *Bible* are metaphor. When the science of geology first hit, Christians were forced to abandon a literal interpretation of Genesis. When science demonstrated that the global flood couldn't have taken place, once again, Christians were forced to adopt a poetic interpretation of that narrative and so on. As time moves forward and we acquire more knowledge, I imagine that the central character of the entire *Bible* will eventually be relegated to the more rational realm of metaphor.

◆

Why did an all-powerful god need to rest on the seventh day?

Did he create the universe with one long six day word or a bunch of words that took six days to say?

What language was that word? It wasn't Hebrew, because that language wasn't invented until at least the tenth century BCE.

Why did he create light before he created the source of light, the sun?

Why wasn't he able to document his own creation without contradicting himself?

Why did he have his chosen people steal the creation myths of their captors, the Babylonians?

Why did he build a garden for his first two ignorant humans and leave them alone with a walking, talking and cunning snake?

How did Noah circumnavigate the entire earth in a week?

Why did God ask Noah to take two of every animal and then change his request in the next chapter?

Why did he bear a child to slaughter him in order to eradicate sin, when he could have clicked his fingers and achieved the same result?

Why did he like virgins?

Why did he allow his son to reverse laws, for the breaking of which he had previously killed people?

I have so many questions, for which there seem to be so few rational and reasonable answers.

If you read the verses in the *Qur'an* which form the foundation of the tradition that prescribes the *burqa* and the *hijab* for women (Surah 24:31), it becomes clear that both the compilers of the *Qur'an* and the founders of the tradition, didn't trust the male proponents of their religion to exercise restraint in the face of feminine beauty. What does this say about their confidence in the teachings of the "divine" *Qur'an*? It says that they believed it to be impotent in the face of natural forces.

There is not a being more frightening and dissonance producing to a theist, than a happy, moral and intelligent atheist, for such a person completely undermines the propaganda upon which the theist has built their entire worldview.

The Pope: Atheists can now go to heaven.

Atheist: Thanks, but I wouldn't want to intrude upon your fantasy.

The Pope saying that atheists can now go to heaven is like a crazy person saying; people who don't believe in magic are now allowed to wear my magic invisible hat.

There are four primary ingredients of god-belief:

Uncertainty

Fear

Credulity

Imagination

Combine these four ingredients and you will be ready to see black as white, white as black and the Church as wise.

When a religious person tells you that the reason you don't understand their faith or believe the fictitious stories in their scriptures, is because you are not looking at the issues with your "heart;" what they are really asking of you is to suspend your reason and use your imagination. Now, I would suggest that if you have to use your imagination to see their god, then their god is probably imaginary.

◆

God is no academic/A Book Review of the *Bible*

If, by some freakishly remote chance, the god of the Christians is real, we can safely conclude that he is no academic. His "Word" is largely unhistorical, profoundly unscientific and riddled with illogicality. It contains errors with regards to geography, astronomy, ancient demography, anthropology and, worse than all of that, much of its contents are plagiarized from earlier authors. In short, God's Word is sloppily researched, unethical and ill-contrived. Its poetry is about the only thing which drags it from the gutters of banality and even then, I must say, I have read better.

◆

A poor creator blames his tools and an even poorer one blames his creation.

◆

Dear Oprah,

You say that atheists cannot experience the awe and wonder of the natural world, but I say; if you need to supersize reality, load it with artificial additives and superimpose superstition onto nature, then it is you and those like you, my dear Oprah, who are incapable of experiencing the awe and wonder of the natural world.

◆

Do you imagine that your god created this entire universe, the earth and our species, so that he could satisfy some base need to be worshipped like some egomaniac? Such thinking is surely rooted in both geocentrism and egocentrism and demonstrates with near certainty, that God is a construct of your mind, or more accurately, of some other person's fertile imagination, which has been implanted via sociological causes, into your less than fertile one. Don't you think, if your fantasy were true, it would have been better for God to construct a mosaic of himself in the stars and gaze upon it eternally to fill that desire to love himself through his own creation?

◆

9

If the doctrines and proponents of the Abrahamic religions admitted that they were just beliefs and that they could be wrong, I would have no problem with that, but they don't. They threaten, attack, persecute and otherwise molest people who don't share their egocentric and narcissistic delusions. Of all the ridiculous religions existing on the earth today, I find this venomous collection of superstitions the most offensive. How dare you cast both stones and aspersions at all those who don't share your ludicrous beliefs! Get over yourselves, you selfish little children.

◆

There is nothing new about the New Age Movement. It is simply old and static superstition, repackaged for modern consumption.

◆

Once we, as a species, conquer our fear of death, religion will become obsolete and the mind of humanity will spring forth new buds of wisdom, love and pure altruism.

◆

What would an all-powerful, wise and all-knowing god, who is complete in and of himself, want, or even need with our worship? What does he really have to gain from our complete obedience and worship? Is he a former public servant disgruntled with his lot in life, wielding power over those subject to him to alleviate his deep-seated feelings of inadequacy? Is he so insecure that he needs his own creation to grovel at his feet daily or weekly as the case may be? Is that why he created us? If you are a parent, do you expect and need your children to grovel at your feet and give constant thanks, praise and money to you, for creating them, even though they had no choice in their manifestation? Or, are you satisfied with their wellbeing and happiness? If all you require from your children is their wellbeing and happiness, then you are nobler, wiser and more philosophically enlightened than the god of the Judeo-Christian Scriptures.

◆

What if I were to tell you that I am reading my five year old son a book, in which rape, murder, human sacrifice, war, genocide, misogyny and all manner of fiendish behaviour is central to many of the narratives in that book? Perhaps, being the good Christian that you are, you would advise me not to be such an irresponsible parent. That is of course, until you learn that the book I am reading him is the *Bible*.

◆

The more we begin to understand what belief is and how it works, the more we begin to understand religion and subsequently, the less we need to believe in it, and the more intelligent we become.

◆

Am I the only one who is unimpressed by the fact that it is alleged to have taken close to a full week for an omnipotent and omniscient deity to create the universe, considering that science has established that natural forces were able to complete this task within a split second?

◆

If you could be trusted to keep your delusions of both grandure and god to yourself, then I dare say, not too many atheists would waste a single minute debunking them.

◆

Don't you find it to be a rather odd coincidence that your god shares all of your own values, beliefs, opinions and in fact, your entire world-view? Doesn't this fact help you to draw back the curtain covering his tabernacle, to reveal nothing more than a reflection of your own ego-centric image?

◆

We first arrived in the country you now call Australia, roughly 36,000 years before the authors of your dreamtime allege that Adam was created by your father spirit. Try seeing your myths through our eyes.

◆

Islam did not become a major religion by the quality of its truth, but by the quantity of its violence and the same can also be said of Christianity.

◆

When judging the word of a person who is mentally impaired, we should make allowance for the appropriate amount of error. When judging the word of a fully functioning individual, we may also make allowance for a certain amount of error, for the individual is only human and humans make mistakes. But in judging the word of an all-knowing and all-powerful god, we would surely be guilty of blasphemy if we were to contend that such a being could be responsible for, or even associated with, error. For error is committed not by the omnipotent, but by the impotent and in contrast, perfection, is not begotten of impotence, but of omnipotence. In other words, perfection can only produce itself and nothing less, for if it does, no matter how slight, it is imperfect. Upon this logic, if we are to examine the wide range of errors and contradictions found within the *Bible* and at the same time assume that God inspired or directed these works, then we must also consider the possibility that he is mentally impaired.

◆

Religions are a lot like cheat sheets. The only problem with these cheat sheets to life is that people become so hopelessly dependent upon their particular cheat sheet, that when the answers on it are shown to be incorrect, they still use it anyway. Furthermore, there are literally thousands of these cheat sheets out there, all with different answers to the same questions; they cannot all be correct. The one thing they all have in common, though, is that they encourage laziness and foster chronic dependency in those unwilling to study for life. Who needs to read, learn and grow, when you can just close your eyes and pray for answers?

◆

I honestly don't know whether it is money or myth that has provided our species with the strongest motivation for murder.

◆

I have been toying with a business idea for some time now that I think would be quite lucrative. I want to open an anti-venom store across from the Appalachian snake handling church and charge exorbitant rates for each treatment. As part of the treatment, the patient would be told that for the medicine to work, they will have to renounce their faith, click their heels together three times and chant; "I have faith in science," for theists constantly tell us, science requires just as much faith as religion.

◆

Why do I ridicule your beliefs? Firstly, because they are only beliefs and secondly, well, they are ridiculous. I thought that would have been obvious.

◆

You claim to have reason for your faith, but I think you are confusing reason with rationalization.

♦

It is so convenient to imagine that the devil is responsible for your short-comings and even more terrifying to realize that he does not exist.

♦

Most religions contain within their whole, portions of valuable philosophy. The trouble as I see it is that this portion is mixed with the artificial preservatives of rampant emotion, chronic dependency, rigid dogma and superstitious ignorance. Moreover, these valuable portions, as minimal and meagre as they often happen to be, form the sales pitch by which the toxic theology as a whole is spread to well-meaning and benevolent human beings, who become poisoned and embittered by the entire package.

♦

The universal criteria common to all apocalyptic religions is the submission to those who herald its coming.

♦

That is not the devil corrupting your mind, it is religious paranoia.

♦

Religion has an amazing ability to transform our natural love for life into a zeal for death.

♦

Religious conspiracy theorists who seek to expose:

Powerful cults that attempt to practice "magic" to control the masses

Unelected bodies that unduly influence our political systems

Organizations that practice psychological manipulation/mind control

Lies

Disinformation scams

The ritual abuse of children

Are like sheep in search of wool.

♦

Christian: Newton believed in the *Bible*, so it must be true and scientific.

Atheist: Newton also believed that the earth was 6,000 years old and that he could use magic to turn lead into gold…Nobody's perfect. Even great minds can be held to ransom by stupid beliefs.

♦

In the Gospel of Matthew the fake author alleges that Jesus advised:

Neither do people pour new wine into old wineskins. If they do, the skins will burst; the wine will run out and the wineskins will be ruined. No, they pour new wine into new wineskins, and both are preserved.

~Matthew 9:17

What a fabulous irony we have here, for the entire religion of Christianity is made from the old wine of paganism and Judaism, which has been merely poured into the new wineskin of the Christian religion.

♦

If your beliefs were true and justified, you wouldn't need to knock on people's doors, they would be knocking on yours.

♦

It saves so much wear and tear on the mind to just say "God," every time we cannot answer a problem easily.

♦

Living your life according to the dictates set out in the *Bible*, is like employing a Bronze-Age life coach to help you make decisions.

♦

The most effective way to veil and protect an absurdity is to turn it into a religion.

♦

A wise person doesn't pretend to know that, which they do not, and for this reason it is only possible to be wise if you are an intelligent atheist.

♦

"Just because you can't see God, doesn't mean he doesn't exist!"

Whenever I am faced with the theist argument that I cannot see oxygen either, so how do I know that it exists, I become besieged with an overwhelming urge to administer the sleeper hold for a little while.

♦

1. The *Bible* is the Word of God
2. God is all-knowing, all-powerful and perfect
3. Therefore the *Bible* cannot contain mistakes

4. But we observe that the *Bible* does contain mistakes
5. Therefore the *Bible* is not the Word of God

♦

If we are to lay the blame on Judaism for crucifying Christ, a charge for which the evidence is in serious want, then we must not neglect, as the overwhelming amount of historical evidence illustrates for us, to lay the blame on Christ for crucifying the innocent.

♦

Generally speaking, where the *Bible* speaks, history is silent and where history speaks, the *Bible* is silent. This coupled with the incredible and impossible tales contained within this library of religious literature, leads to only one logical and rational conclusion. The *Bible* is a collection of myths cloaked in the garb of history.

♦

Logic dictates that in order to establish that your religion's god is the one true God, you must first establish the existence of a god and then you must prove that the aforementioned god is in fact, the one described by your religion. As no religion to date has even established the first proposition i.e., that a god exists, no one has the right to claim exclusive possession of the one true God. This seems to me to be one of the most overlooked flaws of exclusivist religions and religion in general.

♦

Nothing has revolted me as much as the contents of both the *Qur'an* and the *Bible*. Had these books been kept as mere records of our superstitious and brutal past, I would have been left with simple disgust, but because they are still held in high regard by a large portion of our species, my disgust has been compounded by pessimism.

♦

If you were an omniscient and omnipotent creator who despised evil, in what ways, other than bearing a son for the purposes of brutally sacrificing him to remedy that evil, would you go about fixing your mistakes? If you can come up with even a single more humane method than that, which the God of the Jews and Christians employed, then you are both wiser and more compassionate than their god.

♦

Logically speaking, if Jesus couldn't foresee the extreme suffering that would ensue as a result of his word then he wasn't an aspect of an all-knowing triune god, nor even a competent prophet.

♦

What people may not know is that many religious rites and ceremonies release a powerful neurotransmitter in the brain, known as dopamine. This neurotransmitter is also released when people take drugs or have sex. It is responsible for creating intoxicating feelings of excitement and arousal. Even more illuminating is the fact that when dopamine levels rise and serotonin levels drop, the result is what people call, the "religious experience." I guess Karl Marx was closer to the truth than he realized when he said; "religion is the opiate of the masses."

♦

If you met a man who had the same criminal record as both the religions of Christianity and Islam, I am almost certain you would not entrust your children's education to him.

♦

This may come as a shock to many religious people, but you do not need to believe in ghosts, goblins or gods to be a moral human being.

♦

To keep religious beliefs intact, people will commonly renounce the use of both logic and reason and forgo truth, only to replace it with its inferior cousin, belief.

♦

Christian apologetics is founded upon little more than creative mental gymnastics, desperate rationalizations and superstitious supposition.

♦

The most humane Christians and Muslims I have met have been the worst Christians and Muslims. This seems to indicate that their scriptures, if adhered to correctly, are contrary to humanity.

♦

If, as Christians assert, God is unfathomable, that is to say, if we can never truly know what God is, I see little to no value in asking whether or not such a creature exists and subsequently, I see no rational need to believe in God.

♦

Before Jesus' alleged advent there was rape, murder, war, corruption and all of the other insidious deforms of human behaviour and some two thousand years later, nothing has changed. The only logical conclusion to draw from this fact is that he has neither saved nor redeemed anything.

♦

Forgive them father, for they know not that we are myth.

♦

Despite strong prostrations to the contrary, open almost any religious book and you will find the root of unhealthy egocentrism. This is one of the major hypocrisies of religion.

♦

I do apologize for causing you distress, it's just that I am not in the habit of worshipping possibly imaginary beings who discriminate, perjure, injure, imprison, slaughter and otherwise unjustly punish the innocent. Further, if your god behaves in this manner and then has the gall to send to the eternal flames of hell, all those who despise such villainous qualities, then my dear believer, you may keep your god.

♦

Calling all those who do not believe as you do, sinners, is in my opinion, one very small step on the evolutionary ladder above jumping up and down and throwing your excrement at anyone who makes you feel threatened.

♦

The mythical Christ was not constructed from a single ancient source, but many. He was the healing god Aesclepius; the solar hero Hercules, who ascended to heaven amidst a number of witnesses. He was the man transformed by an apotheosis death, like Romulus of ancient Rome, the dying and rising Osiris, king of kings, whose treacherous brother betrayed him at his last supper. He was the dangerous child who posed a threat to the local tyrant and was hastened to safety, as was also the case with the more ancient Krishna of India, Moses of Israel and Sargon of Babylonia. He was the twice-born giver of wine and life, Dionysus. He was the child whose imminent birth was announced by divine dreams, oracles and angels, as was the case with Pythagoras, Buddha and Alexander the Great, to name just a few more ancient examples. He was a composite of all the literature available to the first century ex-pagan Christian mythographers. Yet and still, beyond these shallow and super-ficial edifices, he was the sun personified in myth. One thing we can say with near certainty is that he was not an historical son of a god.

◆

What you call a crisis of faith, I call an epiphany.

◆

Certainty erases the need for faith and faith implies a lack of certainty. Therefore, you cannot be both certain of something and have faith in that thing, at the same time. So, either you know your religion is right, in which case you have no faith, or you have faith and are uncertain of its truth.

◆

Your religious beliefs are wants, not necessities.

◆

You can project your anger onto me as much as you like, however, the fact is that your religion has infringed, and continues to do so, upon the rights of a large portion of our species, and I am not in the habit of putting the fantasies of fools before the rights of real human beings.

◆

If we were to compare the gods to any natural and observable phe-nomenon, it would have to be the apparent motion of the sun. For the gods rise, shine brightly in the minds of the gullible and then recede into the horizon of history, to be reflected upon as mere credulities of a more ignorant past.

◆

Women are to be seen and not heard. They are not as important as men. Women are an inferior gender, made for the sole purpose of serving their superior male captors. This is the message underscoring not only the *Old Testament* and the New, but the *Qur'an* too. I think it is well time we put these misogynistic religions to bed.

◆

According to Dr. Jerome Engel and a number of other neuroscientists, Joan of Arc, Saint Paul and the Prophet Muhammad, may have suf-fered from Temporal Lobe Epilepsy; a neurological disorder that causes auditory and visual hallucinations, as well as seizures and an increased sex drive; all symptoms which these three characters were alleged to have suffered. If such is the case, then over half of the earth's population is spending their entire existence chasing the hallucinations of epileptics.

◆

Prayer, in my opinion, is an act of doubt, not an act of faith, for if you truly trusted your god's plan, you wouldn't pray for anything.

◆

I have found that the most effective…no, let's be honest, enjoyable way to demonstrate the Illusion of Design to a Christian apologist, is not by explaining Emergent Systems or anything too complex, but to simply highlight how they themselves are using the illusion of logic to argue for the existence of fairy tales.

◆

Religions are not truth systems, they are belief systems. You would do well to keep that in mind before you go and vomit your religious madness all over the place.

◆

For obvious reasons, I do not fear a divinely incited Armageddon, but a human inspired one, an Armageddon which might be instigated by religious zealots and brought about by what psychologists refer to as a self-fulfilling prophecy.

◆

The story of Jesus walking on water is not proof of a miracle, but evidence of a lie.

◆

In my opinion, "we don't know, therefore God," is one of the severest thought hinderers existing amongst theists and goes a long way to explaining why scientific progress has dramatically increased since the separation of Church and State. We gain nothing as a species by throwing our hands up and saying; "well, we don't know, we give up, God must have done it and it is not my place to resolve the matter;" a theme (intellectual complacency) all too prevalent within the *Bible*.

◆

Pareidolia: A psychological phenomenon in which a vague and random stimulus is perceived as significant, like seeing the Virgin Mary in a piece of toast. This happens because the brain has been hardwired to fill in blanks based on both beliefs and experience, which alters and ultimately distorts one's perception. This also impacts upon the way in which believers distort the physical world around them to accommodate their superstitions.

◆

Using guilt to control people is emotional manipulation and anyone who needs to emotionally manipulate another human being, is unlikely to be in possession of any grand truth.

◆

Throughout much of the twentieth century, most of the churches in Australia were stealing Aboriginal infants and young children from their parents, to place them with white Christian families and various Christian institutions. Many of these young children were sexually, physically and mentally abused. This practice continued till the 1970's. What most people may not know is that this practice was common throughout the history of the Church. In the seventh century in Spain, for example, at the Church Council of Toledo, a law was enacted to take Jewish children away from their parents.

The law read:

"We decree, that the sons and daughters of Jews are to be separated from their parents, lest they be involved in their errors. They are to be placed in monasteries or with Christian men and women who fear God, that by their society they may learn the worship of the true faith, that, being thus better instructed, they may improve in morals and belief."

This situation appears to support the notion that strong and irrational beliefs often beget injustice.

◆

There is one thing that I love more than peanut butter and that's when Christian apologists attempt to use logic to defend their superstitions.

◆

If your courts are inscribed with the motto, *In God We Trust* and not, *In Evidence We Trust*, and if they make witnesses swear oaths on a *Bible* when a) The truth has nothing to do with the *Bible* and b) The *Bible* expressly forbids the act of swearing oaths, then your legal system has earnt my complete and utter contempt.

♦

Atheists think more about God than believers, for the same reason that doctors think more about cancer than cancer cells do.

♦

So none of your holiest books were written by whom they claim to have been written and were composed an entire generation after the events they allegedly descibe; they contain forgeries, contradictions, errors and assert revelation with regards to philosophies and teachings that were already in existence for centuries, along with the myths that impart those so-called revelations. Oh yes, and they are full of magic and supernatural nonsense. And you wonder why I think your religion is ludicrous.

♦

An effective lie is like a magical spell; it has the power to entrance and transform the mind of the listener, and the most effective lies contain a portion of the truth. I think this is why the authors of the myths which form the foundation of the Abrahamic religions, sought to weave their supernatural fictions into the very fabric of real human history.

♦

I agree with Christopher Hitchens; religion does poison everything. To prove this we need only glance upon the beautiful philosophies of Plato, Aristotle, Zeno and other pre-Christian philosophers, which were stolen by the Christian mythographers, blended with bollocks, set into rigid doctrines and violently cast at all those who begged to differ with credulity. We may see how Muhammad, an armed robber from the Quraysh Tribe, took equally beautiful teachings and blended them with pernicious paedophilia, malignant misogyny and silly, superstitious dogma. Further, we see that religion poisons everything by examining the way in which the Jews of the exilic period, stole the Babylonian *"Eye for an Eye"* or *"Lex talionis"*, originally designed to place a cap on restitution claims, and turned it into a vicious and destructive doctrine for revenge. Finally, if we are to read about all the religious wars and crimes since the birth of this psychological virus, we discover that "religion poisons everything" is not a statement of opinion, but a matter of fact.

♦

I have finally solved one of the greatest mysteries of human society. I now know why religions collect money from gullible believers. It is a redundancy package for God. As science advances, God is being pushed further and further into redundancy. I can only imagine that in the future, once he has burnt through all of the alms collected on his behalf, we will see him on the street begging for change.

♦

How much blood does your religion have on its hands? If it is beyond easy measure, then your religion is not only mindless, but dangerous and malignant.

♦

When Muslim apologists attempt to convince us that the *Qur'an* is supported by modern science, despite the great lengths, to which they have to go, to twist, re-interpret and misinterpret their own Scripture, they tend to leave out the part with the talking ants, because we might think that they are spouting nonsense…I stand corrected; they are now trying to convince us that ants speak using audible words.

♦

The cross and the crown, figuratively speaking, have always been partners in crime. Since the earliest times in ancient Sumer, the priest has been charged with keeping the masses in a state of docile and religious servitude to political tyrants.

♦

Creationism, or Intelligent Design, as it has been shrewdly rebranded, is not an alternative to evolution, it is a sideshow.

♦

God is a word you use when you cannot find the word you are looking for.

♦

Arguing with a theist is like playing tennis with someone who refuses to believe that the ball has dropped on their side of the net. If you want to keep playing, you have to walk over to their side, pick the ball up, show it to them, even though they are now gazing up at passing birds, take it back to your side and serve again. In most cases, this is how the entire game will play out.

◆

Can you truly love humanity if your religion teaches you that we are all inherently evil and that the evilest of all, are those who do not share your beliefs? I don't think so.

◆

Four Historical Problems in the Gospel of Luke

He has Jesus born at the end of King Herod's reign (4 bce) and at the time Quirinius was governor of Syria (7 ce), simultaneously. These two events were over a decade apart. He has two high priests serving together, which was not only contrary to Jewish law and custom, but historical records show that the High Priest Annas, served from 6-15 ce, whilst the other, Ciaphas, began his duties in 18 ce.

He alleged an empire wide census, undertaken by Caesar Augustus, which purportedly required people to travel back to the towns of their ancestors of 1000 years into the past, which, given the size and population of the empire, would have been an impossible census to undertake and administer, not to mention that it is nowhere recorded in history. In short, it never took place.

Luke was not an eyewitness; instead he relied on second-hand manuscripts to write his Gospel, (see Luke 1:1-4) well after the alleged events his Gospel described.

◆

I have dear friends who ask me; "what would your religious friends think about your work," to which I respond; if I lived my life confined and strangled by the dictates of the opinions of others, I would hardly be an honest individual now, would I?

◆

Instead of praying for someone because they do not believe as you do, just grab yourself and make passionate love to yourself, for that is all your prayer truly represents.

◆

If you are a Christian and you have not:
    Read the entire *Bible*;

Acquired Hebrew and Greek to read the books of the *Bible* in their original and unadulterated languages;

Studied the oral and textual traditions that comprise the *Bible*;

Studied the *Bible* from an historical perspective by employing the historical method to assess the alleged validity of Biblical history;

Become proficient in archaeology, so as to examine the archaeological evidences for each and every biblical narrative for yourself;

Read all of the extra-biblical literature, from the Apostolic Fathers, the Ante-Nicene Fathers, to the Post Nicene Fathers, up until the latest scholarly opinions on both the Old and *New Testaments*;

Read all of the opposing works that seek to debunk the *Bible* as the "Word of God" and valid history;

Then, your faith is, at least to an extent, blind. Think about it this way. You wouldn't mind putting this much research into a company that you might want to invest your entire life savings into, yet, when it comes to your life, your mind and your existence here on earth, you have no problem throwing the dice and trusting the advice of an institution that has been proven throughout history, to be a lying, manipulating and otherwise unreliable investment.

◆

The two primary commandments of Christ were to love YOUR god with all of your heart and treat your neighbour as yourself. The trouble with these two commandments is that the first has usually prevented the second.

◆

Theists have done a fantastic job of undermining Darwin's theory of Evolution; not by their arguments, but by their mere existence.

◆

The *Bible* was either planned by Jesus/God to be used in the gruesome manner that it was throughout history, or it was being selectively interpreted by his power hungry followers, who found loop holes and justifications within his teachings, to behave in such a cruel manner. If so, these loop holes were either not foreseen by the Christian god, or were foreseen and thus part of his plan. Either way, Jesus was either brutally savage or pitifully negligent; there is no alternative if we are to take the Christians at their word.

♦

The other day a man showed up on my doorstep trying to sell me a jar of peanut butter. He pointed out all of the good things about peanut butter and warned me that if I didn't start eating it, I would suffer terribly. Ok, I lied, it wasn't peanut butter, it was Jesus. I only said peanut butter because it sounds less ridiculous.

♦

Am I a negative person because I criticise negative religions? If I stand for the rights of every human being and place them above the myths they have manufactured, is this really negative? Ok, let me give you an analogy. If you see a group of men raping a girl and you criticise and even try to stop them, are you being negative? Perhaps we should cheer the rapists on and say, good job, keep raping! No, because that would be absurd and contrary to humanity and so now, hopefully, you see why criticising your hateful religion is positive.

♦

Seven Things Priests And Preachers Never Tell Their Parishioners.
1. The Gospels are pseudonymous, meaning; the names of the authors are false.
2. The Gospels contain forgeries, like the story of the woman taken in adultery and almost the entire final chapter of Mark.
3. The Gospels contain errors with regards to history, geography and contradict one another in many areas.
4. Most of Jesus' revelations were already in existence amongst both Jews and pagans, centuries before his alleged arrival.
5. Most of the mythical motifs of Jesus' life existed amongst earlier pagan religions, like his virgin birth, the divine announcement of that birth, his narrow escape from a brutal tyrant, the nature of his miracles, his apotheosis death and his promise to return, among many others.
6. None of Jesus' proximate and literate contemporaries even knew he existed.

7. If it were not for the horrendous violence of tyrants like Constantine, Theodosius "the Great," and the like, Christianity would not have become a major religion.

◆

If I must stay my rational mind and forgo reason to experience your religion, then I am forced to conclude that your religion is irrational and unreasonable.

◆

The difference between a thinking atheist and a mindless one, in my opinion, is that the latter asserts without equivocation, "there is no god," whilst the former, more cautiously and intelligently says, "I have insufficient reason to believe in the existence of a god."

◆

Given the historical and archaeological evidence, I think it is likely that the original "prophets" of ancient Babylonia, who influenced the development of the prophetic tradition within Judaism, were nothing but glorified meteorologists, who studied the movements of the stars and the seasons and could predict with proficient accuracy, when to plant and when to harvest. With this knowledge, they ruled over a credulous and superstitious people, who believed that these educated charlatans were communicating with the gods.

◆

Dear believer, you are free to vomit verses of the *Bible* at me in response to the questions and criticisms I raise, but please know this, they have no impact on me whatsoever. I am not a believer and subsequently, you would be better off showing me a photo of you sacrificing a chicken, in a bid to make me believe as you do.

◆

The Historicity of Jesus

The entire corpus of literature that testifies to Jesus' earthly existence are four short and conflicting biographies, Matthew, Mark, Luke and John. The earliest Christian writings, the Epistles of Paul, say virtually nothing about his life, so impeach these four alleged eyewitness testimonies and you have debunked his alleged historicity.

The Gospels are pseudonymous, meaning they weren't written by the authors whose names appear on the works.

They fail the historical test of contemporanity, meaning, the earliest Gospel, "Mark," was written an entire generation after his alleged crucifixion.

They are affected by bias, meaning, they are not impartial accounts of history.

They are hampered by arguments from similarity, meaning, pretty much all of the miracles and motifs contained within these Gospels existed amongst earlier religions, including the alleged revelations, or teachings of Jesus.

Their testimony pertaining to Jesus are further impeached by arguments from silence, for no contemporary witnesses, but for two brief mentions in the works of a first century Jewish historian, Josephus, exist, and these two references have been shown, at least in large part, to be Christian forgeries.

The Gospels contain forgeries or interpolations, as it is more politely referred to by textual scholars.

People are not born of virgins and ghosts, turn water to wine, walk on that water, etc. Therefore, to keep the validity of these "historical testimonies" alive, historicists, those who argue for the historicity of Jesus, the human, argue that the genre of ancient biographies often included legendary elements, but this strips the "Christ" from the Jesus.

There is no archaeological evidence for Jesus or his alleged disciples, but that is not a major hurdle for historicists, for archaeology isn't the proper tool for examining the evidence of these kinds of characters, although it does help to kill the certainty of his existence.

◆

Your God is but a mere shadow cast upon the cave wall, to which you have perpetually faced.

◆

A closer examination of YOUR God, an examination beyond your egocentric belief, may just reveal a most disturbing truth. Your God is merely a projection and reflection of your own psyche.

◆

The world would probably sink into the gloomy abyss of mindless orthodoxy if it weren't for blasphemy.

♦

I am sorry to tell you this, but your "profound" religious experience boils down to excited dopamines and depleted serotonin levels, occasioned by your belief-induced euphoria. Perhaps now you won't mind joining the rest of us here on earth.

♦

For too long tradition has shielded religion and given it a free pass. It is like a spoilt child that believes the rules do not apply to it. Ask it to prove itself historically and it blatantly exhorts, "I am historical but the normal rules of historical evidence do not apply to me;" beg it to prove itself scientifically and it mutters, "faith is all I offer you," attempt to hold it accountable for its crimes and it will invoke tradition as a legal defence; and should you commit the crime of asking it to conform to the rules of logic, it will simply smile at you and hand you nothing but illogical arguments wrapped in a thin veneer of misappropriated logic. For too long religion has hidden beneath the emotional bonds of an intellectually dark tradition, but no more. From now on, let's hold it accountable.

♦

Religious people are generally less intelligent than non-believers, but don't take my word for it. In a recently released scientific study (2013), a systematic meta-analysis of sixty-three studies conducted between 1928 and 2012 showed a significant negative association between intelligence and religiosity. Are you really that surprised?

♦

If the *Bible* were to be turned into a movie, a film that depicted every scene and every story, it would be rated XXX and would be banned in most countries. Just imagine the scenes of fathers having gratuitous sex with daughters and impregnating them in drunken stupors, the raping of thousands of young women, the ripping open of pregnant women's bellies and the dashing of foetuses and new born babies against rocks. Genocide, murder, macabre human sacrifice and the manipulation of human remains would be just a few of the horrific scenes from this foul and disgusting movie. Now, consider that the majority of Western children are indoctrinated with this horrendous book.

♦

Egocentrism: Having little or no regard for the beliefs of others. You cannot be a good Christian unless you are egocentric.

♦

Religion is organized escapism.

♦

Why are there four Gospels in the Christian Canon? I know the answer, but if I told you, you may not believe me. Well, according to Irenaeus (late second century), the proto-Orthodox father who made official the selection of the four Gospels we know today, there are four corners of the earth, four pillars upon which the earth rests (flat earth thinking) and Cherubim have four heads. Now, I don't mean to mock you, but if your religious Scripture is built upon the idea of four headed flying hybrids, presiding over a four cornered flat earth, supported by four large pillars, then excuse me for dismissing your insane beliefs altogether.

♦

If your religion attempts to appeal to men with promises of multiple married sex partners and sex slaves here on earth and even more naked virgins in the afterlife, your religion is no deep source of profound wisdom and truth, it is a base and profane sex cult, built upon and propagated by, the exploitation of tawdry carnal thrills.

♦

If your religion would have me hold belief over free and open minded thought and offer benefits to portions of our species and punishments to others, I cannot, intellectually and morally speaking, support it. Here's an idea, let's build a free, intelligent and equal world, where women are not seen as inferior to men and gay couples are treated equally and their lifestyle seen in its proper context, natural.

♦

If the alleged crime of two remote individuals, Adam and Eve, has been imputed onto our entire species, then it is only logical to hold all Christians responsible for the actual crimes committed by their

29

theological ancestors. It's a good thing that no rational person believes in original sin.

♦

Any religion that would encourage a husband to treat his wife as a punching bag when she refuses to be treated as a sex slave as is the case with Islam, is an indelible stain on our species.

♦

In the Gospel of John, Peter asks Jesus where he is going, to which Jesus replies: *Whither I go, thou canst not follow me now; but thou shalt follow me afterwards* (13:35). Shortly after, Thomas asks Jesus the same question, with Jesus replying on this occasion: *I am the way, the truth, and the life: no man cometh unto the Father, but by me* (14:6). Ok, so you are going to meet your father in heaven, that makes sense, you could have just said that! Following both Peter's and Thomas' inquiries as to where Jesus would be going, he scolds them, saying: *But now I go my way to him that sent me; and none of you asketh me, Whither goest thou?* (16:5). I'm pretty sure both Peter and I just asked you that very question. Go home Jesus, you're drunk!

♦

Christianity is little more than hero fetish with a little symbolic cannibalism and vampirism, added to appeal to the insane.

♦

If your religion permits men to marry children and encourages husbands to beat their wives, as does Islam, your religion is both unnatural and immoral.

♦

"Stop disparaging my beliefs!" I hear this so often from believers, but what is a belief and why should it be safe from inquiry and criticism? If your beliefs are true, then what possible harm could I do to an all-powerful and all-knowing creator? No, the reason you don't like me criticising your beliefs is that somewhere deep down, you know you are lying to yourself, but your rampant ego protects you from this horrifying revelation. Furthermore, can you imagine hearing this benign and egocentric statement from a competent scientist, or from someone with an ounce of humility?

♦

I see religion as being a lot like a weight loss wonder pill. It doesn't work and only appeals to the lazy.

◆

Christianity was one of the first religions to target the meek and lower strata of society for conversion. When you take this fact into consideration, you begin to understand why heaven was described as being littered with golden thrones, precious stones and trees that bear fruit monthly, and why it is harder for the rich to enter. It's just good marketing.

◆

What Voltaire achieved with his wit and mastery of language, Darwin accomplished with his keen observations. We all have different gifts; the trick is to find it, aim it at religion and express it to our fullest capacity.

◆

Religion is a house of cards. With a tiny dose of information, mixed with a dash of common sense, it will crumble under the sheer weight of reason.

◆

By definition, a miracle is the least probable event, which leads me to conclude that they probably don't happen.

◆

Before converting to any of the proselytising faiths, I highly recommend that you thoroughly read their scriptures, beforehand. If after you have read them, you still want to convert, then at least you will be an informed idiot.

◆

The *Bible* is full of examples of intellectual complacency, from the sanctioning of Eve to God's murder of Lot's wife, to the doubting Thomas of John's Gospel. Don't question, don't inquire, just believe. This is what the *Bible* teaches and it is what has stifled the intellectual and moral development of all those societies that have been oppressed beneath the yoke of this beguiling collection of books.

◆

What is the difference between "the past" and "history?" The past, we might justifiably conclude, refers to actual events that transpired and real people that existed, prior to the present. History on the other hand, is the record of those events and people, often infringed upon and distorted by, the biases, motivations and general fallibility of the recorder. When we understand the difference between 'the past' and 'history,' we gain even more justification to look sceptically upon the alleged histories of religious legends and myths.

◆

The belief in the existence of a god is certainly the majority opinion, but a delusion doesn't become a fact simply because the majority believe it. Likewise, a fact doesn't become a delusion because only a few can see it.

◆

Religion is a psychological dictatorship, enabling tyrants to control unthinking populations in the same way shepherds control their flocks of sheep. The choice is ultimately yours; do you choose freedom or servitude? I choose to be free, at least psychologically, anyway.

◆

Christ Causes Skin Cancer.

I am the light of the world and the Sun of Righteousness. I send rain down upon the just and the unjust alike. My father is the great and mighty sun of the previous cycle, and only through me can one get to him, who, having grown old and tired, impregnated my mother, the ever-virgin, Virgo, who gave birth to me in humble and dire circumstances. I am the new born king, as yet frail and subject to the dangers of that great tyrant (Herod/Set/winter). I am the twice born giver of life, able to ferment the grapes and turn water into wine with my rays, born and reborn at both the winter solstice (December 25th) and the spring/vernal equinox (Easter), on the cusp of both Aries (The Alpha – first sign of the zodiac) and Pisces (The Omega – last sign of the zodiac), so, I am the Alpha and the Omega, the eternal giver of fish and the Lamb (Aries) of God. My father, the great king, who art in the heavens (space) and whose mansion contains many houses (twelve), having been betrayed by his closest brethren (Set/Judas/the autumnal equinox/darkness) was nailed to his coffin/cross and ultimately had his body (rays) broken into pieces, so that he could nourish the multitudes with his eternal and cyclical sacrifice; this is my body, eat and be fulfilled. I and my father are one and despite the varying descriptions of me given by my four biographers

(Spring, Summer, Autumn and Winter), I am the one and only re-deemer. I was crucified between two thieves, the autumnal equinox, who steals the light to further the darkness and the vernal equinox, who, conversely, steals from the darkness to further the light. The vernal equinox is the loyal thief on my left; he is faithful to me, joining me in paradise (space) on the day of my resurrection. Although I die and descend into the underworld for three days (winter solstice), have no fear and do not cry for me my child, for I promise to return in the future, (next year) but take heed, those who do not abide in me, walk in darkness and the darkness cannot prevail over me, because I am the light of truth, the guider of the way and the giver of life. Whichever name you wish to ascribe to me, whether you call me Osiris, Horus, Helios, Herakles or Christ, and through whatever reli-gion you want to worship me, know this; I am the sun personified in myth and all those who do not protect themselves against me in the summertime, may get skin cancer.

◆

Why don't I believe in the existence of a god? Well, because I am not in the habit of pretending to know things that I don't.

◆

The *Bible* is like a crowded intersection of ideas and beliefs with no traffic lights.

◆

According to the *Qur'an* (4:89), the Hadith (Sahih Bukhari 84:57, 89:271, 84:58, 84:64-65), the majority opinion amongst Muslim scholars and Sharia Law, the religion of Islam prescribes the death penalty for apos-tasy. Apostasy simply means, leaving the religion. This is akin to a no refunds policy, which begs the question, why would they need a no re-fund policy if their product is sound? Also, we have to ask, why did they anticipate people wanting to refund this religion in the first place; a reli-gion started by the alleged hallucinations of a madman wandering the desert, defiling children and beating them when they refused to gratify his insane and depraved lusts; a religion that was forced onto nations by the sword, nations who now proudly wave the Ottoman moon and star for their captor, Islam? Surely this no refund policy is indicative of a sys-tem of beliefs that cannot stand the test of time and truth without the aid of the threat of death to keep its adherents loyal to one of the most pernicious religions this earth has had the misfortune to host.

◆

Beyond the Bounds of Immediate Perception.

There are truths which sit just beyond the bounds of immediate perception and I am not talking about faith-based supernatural nonsense, but logical, testable and demonstrable truths. In my work, whenever I speak about such things, I am speaking about real and rational probabilities with regards to the truth. I will give you an example.

All of the major religions; Christianity, Islam, Hinduism, Buddhism, etc, preach the renunciation of material wealth, yet the very authors of these Scriptures belonged to wealthy classes, rich enough to afford the education necessary to endow them with the skills required to write such poetry, prose and parable. The institutions charged with administering these faiths are likewise, wealthy. So, to whom are they speaking when they beg people to renounce their earthly estates? They are speaking to the masses of adherents, whose constituency forms the powerbase, upon which these popes, preachers, sheiks, monks and gurus sit. Why? Well, once you have established the first part of the equation, the probable answers as to why they beg us to renounce our earthly possessions, become whittled down to a few natural and observable motives.

◆

If I was God, I would make ignorance a sin, punishable by learning. I wouldn't suffer emotional pain when people failed to believe in me because I had provided them with no tangible evidence for my existence, but I would gently frown upon anyone who believed in me without sufficient reason to do so. I wouldn't merely heal a few blind and sick Jews in Judea, I would eradicate blindness and sickness altogether. I would eliminate suffering and do away with hell. I would bestow upon my creation free will and the intelligence to make proper and responsible use of it, thereby doing away with the need for mindless obedience. In short, if I was God, I wouldn't be rude about it.

◆

If power corrupts and absolute power corrupts absolutely, what does that say about an all-powerful God?

◆

Dear Religion,

I promise not to laugh at your answers if you promise not to stand in the way of my questions.

◆

Drawing upon the saying in Deuteronomy (6:16), the pseudonymous (fake) authors of both Matthew and Luke assert; *Do not test God* (Matthew 4:7 & Luke 4:12), but I say, if it can't be tested, it can't be trusted.

◆

Just because a delusion is popularly held by a majority, doesn't lend weight to that delusion, but merely to the fact that most people are deluded.

◆

Once upon a time there was a man named Jephthah, who really wanted to slaughter his enemies. He was so desperate to spill their blood that he called out to God and promised to kill his only daughter if God would help him slay these other men, women and children. The Lord helped Jephthah commit this mass murder and Jephthah fulfilled his promise to the Lord by butchering his only daughter. (Judges 11:1-39)

Now go to sleep, the Lord is watching you!

◆

An altruistic act is one that is performed absent any threat of punishment or promise of reward. Taking responsibility for one's own behaviour means not blaming or crediting someone or something else, for one's own conduct. These two criteria, altruism and personal responsibility are essential to what we might loosely term, morality and yet, they are impossible to achieve for theists.

◆

I always chuckle when I see pro-lifers on the TV with their *Bible* banners. I chuckle because I think it would be hilarious to have advocates for pro-choice show up with *Bible* banners too. Like 2 Kings 15:16 in which God allows Menahem to *rip open the bellies of pregnant women* or

Hosea 13:16, which has God promising to dash to pieces the infants of Samaria, exhorting, *their women with child shall be ripped up.* Little do they realize that in being pro-life, they are rallying against their own fictitious Lord, who, in Numbers 5:11-21, is alleged to personally perform abortions on unfaithful women.

1. Human beings are fallible
2. Beliefs are human constructs
3. Therefore beliefs are fallible
4. The existence of God is a belief
5. Therefore the belief in God is fallible

Once you cast off the crutches of religious faith and after your ego has healed from the painful bruising, you begin to realize that the crutches were the one thing that kept you in a state of cognitive dependency, and that now without them, you are able to move much more freely.

It's possible that a god exists and it is also possible that my children's toys come to life when we are all sleeping. In either case, I reserve the right to disbelieve until I am presented with sufficient evidence, at which time and after a thorough psychiatric evaluation and numerous MRI scans, I will not need to believe, for I will know.

Seven Signs That Your Religion May Have Warped Your Mind
1. You believe that all those who don't believe as you do, will be burnt by fire and tortured.
2. You teach your children that they will be burnt by fire if they don't believe the things you believe.
3. You sit down to dinner and thank an imaginary friend for the food, over and above the people who have actually bought and cooked your dinner.
4. You see difference of opinion as evil.
5. You see certain groups of fellow humans as inherently evil or more prone to evil, like women, Jews, homosexuals, etc..

6. You trust your morality to brutal and superstitious books written between the Bronze Age and up until 2000 years ago.
7. You see creationism as being on par with evolution.

♦

To educated Christians it has been revealed that the Gospel of Matthew is not the word of Matthew, the Gospel of Luke is not the word of Luke, nor is Mark the word of Mark or John the word of John. Further, it has been revealed that many of the Epistles of Paul are not the word of Paul. I think we all know what the next great revelation will be.

♦

The specific beliefs of a believer are a lot like fingerprints, in that each is slightly unique. This is a great point to use when debating believers. Find out how their beliefs about God and their doctrines of faith differ from other members of the same faith and then pit them against the others. It is a great way to demonstrate to the believer that their beliefs are just that, beliefs.

♦

Just as hindsight is 20/20 vision, so too is history the great teacher. What does history teach us about religion? It teaches us that religion is a dangerous tool of oppression and a propagator of ignorance. I am not asking you to believe me, but I challenge you to read any of the great annals of European and even Middle Eastern history and see for yourself.

♦

Christian Apologetics 101 Series

Christian Apologetics 101 – Lesson 1: The Apologist's Mirror

The apologist's mirror is a common technique employed by Christian apologists to shift the burden of proof and level the otherwise unbalanced playing field in a debate.

It may take the form of arguments like:

"I know I can't prove the existence of God, but you can't disprove it."

"I know I can't prove that Jesus was the Son of God, but you can't disprove it."

"Just because there is no real historical proof that Jesus existed doesn't mean anything, as there is no historical proof for Socrates and Pythagoras, either."

"You have unsubstantiated beliefs too."

Be sure to explain to the apologist that the burden of proof rests with them, as they are the ones defending an assertion of truth. The bottom line is that if a person cannot reasonably defend a statement of belief with reasonable evidence but resort instead to tactics such as the mirror, then you can rest in the knowledge that they have lost the debate.

♦

Christian Apologetics 101 – Lesson 2: The Apologetic Merry-Go-Round

This technique is one of the weakest and is usually only employed by unseasoned apologists. It goes like this:

Apologist: The *Bible* is the Word of God!

Atheist: How do you know that it is the Word of God?

Apologist: Because it says so!

Atheist: How do you know it is right?

Apologist: Because the Word of God is infallible, like God!

Atheist: How do you know that it and he are infallible?

Apologist: Because He is God and the *Bible* is his word!

Before becoming dizzy from such circular argumentation, you can stop the apologist merry-go-round at any point by bringing into question the reliability of the texts that form the foundation of the *Bible*. The wealth of scholarship that has been done in the areas of textual criticism and biblical history should help you in this area. All you need are a few books by legitimate *Bible* scholars and some good *Bible* Dictionaries and you will find everything you need to stop this nauseating ride. Failing this you can always employ the "napkin technique".' This technique is simple, just grab a napkin and write the following on it. "I am God." Hand the napkin to the apologist and tell them that the napkin is self-authenticating and that it is even better than any of the books of the *Bible*, for they are able to attest to the authorship of this napkin.

♦

Christian Apologetics 101 – Lesson 3: The Apologetic Yellow Brick Road

The Yellow Brick Road is a technique employed when an apologist knows they are about to lose a point on the grounds of fact or reason, an inevitable consequence of arguing for unreasonable beliefs. The apologist will skip to a semi-related topic, leading the opponent down the proverbial Yellow Brick Road. They do this by taking any small and insignificant issue in the present failing argument and use that as a bridge to quickly evacuate the disaster which looms on the horizon. This technique is effective for distracting an opponent who feels the need to address every single point raised, regardless of its overall importance to the central debate. To overcome this technique, you need to "stop and stay". Stop at any point not resolved and stay there until the issue has been fully addressed or until the failing apologist uses their "Get out of Defeat Free Card"; "Let's agree to disagree." Do not let the apologist move on until they have answered all outstanding questions or thrown in their G.O.D.F.C.

◆

Christian Apologetics 101 – Lesson 4: The Multiplication Table Technique

This technique is used to overcome obvious errors in Scripture. If the author of John described the town of Bethany as being on the east side of the Jordan River, when we know that it is actually on the west side of the Jordan River, they will create an entirely fictitious Bethany on the east side of the Jordan, thereby multiplying the town of Bethany by two. If the author of Mark describes the city of Bethsaida as a village, when we know that it was a large city, they will create another fictitious village of Bethsaida, just kilometres away from the real one. Or, if the author of Luke describes Jesus' birth as having occurred during both the reign of Herod the Great and the Governorship of Quirinius, simultaneously, when these two historical events were separated by over a decade, they will claim without evidence, that the Quirinius was governor twice, even though we know he was only governor of Syria one time.

We also may observe this technique when the science of geology debunked the Seven Days of Creation as having taken place six thousand years ago. Here the rationalization was; "Well, between Genesis 1:1 and 1:2 there were two separate creations, and in between that time, billions of years elapsed, which is when the dinosaurs roamed the earth and unshakable fossil records were formed. So, there wasn't just one creation, but two. There are many other instances where this multiplication technique is employed by the desperate apologist.

In creating such arguments, apologists are attempting to hide obvious errors of scripture within the obscurity of multiplicity, but as most people know, multiplying error only compounds it and the truth can be readily discovered with a minimal amount of investigation.

◆

Christian Apologetics 101 – Lesson 5: The Ink Blot Technique

This technique relies on the vague wording of many biblical passages. Due to the ambiguity of scripture, apologists have near free reign to bend, twist and distort various passages and sayings of Jesus, to support interpretations that further their arguments. One example is the failed second coming of Christ, which was clearly alleged in the Gospels to be due in the first century (during the lifetime of the disciples). Wherever these errors arise, the apologist may play upon the linguistic or poetic translations and applications of a word or passage in order to escape defeat. The alleged prophecies relating to Jesus' advent from the *Old Testament* and their application by the fake author of Matthew are a great example of this Ink Blot Technique.

To overcome this technique, simply buy or visit online Hebrew and Greek concordances, read the textual scholarship on these passages and the apologist will be left with the hollow echoes of their own desperation.

◆

Faith cannot be defended with logic and reason, nor can a nail be driven into a piece of wood, with a feather. Trying to do either for an extended period of time is only going to lead to insanity.

Here ends Christian Apologetics 101.

◆

The story of Noah's Ark is about a man who was over 600 years old and…Wait, where are you going? I haven't finished the story yet!

◆

Jesus is the omniscient and omnipotent God; say the Trinitarians, the Nicene Creed, the Gospel of John and a large portion of Christians. If this is the case, why should we thank a God for sacrificing himself, to himself, in order to rectify mistakes, for which he is ultimately responsible? If you believe that Jesus was merely the Son of God, then you are left with the Gospel's claim that he was aware of his fate, and what a fate it was! He suffered a mere day as a mortal, in order to gain an eternity as an immortal. That's not a bad deal. I certainly wouldn't call it a sacrifice.

♦

It seems to me that many religious people feel that loving their god warrants or even obliges them to hate their fellow human being. In this way, they appear to love fiction and hate reality.

♦

You say you need Jesus to live your life, but what was Jesus? Jesus was a mythical or perhaps legendary character, whose fictional life mimics many other ancient characters and who taught the same things as many earlier philosophers and teachers. So when you say you need Jesus, you are saying you need a common myth, who taught common things, to live your life.

♦

The toxic tides of religious bigotry and dangerous superstitions are beginning to recede into the recesses of human history and the cleansing waters of reason and science are on the way in.

♦

Before you have faith in Jesus Christ, you must:

Have faith in the *Bible, New Testament* and *Old Testament*, as a whole; rape, murder, slavery and misogyny included.

Have faith in the anonymous authors of the Gospels and their accounts of Jesus' life, despite the fact that they were written well over a generation after his alleged death.

Have faith in the various forgeries that were written into the *New Testament* well into the second and even third centuries.

Have faith in the texts of the *New Testament*, despite the fact that the manuscripts that form their foundations contain more variations and errors than there are words in the *New Testament* itself.

Have faith in the second century Church Father, Irenaeus, who selected four gospels out of the plethora that existed, based on reasoning which included flat earth thinking and four headed creatures.

Have faith in the handful of fourth century Nicene bishops who decided what Christ should be believed to be and they only reached this decision after the emperor Constantine intervened to stop them fighting with each other.

Have faith in the Catholic Church's version of your faith, a version which forms the foundation of almost every modern brand of Christianity, all 40,000 of them.

If, after all of this and much more, you still have faith in Jesus Christ, you are beyond help.

◆

If a religion threatens the death penalty for apostasy (leaving the religion), which Islam does (see *Qur'an*; Surah 4:89, 9:11-12, Sahih Bukhari 52:260, 83:37, etc..), you can be quite certain that such a religion is insecure of its "truths," for if it possessed the truth, it wouldn't need to threaten people into submission.

◆

Darwin's theory of evolution by way of natural selection wasn't perfect. So what? Since Darwin first proposed his theory in 1859, many advances have been made in the fields of physiology, microbiology, biochemistry, ethology, and we have learned more and more about the fossil record. All these advances have not only vindicated Darwin's original hypothesis, they have improved upon his theory. Such is the nature of science and enlightenment. It is an evolutionary process, by which the humility of the scientist fosters the continual reciprocity of question and answer.

◆

You seem to believe that because science is unable to answer every question about the workings of the universe, there must be a god, but ignorance is only evidence of ignorance, nothing more.

◆

The next time a creationist puts forth the argument that; "the theory of evolution contradicts the second law of thermodynamics (entropy)," ask them the following questions:

What are the other laws of thermodynamics?

Does this second law only apply to closed systems?

What is a closed system?

Can the only closed system we know of (the universe as a whole), contain sub-systems in which the second law of thermodynamics does not apply?

If so, explain the relation between two connected sub-systems and how that relationship undermines your argument completely.

Once you have asked these questions, step back, the creationist may need some breathing room.

◆

I imagine that you would like me to use my imagination to experience your god, but I think you should put some thought into the probability that your god is entirely imaginary.

◆

Jesus allegedly said; *Don't resist evil* (Matthew 5:39), but I say; the minute we stop resisting injustice and ignorance, we begin enabling it.

◆

If it wasn't for the aid of Constantine, Christianity would not be a major religion today. Let me put it another way. If it wasn't for the help of a powerful Roman Emperor who executed his own son and boiled his wife alive, Christianity would not be a major religion today.

◆

Many Christians living today are ignorant of the true origins of both their scriptures and their religion. In many ways the average Christian is like the patron of a fast food restaurant, standing in rank and file, waiting for their meal to be delivered to their hands. They seldom if ever, wonder or even question, the process which has gone on behind the scenes with regards to the preparation of their meal. Like children they wait for the finished product to be handed to them. If Christians were to diligently investigate the origins of their belief system, what would they learn? And would what they learn have an impact on what and how strongly they believe?

◆

When we begin to acknowledge and understand the impact our belief-cluttered egos have on how we treat information that comes into conflict with cherished beliefs, we start to gain an understanding of how we manipulate ourselves in order to protect outdated and thoroughly debunked beliefs, like our belief in God, for example.

◆

I'm looking for a word that begins with "R" and describes something that is dependent upon the suspension of critical thinking, logic and reason. It has been responsible for countless wars, genocides and the oppression of various groups of human beings; is contrary to the psychological evolution of our species and is something the majority of our unthinking populations are desperately addicted to.

I'll give you hint. It's not Road Rage or the Republicans, although the latter is very close and heavily tied to it.

◆

You want me to have faith in an outdated collection of superstitious books that would teach me to:

Hate women (Genesis 3:16 & Ecclesiastes 3:28)

Hate Same Sex Couples (Leviticus 18:22)

Hate Knowledge (Genesis 3 & Genesis 11:7)

Hate Evidence (John 20:29)

Hate the earth (Ecclesiastes 3:16)

Hate my parents (14:26)

Hate myself (Luke 14:26) and;

Love Slave Masters (Ephesians 6:5) and Tyrants (Romans 13:1-2).

I am sorry, but my humanity prevents me from having faith in your misanthropic myths.

◆

If you are not going to obey the voices in your head, you may as well give up your religion today.

◆

Although I respect all forms of education, let's be honest, having a degree in theology is no different to obtaining a degree in witch-doctory, or spiderman-ology. It just means you are certified to talk about ghosts, gods, ghouls and demons.

◆

According to the Gospels, Jesus was crucified on a cross (John 19:17-18, Mark 15:25, Luke 23:33, Matthew 27:32-35). According to other *New Testament* authors, he was hung from a tree (Galatians 3:13, 1 Peter 2:24, Acts 13:29, Acts 5:30, Acts 10:39); so which is it? My guess is neither.

◆

If you believe the Gospels to be true accounts of a son of God, then you must concede that he was no botanist. Firstly, he became enraged by a fig tree that wouldn't produce fruit out of season (Mark 11:12-14, 11:20-25) and secondly, he asserted that the mustard seed is the "smallest seed on earth" (Matthew 13:31–32, Mark 4:30–32, and Luke 13:18–19), when it is not. There are literally hundreds of smaller seeds on earth, but what would the son of God know, right?

♦

God didn't create Adam and Steve, because God probably doesn't exist, but if by some freakishly remote chance he does and we were created in his image, then he almost certainly carries a gay gene or two.

♦

I think it is fair to say, Christianity and Islam have caused more suffering, more misery and have taken more lives throughout their sordid histories, than both heroin and cocaine, combined. It seems strange to me then, that the latter two have been deemed injurious to the welfare of society, whilst the former have been protected and even enthusiastically propagated.

♦

Whenever theists argue that God is synonymous with morality, I always agree whole heartedly, because both are manmade constructs.

♦

You can't keep using free will as a "Get out of Jail Free Card" for the malignant nature of your fictitious God, especially when you assert that he is the creator and your own scriptures say: *I form the light and create darkness: I make peace, and create evil: I the lord do all these things.*

~ Isaiah 45:7

♦

If you believe that love is contingent on a god, then your love is rooted in selfish and egocentric fantasy. Learn to love without a god and you will have learnt to love in reality.

♦

It seems that pretending to know the answer to something when you really don't, is viewed negatively in all aspects of life, but for religion.

♦

THE BOOK OF FREETHOUGHT

WHAT IS A FREETHINKER?

I don't really know, but I imagine that a freethinker is one whose thoughts would be free from encumbrance, well, as free as possible. They would not perceive themselves or anyone else through the rose coloured glasses of any religion, nation, ethnicity, gender or race. They would be free from the narrow cognitive constructs of societal norms and traditions and they might even see the human race as a single family of kindred beings, all sharing a single earth, with equal entitlements to freedom, regardless of any of the aforementioned categories. A freethinker, I imagine, would not follow the teachings of any one teacher or group of teachers, but would sift through, that which they find to be useful for furthering their own learning and psychological sovereignty. They would not be moved by the emotionally manipulative rhetoric vomited into the ears of their fellow human beings by religious and political mis-leaders, for their minds would be sound enough to see through such base and ill-contrived manipulation. They would be free to follow the dictates of their own mind and at the same time, appreciate the great responsibility that comes with such freedom. Ultimately, I can only imagine, the freethinker would be one of the most hated kinds of people in a society that has been built upon, and maintained by, chronic dependency and ignorance.

◆

Why do you fish from only one small and stagnant pond, when there are oceans of wisdom out there? Put down your *Bible*s, your Qur'ans and your Bhagavad Gitas when you have finished reading them and pick up Paine's *Age of Reason* or Ingersoll's *The Gods and Other Lectures*.2' Browse the ancient tomes from Egypt, Greece, Persia and Mesopotamia; listen to the stories of the Australian Aboriginal Dreamtime and the myths of the Polynesians. Read Dawkins, Hitchens and Sam Harris' works, thumb through Thomas Aquinas' *Summa Theologica*, Jung's great volumes, Joseph Campbell's *Hero with a Thousand Faces* and Voltaire's biting satires. There are oceans of wisdom out there, yet you remain fixated upon and obsessed with one meagre little pond.

◆

Once a belief has taken up residence in our mind, we have arrived at the conclusion of a perceived truth. There is no longer a need to question or seek further information regarding the matter, as we have now produced, or been handed, a manufactured certainty that creates a dead end for our mind to take rest in. We have become dependent upon the thoughts and beliefs of others and stopped thinking for ourselves. Therefore, the earlier we are able to arrive at a conclusion or establish a belief, the less work our minds have to do and so, the less our individual minds become necessary.

♦

Imagine for a moment that the entirety of life is written in a large book, millions upon millions of pages long. In this book, belief systems, beliefs and ideas, each occupy one meagre page each. Now consider how the belief, with all of its emotional components, inhibits the believer from turning that page to read on. Christianity takes up one single page in the book of life and yet the Christian is warned not to turn the page, and if he does, he interprets each individual page through the lens of his favourite Christian page, which obstructs his ability to rationally interpret each page in its own right. More often than not, the believer will forsake millions of pages of wisdom, only to read the same page over and over again.

♦

What if our actual knowledge represents a single grain of sand on a beach that spans the entire universe?

♦

Belief is a matter of choice, not necessarily a matter of fact. The sooner we realize this simple truth, the sooner we might unlock the hidden potentials of our minds and possibly even reach that ideal romantically referred to as, humanity.

♦

This Christmas, whether you spend it prostrating yourself before the God of the Christians or the corporate gods of the secular consumer world, just know that you will be making some charlatan rich.

♦

The mere existence of a possibility in no way testifies on behalf of impossibility.

♦

It has come time for the masses of sleeping souls to wake up and for those who have been awake, but who have remained fearfully silent, to stand up together against religious and political manipulators and say with one loud resounding voice: "I will no longer serve my earthly master. I will no longer render unto Caesar that which is Caesar's, because all that I have rendered unto him is actually mine.

No longer will I stand by and allow you to manipulate and control my most sacred and inner sanctum. My mind is my own. I am awake now. I have been your prey, your ticket and your product. You have distracted me with false spiritual and material rewards and frightened me with your rod. No more!

From now on I choose to be free.

♦

Faith is the great enslaver. It has led more people to persecute, hate, imprison, torture and murder than almost any other device of the mind. Doubt on the other hand, is the noble saviour, freeing the mind of humanity and preventing the chaos and injustice wrought by faith. Is it any wonder that our religious and political masters have demonized doubt to such a dramatic degree? Had they not, they would have lost their oppressive grip on their slaves. Until we teach ourselves to overcome this subversive conditioning, we will remain in a perpetual state of bondage.

♦

Your identity is merely a social and psychological construct. Don't take it too seriously.

♦

Many people become seduced by and infatuated with their own subjective perceptions, leading them to despise an unbiased search for truth. For this reason the true teachers of this world have been some of the most despised and ridiculed people in history. They are the outsiders who think beyond the fences of societal norms and perceptions, the intellectual rebels that refuse the kind offer to join in the "consensus trance"' which underscores human society and they are the brazen heretics, who have possessed both the audacity and the courage, to challenge the mass manipulation of the human mind.

♦

If you want to live an honest life, a life guided by the truth, it is necessary and even inevitable, that you will make some people angry.

♦

49

It is much easier for a belief holder to stretch the very fabric of their own credulity than admit that error exists within their established belief. Herein lies the snare of beliefs and the relief afforded by confirmation biases and adaptational strategies, in dealing with new information that threatens a person's core beliefs. Thus, it is generally confirmation biases and irrational rationalizations which come to the rescue of unsound beliefs, leaving the believer in a state of blissful ignorance.

◆

Ignorance is bliss, until you wake up in the middle of the road and realize there is a truck barrelling toward you.

◆

If you don't know the truth, which you probably don't, then believing that you do is both useless and counterproductive to an honest search for it.

◆

Life is beautiful because it is short. Eternal life is merely the gluttonous fantasy of the profane mind.

◆

Whenever we indoctrinate our children into a belief system, we stifle their ability to express their uniqueness, freely. Of course, every parent indoctrinates their child to a certain degree, but to brainwash them with a rigid set of mutually supportive beliefs, leaves them virtually incapable of thinking originally and thereby suffocates their cognitive development, in my humble opinion. Further, they are effectively turned into clones of their parents and as a result, the insanities of the past generations are seamlessly transferred to the next.

Insanity is doing the same thing over and over and expecting different results.

~Albert Einstein.

◆

In the Gospel of Matthew it is written; *a man [human being] cannot serve two masters*. This is true with regards to belief and truth. A person cannot serve both belief and truth at the same time, for they will either hate the one and love the other, or hold to the one only to forsake the other.

◆

The believer has eyes but cannot see and ears but hears not and even upon beholding reality for themselves, understands it not.

♦

The further you stand from the light of truth, the less you will be able to see and the less you are able to see, the more you will need to believe.

♦

Don't you get tired of editing reality to fit your fantasies? You get one short shot at life and I would advise that you spend it here, on earth.

♦

Uncertainty can bring about fear, which in turn has the capacity to produce belief. Belief may be little more than an attempt to eradicate the terrifying uncertainties of life and control one's psychological environment. If this is the case, then our beliefs are for the most part, fear-induced and irrational.

♦

To superimpose a fantasy upon your real life is unhealthy. To impose it onto others is narcissistic and unjust.

♦

Dear Believer,

Let me start by saying, I understand your desire to want to believe you are right, I really do. Despite this desire, however, you must understand that no matter how much you push and pull the truth, no matter how loud you shout at it, it will not budge. You are not free to command the truth as you see fit. The truth should be your master and not the other way around. The sooner you learn this, the sooner we might all get some peace.

♦

Societies are mobilized by heroes and unified against enemies. It seems to me then, that these two archetypes, the hero and the enemy, are two of the most influential of all the archetypes. If we were to internalize these archetypes rather than externalize them, I think people would be a lot harder to manipulate.

♦

The difference between an intelligent and peaceful society and an unenlightened one is that the former is established and maintained by intelligent and thoughtful cooperation, whilst the latter is held tenuously together by unintelligent conformity. This is why an unthinking and unenlightened society requires religion and ancient traditions to hold it together and why we will never achieve an enlightened and peaceful society, until we learn the difference between enlightened cooperation and mindless conformity, and replace the latter with the former.

◆

Demons don't possess people and cause them to behave badly, beliefs do.

◆

It seems that the majority of our species would rather live within the confines of their false realities than unlock the mental prison of perception and escape the clutches of tyrannical shepherds, who want nothing more than to keep the human race mentally and emotionally incarcerated. When wise teachers have come with the keys to free us from our prisons, we have turned our backs on them only to forsake the freedom of pure thought for the intoxication of ignorance.

◆

When dissonance occurs in the mind of the believer, it is usually the established belief that wins the day. The rationalization processes, adaptational strategies and self-delusions that prevent a believer from growing past their beliefs, has underscored some of the most insane thinking and behaviour throughout human history. Yet, its most tragic consequence has been the protection of those who have gained power over the people, by relying on these psychological defects in those they control.

◆

Just imagine the contemplative power of a species united beyond the bounds of the mental prisons we call our beliefs. Absent this limitation, the human race would have a real chance at creating a supremely peaceful and enlightened world, the likes of which we have yet to witness.

◆

I don't know what the truth is, but I know this much; the truth does not become angry when ridiculed, it does not ignore unpleasant information, it doesn't employ rationalizations to keep itself intact and above all, the truth does not fear questions.

◆

Before you can begin to change the world for the better, you must first change yourself and to do that, you must know yourself beyond the illusions of your unoriginal and adopted beliefs.

♦

The certitude afforded to us by our beliefs, in a world full of uncertainties, is a lot like a warm and comfy bed. The only trouble is that there is so much work to do and so little time to do it.

♦

Until we learn to foster a greater regard for questions rather than answers, we will continue to choose false and dishonest certitudes over honest uncertainty.

♦

The more we use faith as a substitute for evidence, the more momentum faith gains, forming a black hole in the mind, into which, reason, truth, logic and rational thought are consumed.

♦

Possibilities may be infinite, but reasonable ones are certainly finite.

♦

Our emotions are quite often easily manipulated and our beliefs are emotional creatures. As a result, leaders have little trouble pushing the right buttons in a society full of believers, for all they need do is instil, pander to, or manufacture a threat to our beliefs and we will do what they want us to. Cut the strings.

♦

All I want is for my children to grow up in a world that doesn't persecute on the basis of belief, nationality, ethnicity, race or gender. I want my children, and by extension, your children to enjoy a peaceful existence. As Epicurus once said; "To love one's child is to love all children," I want to tell my grandchildren that wars used to be fought because we as a species were easily manipulated by our emotions, but now we know better. I want to tell my children that corporations lost their grip over our leaders and as a result, we now live in a real and peaceful democracy, one which considers the means and not just the greedy and pathological ends. I want to tell my daughter that there is no need to remain silent or obey her husband when he is wrong or abusive, because those Abrahamic religions are now a thing of past. I want to pass a world onto my children that is free from the belief-induced insanity that ours is plagued with; I want the poor to be fed, the weak to be protected and supported and more than anything, I want humanity to prevail against the egocentricity inherent in every belief system, so that all of our species have a chance to enjoy life.

♦

As it presently stands, in my opinion, the education system does not teach children how to think, but rather, what to think. Until we remedy this, we will continue to live within the suffocating bowels of an idiocracy in which, the stupid govern over the intelligent.

♦

If your friend told you to go and kill someone he didn't like, would you do it? So why do you think it is ok for greedy politicians and selfish corporations to do it?

♦

The Freethinker living in a society saturated by believers of every hue is a lonely person indeed.

♦

If one is to look back through the annals of history and observe our current state of affairs, it becomes apparent that the process of change and transformation is met with great resistance. One need only look back to the official introduction of the "Germ Theory" which caused much tumult in the mid nineteenth century, when scientists of the day proposed a "crazy hypothesis!" These "devil worshiping" scientists were claiming that diseases were the result of germs and not sins, demons, witches and warlocks, which up until that time, was the Christian Church's learned position on the matter. We may also observe how, during the eighteenth century, those evil scientists created smallpox inoculations, much to the dismay of many Christian churches, who protested against them, arguing that they would disrupt "God's" natural order by sparing those who were meant to die. History is littered with these kinds of examples, demonstrating beyond any reasonable doubt, that it has often been the preferred option of the many to cling to outdated and logically flawed beliefs, in spite of the best and most desirable outcome for themselves and society at large.

♦

We live in a society in which the poor are imprisoned for stealing crumbs and the wealthy worshipped for stealing estates.

♦

Mystery breeds both credulity and curiosity, but the decision is ultimately yours as to which one you choose to foster within yourself. Should you choose curiosity, you will learn, grow and earn the right to be called an individual. However, if you choose credulity, you will spend your short life on your knees in service to the beliefs and thoughts of others.

♦

I have no doubt that the leaders in democratic nations are selected by the people, but just what constitutes "the people," is where our modern democracies converge with the oligarchies of old.

♦

True forgiveness is not derived from the grace of some holy fictitious phantom, but through sincere regret, reconciliation and thoughtful contemplation. Learn to truly forgive yourself for whatever trespasses you may have committed in the past and forgiving others will come easily to you.

♦

The concept of the external enemy, the enemy outside of the self is a myth, a manipulative projection. Conquer the internal enemies that reside within yourself and your external ones will evaporate into thin air. Conversely, the same is also true of the hero.

♦

Faith cannot move a single pebble, let alone a mountain. Such endeavours are always the result of human ingenuity, which is exclusively the result of mindful thought, not mindless faith.

♦

A true sceptic cannot be told what to think, because they have taught themselves how to think.

♦

Figure out how far you will go to protect and serve your beliefs and you will discover to what extent your behaviour is manipulated by your emotions.

♦

The search for knowledge and truth is one of the only journeys in life for which there should be no destination.

♦

Imagination is healthy until you begin to mistake it for reality.

◆

I cannot disprove the existence of a creator, but does that mean I should believe? You cannot prove the existence of a creator, so does that mean you should believe? To both questions the answer is, in my opinion, no.

◆

Too many people are too quick to kill and die for their beliefs and too slow to examine them. I think once we reverse this insanity the world will be a much more peaceful place.

◆

It is usually the stupid who view themselves as intelligent and the intelligent who view themselves as stupid.

◆

Evil is a myth, but error is a reality. The sooner we stop mistaking error for evil, the sooner we will stop demonizing and begin rectifying the problems that ail our species.

◆

I am joyfully plagued with doubts and I wouldn't have it any other way. For my doubts breed questions and the more questions I have, the humbler I become.

◆

Life has a way of kicking us to the ground and when it does, we have two choices, kneel and pray, or get back up, think and fight with every cognitive resource at our disposal. We can succumb to pain or we can use it as fuel for life and growth. It is all about choice. God is a cop-out, a declaration of defeat and we can no longer afford to admit defeat, we can no longer let our pain impact on the survival of our species. We all bear the burden of furthering the next generations and in carrying such a heavy burden, we can become self-indulgent, selfish and fearful, but we must never give up, we must not falter and fall to faith. We must persevere.

◆

A society that makes it a social offence to criticise religious beliefs and at the same time makes it a norm to attack non-belief, leads to the protection and veneration of stupidity. This naturally results in a society in which the stupid rule over the intelligent.

◆

If you cannot manage to move beyond your own egocentric beliefs about life, love and truth, how will you ever truly love another, other than yourself?

◆

Beliefs, generally speaking, are mindlessly inherited, whilst critical thinking is tirelessly and independently achieved.

◆

It is more important, in my opinion, to address the errors of the multitude, than to merely focus on the opinions of an enlightened minority.

◆

How can we build a free and peaceful future if we continue to remain slaves to a brutal past?

◆

1. Nothing is a coincidence.
2. A lack of coincidence implies coordination.
3. Therefore, such coordination requires an overarching mind/consciousness.
4. Without proof of this mind, which we do not have, we are left with the probable existence of coincidences.
5. Therefore coincidences probably do happen; at the very least, we lack the evidence for the first proposition.

◆

The more we believe, the less we learn and the less we learn, the slower we advance. Conversely, the less we believe, the more we learn and the more we learn, the faster we advance.

◆

The more you believe, the more you distort reality to conform with your beliefs.

◆

There is nothing so uninspired and profane, so dangerous and deranged, as a believing population. Such a population doesn't think, it merely believes and follows, regardless of who is leading it. For this reason, an emotionally driven and unthinking population is the tyrant's greatest asset.

◆

It's certainly possible that a closed mind doesn't see things as they really are, but as they want them to be.

◆

The mind of the believer is like the paranoid inhabitant of a dark and dank basement. It has locked itself in and covered every possible crack and crevice that may shed light into this gloomy and festering habitat. Should someone come along and offer to open a window or clean up, the believer will often become agitated and in drastic cases, they may even employ violence to prevent any further attempts to open their shady room to the light.

♦

My faith in the human race is but one small degree above my faith in God.

♦

Your beliefs are a lot like buttons. Now, if someone as simple as myself can push them and get you to react, what do you think a cunning politician could do with them?

♦

I don't profess to know the truth; all I assert, with some confidence, is that you don't either.

♦

Scepticism is healthy as long as it is employed in every direction and tempered with reason. That is to say, if you simply employ scepticism to protect your established beliefs, you are not an intelligent sceptic, but a blind and desperate believer.

♦

I think morality is subject to time and space and is therefore evolutionary in nature. What was considered moral and immoral at various points in history has changed over time and what is presently considered moral in one society, may not be so in another. If this argument is acceptable, then it is also fair to say that many animals are moral creatures too, as morals according this line of thinking, are simply a set of rules agreed upon by social creatures, who share a given environment, an environment that also dictates morality, at least to a degree.

♦

Thought is what separates us from the brute. Therefore, any religion or fixed system of beliefs that would seek to subtract the individual from the process of thought represents a system by which that disenfranchised human being is turned into a brute.

♦

The attainment of truth, whatever that may be or mean, might well be an impossible task, but it is, in my opinion, certainly worth aiming for.

◆

As most cognitive psychologists hold, our thoughts dictate our emotions and feelings, so if one could change thoughts that cause one to experience unnecessary grief, guilt, self-loathing, anguish, paranoia, etc, that person could develop a healthier and happier psyche. But how can one change these thoughts if they are fixed in place by emotionally driven and tradition-protected beliefs? If we could only let go of our beliefs and dethrone the traditions which have shielded these beliefs from rational inquiry, we may just create a more fluid cognitive platform in the mind, which could lead to a healthier state of mind, not only for the individual, but for the society as a whole.

◆

You are foolish if faith is your fuel, credulity your crutch and evidence your enemy.

◆

Because men and women's brains are different, both genders exhibit skills and intelligences in different areas of life. For this reason, if we oppress one of the genders, we effectively cut the potential of our species in half.

◆

Faith is merely credulity with bells and whistles and credulity is only capale of producing nothing but the sum of its own parts.

◆

Most of us are raised to believe that it is important to be polite and to a limited extent, I think this is a good thing, but the scope of this word is determined by the society and as such, politeness can become a tool for perpetuating insanity. For example, a polite person doesn't criticise another person's religion, no matter how dangerous or absurd, they don't seek to disrupt the political status quo, regardless of how inhumane and unjust it might be, and they do not discuss contentious matters in public forums, even though such matters may be in need of discussion. Needless to say, I am not a polite person.

◆

I could be wrong, but when I look at the various political systems in our world, they all bear a striking resemblance to one another. Whether they be capitalist, communist or aristocracies, they all seem to thrive on the collective ignorance of the masses and their lifeblood appears to be social inequality.

◆

If no amount of evidence can get you to admit that your beliefs are possibly errant; then in my opinion, you have a psychological problem.

◆

If you are under the misguided notion that being an atheist automatically endows you with wisdom, character, intelligence and all the pretty things, I would urge you to reconsider. For such qualities are the result of hard and painful self-examination and work, not merely non-belief in a deity.

◆

Your beliefs make you the resident expert and the guest of honour, but the truth asks you kindly to sit at the back of the room, be quiet and listen. Is this why you fear the truth so much?

◆

Two of the most devastating weapons of mass destruction man has created have been money and myth.

◆

Nationalism is a religion. The God of nationalism is a phantom ideal, the scriptures are the laws, the hymns are national anthems and the prophets are the founding fathers. The priests are the politicians, the holy days are the national holidays and the flags are the emotion evoking idols, before which, believers prostrate themselves in fits of emotional idiocy. The churches are schools, the military, the crusaders and the true believers are the mindless xenophobes who have sacrificed their psychological sovereignty, only to have replaced it with an ill-gotten and ridiculous form of pride.

◆

To be a sceptic in a world full of believers is a hard thing to be. Scepticism is seen as a negative thing, but what is it to be a sceptic? We question, criticise and critique the beloved beliefs of our fellow human beings and this, they say, is a bad thing to do. Really? Shouldn't we encourage inquisitiveness in our children? How will they learn? Don't you think that we will advance quicker if we challenge and seek out holes in the current status quo? Where would we be without sceptics? Perhaps we would all still be cowering from thunderstorms in caves and beneath trees, to which we would be paying fruitless superstitious homage? Or maybe we would be burning and destroying those who disagree with our beliefs, as the Church and Mosques have enjoyed doing for the majority of their histories? But you say that we sceptics are selfish and rude. The sceptic is not a selfish person, but a selfless one. For the sceptic there is no rest, we cannot afford the decedent psychological luxuries occasioned by the certitudes of lazy and acquisitive belief and we are granted no fame, for everyone hates a sceptic. Having said all of this, I will be completely honest with you. I would rather be a hated sceptic, than a beloved and believing moron. I would rather think; I would rather live a life, in which I struggled, suffered and grew, than one that would relegate my mind to the vacuous vacancies of ill-gotten beliefs.

◆

A person can be born with a thousand talents, but if they employ those talents to the sole benefit of their pre-established beliefs, they have squandered them, in my opinion.

◆

If I were asked to describe Plato in a few words, I would say that he was a noble and intelligent fascist.

◆

When I say that we live in an insane world, what do I mean? I mean we live in a world in which the poor are imprisoned for stealing crumbs and the wealthy are worshipped for stealing estates. I mean, in the 21st century, we are still plagued by Bronze Age superstitions, despite the scientific and academic evidences against such primitive idiocy. I mean we are living in an idiocracy which has just emerged from the profanity of religious credulity and been seamlessly transferred to a secular celebrity, consumer and pop-culture based idiocy. Finally, many of us are still irrationally tribalistic, nationalistic and xenophobic, viewing our birthplace as something to be proud of, when the truth is it is merely a single location, on a single planet.

◆

Try not to embrace beliefs, but instead, place ideas on a scale from least possible to most probable. However, if you feel you cannot avoid embracing a belief, try doing so with only one hand; this will leave your other hand free to explore alternatives.

◆

Generally speaking, to hold onto your beliefs, you must be willing to let go of truth and to hold onto truth, you must be willing to let go of your beliefs. You cannot hold both in equal esteem, for when they come into conflict, which they frequently do; you will be forced to forsake one for the other. This is exactly why I am not a believer, because I love the truth, whatever it may well be.

◆

I find questions to be far more useful than beliefs.

◆

I am the one you have been trained to fear; the forbidden fruit that has laid waste entire theocracies. I am the anti-Christ, the anti-Muhammad and the anti-Krishna. I am the one who met Buddha along the road and killed him. I go by many names and express myself in a variety of forms. I am the source of humility, love, compassion and equality. I am the primary source of fuel for reason, wisdom, light and logic. I am the one who strikes fear into the hearts of all those who have forsaken me and I cause immeasurable dissonance in the minds of all those who call themselves religious. I have remained painfully patient, sitting in relative silence for millennia, plotting my uprising in the minds of the meek and through science and in secular societies my voice is only now beginning to be heard. I am the atheist's greatest ally and the theist's fiercest foe. I am curiosity…and I cannot be stopped.

THE BOOK OF HERESY

CHRISTIANITY AS UNTRUE MYTH

I BEG TO DIFFER WITH C.S. LEWIS, WHO WROTE: THE HEART OF CHRISTIANITY IS A MYTH WHICH IS ALSO A FACT.

The purpose of this essay is to provide the reader with a cursory understanding of not only what constitutes myth, for the purposes of analysis, but of how the narratives which form the basis of the Christian religion, fit into this category we call myth. First of all, myth, as distinct from mythology, refers to the body of traditional tales told by a given culture, or religious group. Mythology, on the other hand, connotes the theoretical study of that body of traditional tales, or myths. Quite often these terms are used interchangeably, and thus have become conflated to such a degree that one can use either term and be understood. To be perfectly accurate however, mythology, like any other "ology" refers to the study of myth.

In this essay, I will be employing the characteristics of myth, as laid out by one of the world's foremost scholars of classical mythology and classical literature, Professor Elizabeth Vandiver.[1] In her lecture series entitled, *Classical Mythology*, Prof Vandiver sets out a number of criteria for identifying myth. This essay will rest upon the six main criteria, described in Lecture Two of the series, and they are as follows:

1. Traditional Tale
2. Change over time
3. Set in the Extraordinary (remote) Past
4. Myths as True Accounts
5. Functions of Myth: Instruct, Explain, Justify, or Warn
6. Supernatural and/or, Divine orientation[2]

---

[1] http://www.goodreads.com/author/show/151655.Elizabeth_Vandiver; http://www.thegreatcourses.com/tgc/courses/course_detail.aspx?cid=243
[2] Professor Elizabeth Vandiver. Classical Mythology. Lecture 2: What is Myth? The Teaching Company. (2002).

I will analyse each of these elements and compare them to the myths which form the foundation of the Christian religion.

Before doing so however, it would be both useful and prudent, to briefly sketch out a distinction between stories that can be categorized as myths, as against other related and often overlapping categories of narratives, such as folk tales and legends.

Professor Vandiver distinguishes between these three categories, myth, legend and folk tale, by explaining that myths refer exclusively to narratives about gods, whereas legends involve traditional tales built upon historical facts and characters, to varying degrees. Folk tales are primarily focussed on entertainment and contain exaggerated characterizations of both people and animals, like Little Red Riding Hood or Goldilocks and the Three Bears, for example.[3]

Now that we have this clear distinction between these three categories of traditional tales, let us acknowledge that the lines between them can become blurred and that a traditional tale may involve one, two, or all three of these categories, interwoven in the one narrative, or collection of narratives. Such seems to be the case with Christian myths. On the one hand, we have historical characters like, Pontius Pilate, Emperor Tiberius, the Roman Governor of Syria, Quirinius, and possibly even Jesus himself, etc. And on the other, we have the very mythological narratives of the four anonymous gospel authors, who describe supernatural and divine events, set on the backdrop of real history, making these stories a combination of both myth and legend.

1. THE TRADITIONAL TALE

According to Professor Vandiver, a traditional tale which qualifies as a myth can only be in the form of a narrative. It cannot be a series of lectures, dot point instructions, a recipe, etc., it must be a tale. In other words, if it is not a story, it is not a myth. Further, according to Professor Vandiver, the original author(s) of the tale are authors who cannot

---

[3]Ibid.

be identified. In other words; the author of a myth is someone who is unknowable, they are and always remain, anonymous.[4]

Without spending too much time and space on such a self-evident element of myth, as it relates to the Christian story, let us just say that the story of Jesus, as relayed by the anonymous authors of the gospels, is just that, a story. It follows a narrative formula, describing his birth, life, death, and resurrection in a narrative form. Also as alluded to above, the authors of the original Gospel tales are anonymous, or more accurately speaking, pseudonymous (falsely attributed).[5] I think that is all that needs to be said on this criterion.

So already, we have one limb of Professor Vandiver's definition of myth satisfied for the purposes of this comparative investigation. The story of Jesus is one which follows a narrative scheme and was created by unknown and unknowable authors.

2. CHANGE OVER TIME

The second element in Vandiver's list of criteria is change over time. Like the beings that created and propagated these tales, myths almost invariably change over time. Here we need to draw one of the first distinctions, or seemingly distinct characteristics of Christian mythology, as opposed to Classical and other ancient mythologies. In pre-literate societies, and even within literate ones, the details of mythological tales tend to develop and change with time. Of course, in pre-literate societies, the details of a given myth would generally change to a greater degree, than in literate ones, for when we write something down; the details become fixed, well, to a relative degree anyway. Take the myth of the Egyptian God Osiris, for example. Even though Egypt was a literate or, semi-literate society, various details of the myth of the death of Osiris, changed over time.

---

[4]Ibid.
[5]Bart D. Ehrman. Peter, Paul and Mary Magdalene: The Followers of Jesus in History and Legend. (2006). Oxford University Press. pp. 8–10; John Barton and John Muddiman. The Oxford *Bible* Commentary. Oxford University Press. (2001). p. 886; Paul. J. Achtemeier. Harper-Collins *Bible* Dictionary Revised Edition. Harper Collins, (1989). p. 661; Bart D Ehrman. Jesus Interrupted. Harper Collins Publishers. (2005) Pg. 111.

In one of the more popular versions of the myth, Osiris is tricked by his evil brother Set, into laying in a coffin, which his evil brother nails shut and castes into the Nile, or ocean. Following this, Isis, the sister-wife of Osiris, goes in search for her husband, and eventually finds him in a Syrian city called, Byblos, within an Erica tree, that has grown up around his coffin. Isis brings her husband's body back to Egypt where Set, who was hunting by the moonlight, discovers his brother is back in Egypt. Upon discovering this, Set scatters his bones across Egypt, in a bid to finish his brother off once and for all.

Many of the details of this myth changed over time as the society developed. Some versions of the myth relate that Osiris was mutilated and cut into pieces by his brother Set, as opposed to the earlier accounts which described Set as merely scattering the bones of his dead brother Osiris. Even the number of pieces varied, ranging from fourteen, up to forty-two, the number of administrative regions (Nomes) throughout most of the Dynastic period of ancient Egypt.

With regards to the fluid nature of the mythology surrounding Osiris' death, *The Cambridge Ancient History* Series, Volume 1, relates:

The older sources are less explicit. According to the Pyramid Texts Set struck his brother down in Nedyt, wherever that may be, and on the British Museum Stela, No. 797, a late production, but based on documents of the Pyramid Age, Osiris is represented as having been drowned.[6]

Even the nature of Osiris himself was subject to change over time. Edward I. Bleiburg, Associate Curator of Egyptian art, at Brooklyn Museum tells us that Osiris was not originally seen as a positive character, in fact, within the very ancient pyramid texts he was depicted as a dog or with a jackal head and that this form and his very nature, changed over time.[7]

From this example, we observe that myth is subject to change over time and if one is to survey the corpus of Classical and other ancient mythologies, it becomes evident that such change is common, in both

---

[6]J.B. Bury, S.A. Cook & F.A. Adcock. The Cambridge Ancient History. Vol. 1: Egypt and Babylonia - To 1580 BCE. Cambridge University Press (1928). p. 332.
[7]Edward I. Bleiburg. World Eras Volume 5: Ancient Egypt. 2615-332 BCE. Gale Group. (2002) p. 243.

literate and pre-literate cultures. Speaking on the subject of change over time within Classical mythology, the two Oxford Emeritus Professors, Mark Morford and Robert Lenardon, say that the beauty of classical myths is that they are:

"...*retold and reinterpreted with infinite variations, repeatedly and continuously*..."[8]

Ok, so ancient and Classical myths change over time, but the myth of Christ hasn't changed. Or, has it?

CHRISTIAN MYTHS - CHANGE OVER TIME

We have, as a result of various socio-political factors, only four official sources for the myths surrounding the birth, life, death and resurrection of Jesus Christ. Four pseudepigraphical (falsely named) works called; The Gospel "According to Mark," which the majority of modern scholars agree, was the earliest of the four;[9] The Gospel "According to Matthew," The Gospel "According to Luke," and The Gospel "According to John." These are our primary sources for the myths surrounding the alleged life of Jesus Christ. This being the case, we need to briefly examine the origins and development of these manuscripts, to ascertain whether or not the Christian myths have changed over time. How were the stories in these Gospels originally transmitted? Who told them? And where can we find evidence of change over time? These are the issues we need to address.

According to Professor of *New Testament* Studies, Bart D. Ehrman, the Gospels were originally written well after the date of the alleged events they describe. For decades, the stories contained within these Gospels were transmitted via oral tradition, that is, by word of mouth.[10]

Theologians, Gregory A. Boyd and Paul R. Eddy, in their book, *Lord or Legend*, concur with Ehrman's majority opinion on the issue

---

[8]Mark P.O. Morford & Robert J. Lenardon. Classical Mythology. Oxford University Press (2003).Preface xiii–xiv.
[9]John Barton & John Muddiman. The Oxford *Bible* Commentary. Oxford University Press (2007). p. 886.
[10]Bart D. Ehrman. Jesus Interrupted. Harper Collins (2005). p. 144.

and add that first century Jewish culture was dominated by what scholars refer to as an "orally dominant" culture, with most of the population illiterate and therefore dependent upon the oral transmission of history. This is why Boyd and Eddy follow the scholarly consensus on the issue of the Gospels early oral origins.[11]

As mentioned, those myths which were communicated by word of mouth, tended to be more prone to change and variation, generally speaking, than those fixed on paper, parchment, papyri, or stone. Evidence of this can be seen in the variations and contradictions in the narratives, found in and between the four official Gospels of the *New Testament*.

Mark, as mentioned, was the earliest of the four Gospels and contains no details of Jesus' miraculous conception, virgin birth, flight to Egypt, nor any event prior to Jesus' baptism at around 30 years of age. Before this time, Mark says nothing about Jesus' life (see Mark 1). The later Gospel of Matthew, does contain a narrative of Jesus' miraculous conception (Matthew 1:18-2:11), his virgin-birth (Matthew 1:18-23), his flight to Egypt (Matthew 2:13-15), and other miraculous and mundane events from Jesus' youth, up until the age of twelve, anyway. Luke, the next in the series, chronologically speaking, also describes Jesus' miraculous conception, his virgin birth, but it also contains quite a few key contradictions in relation to Matthew's version of events. Here is a short list of some of them:

1. Where did Joseph and Mary live before Jesus was born?
λ   Luke 2:4 – City of Nazareth in Galilee.
λ   Matthew 1 – Bethlehem.

2. Where was Jesus born?
λ   Luke 2:7 – Manger (stable)
λ   Matthew 2:11 - House

3. When was the divine announcement of Jesus' birth?
λ   Matthew 1:18-21 – After conception
λ   Luke 1:26-31 – Before conception

---

[11]Gregory A. Boyd & Paul Rhodes. Lord or Legend? Wrestling with the Jesus Dilemma. Baker Books. (2007). p. 65.

4. To whom was the divine announcement made?
λ   Matthew 1:20 – Joseph
λ   Luke 1:28 - Mary

5. What happened when Jesus was born?
λ   Luke 2:13-14 – Angels sang praises to God.
λ   Matthew 2:1-9 – A star appeared and stood in the heavens above him

6. Who visited baby Jesus?
λ   Matthew 2:1-11 – Wise men (Astrologers) from the East.
λ   Luke 2:8-20 – Shepherds from a neighbouring field.

7. Was Jesus in danger of being killed by King Herod?
λ   Matthew – Yes.
λ   Luke – No.

8. Did King Herod slaughter the children of Bethlehem?
λ   Matthew – Yes.
λ   Luke – No.

9. Did Jesus' parents take him in his infancy to Egypt?
λ   Matthew 2:13-15 – Yes.
λ   Luke 2:22-52 – No. (they stayed in Palestine)

10. What was God's mode of communication?
λ   Matthew 1:20, 2:12-13, 19, 22 – Dreams.
λ   Luke 1:11, 26, 2:9 – Angels

11. Did Joseph and Mary know of their Son's divine nature?
λ   Matthew 1:18-21 and Luke 1:28-35 – Yes
λ   Luke 2:48-50 – No

These are only the variations between Luke and Matthew regarding Jesus' early life. If we were to look at the total number of contradictions and variations within the narratives of the four Gospels, in their entirety, we would find many more, not to mention the variations between the manuscripts of the *New Testament*.

Another interesting discrepancy between the birth narratives we have today, versus a much older second century one, can be witnessed within the writings of the second century church father and apologist, Justin Martyr, who described Jesus' birth as having taken place in a cave.[12]

So, the myths of the Christians changed during the formative years of the religion, possibly due to the fact that their transmission was largely oral in nature. But did it continue to change after it had been written down? The answer to this question is; yes it did. Some of the myths found within the official Gospels were later interpolations (additions), added to the pre-existing narratives, centuries after they had been written down.

One of the most famous Christian tales found within the Gospel of John, that of the woman taken in adultery, is an example of this change over time.

According to the majority of *Bible* scholars, the story of the woman taken in adultery was added to the Gospel narrative centuries later.[13] Within all of the earliest and most reliable manuscripts relating to John, this story makes no appearance.[14] The earliest manuscript (*Latin Codex Bezae*) to contain the story dates from around the late fourth, to the early fifth centuries, hundreds of years after the Gospel's original production. Prior to this, there was no mention of the story within any of the earliest and most reliable Eastern manuscripts, those being, the *Codex Sinaiticus*, the *Codex Vaticanus* or the *Codex Alexandrinus*, nor in the earliest papyri, that constitute the foundations of the Gospel of John, known as *P 66* and *P 75*. As mentioned, the story first makes an appearance within the Western, or Latin Codices, which many biblical scholars agree, are later and less reliable than their Eastern counterparts.[15]

---

[12]Ante-Nicene Fathers: Vol. 1: The Apostolic Fathers with Justin Martyr and Irenaeus; Against Heresies, Book 3. Philip Schaff. Grand Rapids. MI: Christian Classics Ethereal Library. (1885). p. 383.

[13]Paul. J. Achtemeier. Harper-Collins *Bible* Dictionary Revised Edition. Harper Collins, (1989). p. 535.

[14]Carl R. Holladay. A Critical Introduction to the *New Testament*. Abingdon Press. (2005). p. 281.

[15]Bart D Ehrman. Misquoting Jesus. Harper-San Francisco. (2005). p. 72.

The Biblical scholar, James M. Robinson, in his work, *The Gospel of Jesus: A Historical Search for the Original Good News* agrees that this story was not part of the original *New Testament* and that the oldest and best manuscripts do not contain it. Robinson, as with the majority of textual scholars, demonstrates with solid evidence, that this story was added much later by scribes. The reason for its popularity, Robinson says, is that it ended up in the medieval manuscripts used by the King James translators and so became a part of the textual tradition. Robinson also informs us that most modern translations of the *Bible* either leave it out or indicate in some way that it is not a part of the original text.[16]

The Gospel of John itself, being the latest of the four Gospels to have been written,[17] is also of interest to us here, because the very nature of Jesus was updated and advanced from the time of the composition of the earlier gospels. In John's narrative, Jesus has the highest level of Christology (divinity), of the four gospels. Within the Synoptic Gospels (Mark, Matthew and Luke) Jesus is depicted as the Son of God, whereas the author of John's Gospel, implied that Jesus was God, thereby advancing his divine status.

John emphasized Jesus' Cosmic mission, illustrated by Jesus saying things like; *my kingdom is not of this world* (see John 18:36), and by identifying himself as *I am* (see John 8:58), which was Yahweh's ("God's") title in the *Old Testament* (see Exodus 3:14). In other words, John, seemed to be implying that Jesus was not just a messenger, or a prophet, or a Jewish messiah, or even the mere son of God, but God himself. In John's Gospel, Jesus openly describes himself as having *come down from heaven* (see John 6:51). Such open declarations of divinity are in stark contrast to the earlier Gospels, like Mark, for instance, in which emphasis is placed on Jesus' human qualities.

---

[16]James M. Robinson. The Gospel of Jesus: A Historical Search for the Original Good News. Harper Collins, (2005). p. 65.

[17]John Barton & John Muddiman. The Oxford *Bible* Commentary. Oxford University Press (2007) p. 973; Ismo Dunderberg. The Beloved Disciple in Conflict. Oxford University Press. (2006); p. 1, 117 &174; Louis A. Ruprecht Jr. The Tragic Gospel: How John Corrupted the Heart of Christianity. John Wiley and Sons. (2008). p. 34.

A final example of Scriptural change over time, within the Christian myths, relates to the final twelve versus of Mark, which has been established beyond a reasonable doubt, to have been a later interpolation.[18] The original ending of Mark's Gospel, finishes with the resurrected Jesus telling some of his female followers to go and tell everyone he has been resurrected, at which point, they run away in terror, and tell no one (Mark 16:8). This narrative was eventually expanded and changed over time to include Jesus meeting up with his disciples again and promising them that, those who believe in him will be able to work miracles in his name, like handling deadly snakes safely, drinking deadly poisons with no ill-effect, and so on (Mark 16:17-18).

With regards to the interpolated ending of Mark's Gospel, the late great, Bruce Metzger, *Bible* scholar and Senior Editor of the NRSV *Bible*, remarked:

> *Four endings of the Gospel according to Mark are current in the manuscripts. (1) The last twelve verses of the commonly received text of Mark are absent from the two oldest Greek manuscripts, from the Old Latin codex Bobiensis, the Sinaitic Syriac manuscript, about one hundred Armenian manuscripts, and the two oldest Georgian manuscripts (written A.D. 897 and A.D. 913). Clement of Alexandria and Origen show no knowledge of the existence of these verses; furthermore Eusebius and Jerome attest that the passage was absent from almost all Greek copies of Mark known to them. The original form of the Eusebian sections (drawn up by Ammonius) makes no provision for numbering sections of the text after 16:8. Not a few manuscripts which contain the passage have scribal notes stating that older Greek copies lack it, and in other witnesses the passage is marked with asterisks or obeli, the conventional signs used by copyists to indicate a spurious addition to a document.*[19]

For the sake of brevity, I have forgone discussions on the Apocryphal (unofficial) texts, along with the various interpretations of Christ,

---

[18]Joel F. Williams. Literary Approaches to the End of Mark's Gospel. Journal of the Evangelical Theological Society. 42.1 (1999).

[19]Bruce Metzger, A Textual Commentary on the Greek *New Testament* . Stuttgart, (1971). pp. 122, 126.

which developed and changed over the span of Christian history, in and between the various denominations of Christendom. If, however, one were to add these excluded versions of the Christ myth to the investigation at hand, much more weight would be added to the argument that the Christian myth has changed over time.

Even though Christianity was and still is, a "religion of the book", so to speak, having written its myths down relatively quickly, this did not prevent those myths from being altered over time, thereby establishing this element of Professor Vandiver's definition of myth.

3. SET IN THE (REMOTE) PAST

With regards to this limb, Professor Vandiver informs us that myths are frequently set in the remote past and that, we never have myths that describe currents times.[20]

We need to establish what exactly constitutes the remote past, and what the likely purpose would be for setting a myth in the remote past.

The word, "remote", as it relates to the term, "remote past", is defined by the World English Dictionary, as being: *distant in time*[21].

This is a rather vague definition and doesn't really help us define what Professor Vandiver meant when she said; a myth is often set in the remote past. The etymological root of the word, remote, may be of more assistance. The English word "remote", stems from the Latin, *remotus*, being the past participle of the English word, "remove".[22] So, the remote past is a time in the past which is removed from the present. If one accepts this definition of the "remote past", then we could say that myths are often set in a time in the past, which is removed from the present. This makes sense when we look at the creation myths of the Egyptians, Babylonians, Hebrews, and many other cultures, it also fits the descriptions of myths such as Hercules/Herakles,

---

[20]Professor Elizabeth Vandiver. Classical Mythology. Lecture 2: What is Myth? The Teaching Company. (2002).
[21]Collins English Dictionary - Complete & Unabridged 10th Edition 2009 © William Collins Sons & Co. Ltd. 1979, 1986 © HarperCollins Publishers 1998, 2000, 2003, 2005, 2006, 2007, 2009; cited at: http://dictionary.reference.com/browse/remote
[22]Ibid.

and his twelve labours, Demeter and Persephone, Osiris and Isis, and even Noah and his Ark, all being set hundreds and sometimes thousands of years from the time they were transmitted.

But the Christian myth was written down just over half a century after the purported events were claimed to have transpired. So is this shorter span of time long enough to qualify as, "remote"? Keep in mind our definition; a time removed from the present. To provide some context here, we should acknowledge that what qualified for the remote past 2,000 years ago is different from what would sufficiently describe the remote past, today. The reason for this difference is that today and over the last few centuries, there has been a proliferation of chroniclers and chronicles. Since the advent of Gutenberg's printing-press in the fifteenth century, history has been increasingly and more accurately documented, as a result of the increased media capacity of the modern era. Thus, fifty years ago, during the 1960's, would not be considered the remote past, as we are not removed from it. We have video footage, newspaper archives, books, poems, and a plethora of various forms of media that serve to keep us in touch with that time. 2,000 years ago however, this was not the case.

One of the reasons we should distinguish between what constituted the remote past 2,000 years ago, from what we would consider the remote past, today, is that literacy rates 2,000 years ago were much lower than they are today. This means that there were less people to record history or keep people in touch with the past, during the first part of the first century, especially in such a rustic and remote location as Palestine.

According to Ehrman, illiteracy was widespread throughout the Roman Empire, with about 10% of the entire population able to read and write, and this 10%, according to Ehrman, was the wealthy class or else the slaves of the wealthy, who were trained in these skills for the benefit of their masters[23]

Naturally, such extreme illiteracy, coupled with the lack of media technology, meant that there was comparatively less literature and means of chronicling events, resulting in a situation, in which many

---

[23]Bart D. Ehrman. Jesus Interrupted. Harper Collins (2005). p. 105.

things would go unrecorded, especially outside of the major metropolises of the Roman Empire.

This brings us to an additional aspect of remoteness. The myths described in the Gospels were set, not only in the remote past, but in a remote location. Unlike many of the Classical myths, which described a dreamlike world, almost entirely dominated by supernatural forces, events and people, the Christian myth localized its supernaturalism around a small insignificant figure who, lived in a small insignificant region, at a real definable point in history. For this reason, many scholars refer to the stories about Jesus as, legends, rather than myths. They are composed of unreal events, superimposed onto an historical canvass. Despite the legendary components of the Christian narratives, they also contain many mythical aspects as well, remembering that a traditional tale can contain elements of legend, myth and folk-tale, all combined. The myth underscoring the Christian religion is one such tale, as we have seen and will see; it contains all the elements which comprise a myth, according to Professor Vandiver's definition.

Returning to the issue of the remoteness of the location of the Christ myth, apologists love to hide behind this when sceptical inquirers come storming in with demands, not only for proof of Jesus' earthly existence, but for the miracles which he was alleged to have performed and the supernatural events surrounding his birth, life and death. Apologists often argue that Jesus' contemporaries did not mention him in their vast and voluminous chronicles, because he was an insignificant figure, living in an insignificant region of the empire. He was, in other words; a nobody from nowhere.

Regarding Jesus' obscurity, Ehrman says:

> *What do Greek and Roman sources have to say about Jesus? Or to make the question more pointed: if Jesus lived and died in the first century (death around 30 CE), what do the Greek and Roman sources from his own day through the end of the century (say, the year 100) have to say about him? The answer is breathtaking. They have absolutely nothing to say about him. He is never discussed, challenged, attacked, maligned, or talked about in any way in any surviving pagan source of the period. There are no birth records, accounts of his*

trial and death, reflections on his significance, or disputes about his teachings. In fact, his name is never mentioned once in any pagan source. And we have a lot of Greek and Roman sources from the period: religious scholars, historians, philosophers, poets, natural scientists; we have thousands of private letters; we have inscriptions placed on buildings in public places. In no first-century Greek or Roman (pagan) source is Jesus mentioned.[24]

The popular apologetic opinion on this issue is that Jesus was an insignificant figure of his time, whom the great recorders and commentators would have had no reason to record. One of the most popular apologetic websites on the internet, *Tektonics*, says:

As far as the historians of the day were concerned, he was just a 'blip' on the screen.[25]

So, let us now look briefly at a possible reason why mythographers seemed to always employ the devise of remoteness to their tales. Why did they set their tales in the remote past, and in the Christian's case, in a remote region of the empire, far back in time enough to also be considered remote?

Looking at the issue critically and somewhat sceptically, it is likely that these tale-tellers set their fictitious stories in the remote past and in remote locations for the sake of apology (defence). By doing so, they could defend the alleged truth of these tales within the obscurity afforded by a lack of witness.

Imagine if someone was to tell you that two years ago, the earth was covered with a great flood and that a 600 year old man, was given a weeks' notice to build a giant boat, upon which, he was told to take two of every kind of animal, from bears to kangaroos, from grasshoppers to snakes? Following this, the storyteller claims that this 600 year old man succeeded in achieving this miraculous task and subsequently the flood covered the earth, and only he, his family and the animals were saved.

---

[24]Ibid. p. 148.
[25]http://www.tektonics.org/qt/remslist.html

First of all, you were alive two years ago and can probably remember most of the events of that time. Surely, you would remember a global flood, or would have not been around to hear the storyteller's tale! Furthermore, you would question the storyteller with regards to the age of the man. Humans do not live this long, let alone build giant boats at such an advanced age. Also, you may, with your knowledge of geography, see the ridiculous nature of the claim made by the storyteller that, this 600 year old man managed to herd two of every animal on the earth, onto this ark, in a week no less. You even may wonder how on earth, he could have built the kinds of refrigeration and heating systems, required to keep the polar bears cool and the tropical animals warm. Ultimately, you would come to the conclusion that, this storyteller is not telling the truth and that what you are hearing is fiction.

But what if, as a storyteller, you localized your myth? You could subtract the universal dreamlike state of the earth and replace it with a more localized supernatural event, one which could not be easily observed and thus, remain safe from refutation? You could set the tale as far back in time as necessary, to separate the audience from the time and place of the tale. You could say that the miracles occurred around one little obscure man, a "blip on the screen," in an equally small and obscure location. This way, your tale would be relatively safe from immediate dismissal and refutation. Finally, you could initially relay it to the meek, unlearned, the illiterate masses, who are prone to credulity, whose hopes can be fanned by the flagrant fantasies, those who wouldn't know who Pontius Pilate was, or that Quirinius could not have been governor of Syria at the same time as Herod the Great's rule. You could sell your tale, not only upon the grounds of remoteness, as it applies to both the location and the obscurity of a single insignificant figure, but also, upon the intellectual remoteness of your audience. This is precisely how I see the element of remoteness, as it applies to the development and propagation of the Christian myth.

4. MYTHS ARE TRUE

C.S. Lewis studied many of the ancient pre-Christian myths and seeing a wealth of parallels to the later Christian myths, he was of the opinion that Christianity, although being founded upon myths that were, in some cases, identical to earlier ones and, unlike its earlier antecedents, was "true myth." But what was it that led C.S. Lewis to form this conclusion? C.S. Lewis was a devout Christian, something he, with his astounding wit and prized intelligence could not seem to fathom.

Discussing this aspect of myth, Professor Vandiver says that within the society or the religion, myths present themselves as true accounts of the past and that only objective observers view these fantastic and superstitious tales as being fictitious myth.[26] Those within the matrix of the belief system see such tales as true accounts of the past. Hercules' twelve labours, the tales of Asclepius' magic healing powers, Persephone and Demeter's trials and separation, all these were believed by those within the relevant cultures, to have been actual accounts of the past or, in the words of C.S. Lewis, "True Myth".

Such is the case not only with these classical religions and Christianity, but almost all religions, especially the Abrahamic ones, which have attempted to weave myth into the very fabric of history. Ask a true-believing Christian whether or not they believe the Gospels describe real history and they may respond with any of the following remarks:

> ...historicity, however, should be determined not by what we think possible or likely, but by the antiquity and reliability of the evidence. As we shall see, as far back as we can trace, Jesus was known and remembered as one who had extraordinary powers.[27]
> ~Father Raymond E. Brown (Catholic *Bible* Scholar)

> The Gospels follow no order in recording the acts and miracles of Jesus, and the matter is not, after all, of much importance. If a

---

[26]Professor Elizabeth Vandiver. Classical Mythology. Lecture 2: What is Myth? The Teaching Company. (2002).
[27]Michael J. Wilkins & J. P. Moreland. Jesus Under Fire. Zondervan Publishing House. (1995). p. 5.

difficulty arises in regard to the Holy Scripture and we cannot solve it, we must just let it alone.[28]

~Martin Luther (Founder of the Protestant Church)

We look at the New Testament documents and, yes, they have an agenda: they're affirming that Jesus is the Messiah, the Son of God. But they also make all kinds of statements that can be evaluated. Are they culturally accurate? Are they true to what we know from other historical sources? Were they written in a time and place that has proximity to Jesus' life? The answers are yes.[29]

~Craig A. Evans (*Bible* Scholar – Professor of *New Testament* Studies)

Now, ask a non-Christian this same question and you will may hear any of the following kinds of remarks:

The prominence, therefore, of the sun and stars in the Gospel story tends to show that Jesus is an astrological rather than a historical character. That the time of his birth, his death, and supposed resurrection is not verifiable is generally admitted. This uncertainty robs the story of Jesus, to an extent at least, of the atmosphere of reality[30].

~M.M Mangasarian (Theologian turned Freethinker)

It is, however, not difficult to account for the credit that was given to the story of Jesus Christ being the Son of God. He was born when the heathen mythology had still some fashion and repute in the world, and that mythology had prepared the people for the belief of such a story. Almost all the extraordinary men that lived under the heathen mythology were reputed to be the sons of some of their gods. It was not a new thing at that time to believe a man to have been celestially

---

[28]Albert Schweitzer. The Quest of the Historical Jesus. Adam and Charles Black. (1911). p. 13.

[29]Lee Strobel. The Case for the Real Jesus. Zondervan. (2007). p. 33.

[30]M.M. Mangasarian. The Truth About Jesus. Is He a Myth? Independent Religious Society. (1909). pp. 37–38.

begotten; the intercourse of gods with women was then a matter of familiar opinion.[31]

~Thomas Paine (Philosopher)

The Jesus of the New Testament is the Christ of Christianity. The Jesus of the New Testament is a supernatural being. He is, like the Christ, a myth. He is the Christ myth.[32]

~John E. Remsburg (Rationalist)

It all comes down to whether a person believes it to be true, or not. In other words, it is all biased conjecture, occasioned by personal experience and subjective bias. Non-Christians call it myth, and in my biased opinion, should be forgiven for doing so, as people are not born of ghosts and virgins, they cannot walk on water, or even turn that water into wine. They do not return from the dead and they certainly do not float into outer-space, well not in my experience, or anyone else's I know. Christians on the other hand, take it on faith that these things happened in an isolated region, in a time long ago, and to a person who was otherwise a "blip" on the radar; a figure whose remoteness has served to spawn justified criticism and the credulous defence of the believer.

5. FUNCTION OF MYTH

Myths, according to Professor Vandiver, will often serve one or more of the following functions within a given culture, or society. They will explain (Explanatory/Etiological Myths), warn (Warning Myths), instruct (Instructive Myths) or they will justify (Justification/Charter Myths).[33] Let us now look at how this aspect of myth applies to Christianity.

Christian Myth as Explanatory

The Christian myth, notwithstanding the first few verses of the Gospel of John (see John 1:1-5) is not an etiological myth in its own

---

[31]Thomas Paine. The Age of Reason. (1796). pp. 14–15.
[32]John E. Remsburg. The Christ. The Truth Seeker Company. Preface p. 9.
[33]Ibid.

right, yet it was built both exoterically and later, esoterically, upon a portion of the Hebrew etiological myth found in the book of Genesis (see Genesis 2 &3: *The Fall of Man*).

In the book of Genesis we are told that the human condition, specifically relating to the existence of evil, sin, suffering and death, stems from Adam's (man's) "original sin," although the *Old Testament* does not expressly support the doctrine of original sin, it being a sin which is universal and inherent, yet a few passages throughout the *Old Testament*, aside from those in Genesis 3, may be seen as implying it (see Jeremiah. 5:23; 17:9-10; Ezekiel. 36:26 and Isaiah. 29:13). Naturally, the doctrine of original sin and the story of the Fall of Man are important etiological myths for Christians, as their entire foundation rests upon them.

Jesus, we are told, was born the sinless son of Yahweh, the great saviour and redeemer, sent by Yahweh to save and redeem his creation in the face of a sinful existence, which stems from the initial "fall of man." Without the original Hebrew etiological myth found in Genesis, the Christ myth would make no sense. Why would we need a redeemer if we had not fallen? Thus, we are begged to believe that Jesus is the yin to Adam's yang, and his virgin mother, Mary, the *most blessed female* (Luke 1:28) in place of Eve, the first woman to be cursed by Yahweh (Genesis 3:16). In the words of the second century church father, Irenaeus:

As Eve was seduced by the word of an angel and so fled from God after disobeying his word, Mary in her turn was given the good news by the word of an angel, and bore God in obedience to his word. As Eve was seduced into disobedience to God, so Mary was persuaded into obedience to God; thus the Virgin Mary became the advocate of the virgin Eve. Christ gathered all things into one, by gathering them into himself. He declared war against our enemy, crushed him who at the beginning had taken us captive in Adam, and trampled on his head, in accordance with God's words to the serpent in Genesis: I will put enmity between you and the woman, and between your seed and her seed; he shall lie in wait for your head, and you shall lie in wait for his heel...That is why the Lord proclaims himself the Son of Man, the one who renews in himself that first man from whom the race born of

woman was formed; as by a man's defeat our race fell into the bondage of death, so by a man's victory we were to rise again to life.[34]

Theologians and church fathers like Irenaeus, have even gone so
far as to attempt to tie Jesus directly into a part of the Hebrew's Genesis myth, claiming that he was mentioned, albeit esoterically, by the
author, Moses, a matter which carries insurmountable evidentiary
problems.

This alleged reference to Christ has been dubbed, *The Proto-Evan-
gelium* and is asserted to apply to the following passage in the book of
Genesis:

And I will put enmity between thee and the woman, and between
thy seed and her seed; it shall bruise thy head, and thou shalt bruise
his heel.

~ Genesis 3:15

The verse above relates to the talking snake in the magical Garden
of Eden that tempted Eve, who in turn tempted Adam, to eat the fruit
of the Tree of Knowledge, thereby condemning our species to a life of
misery and suffering, from which, Christians believe, Jesus came to redeem us. So, we have the charter myth of the Fall of Man, which serves
to explain the presence of suffering, hardship and ultimately human
mortality, and we have the Christian myth, later being tied into that
myth as a kind of promise, or "get out of jail (mortality) free card", attempting to offer hope in the face of this fallen state of affairs. This is
one of the ways Christianity has attempted to further entrench itself
within the etiological myth of the ancient Hebrews and it serves as an
example of how the Christian myth is partially etiological in nature.

Myths that Warn

And woe unto them that are with child, and to them that give suck
in those days! But pray ye that your flight be not in the winter, neither
on the Sabbath day: For then shall be great tribulation, such as was
not since the beginning of the world to this time, no, nor ever shall be.
And except those days should be shortened, there should no flesh be
saved: but for the elect's sake those days shall be shortened.

~Matthew 24:19-22

---

[34]Irenaeus. Against the Heresies. Book 2.

This is just one passage from a multitude within the canonical (official) texts, not to mention the various passages found in the apocryphal (non-official) literature, which forewarn its audience of the terror and hopelessness that awaits non-believers. I could run through all of the various canonical and non-canonical passages that demonstrate this function of the Christian myth, but I think most people are familiar with the Christian myth of the future Apocalypse and Armageddon. The question is however; what function do such warnings really serve?

Following the Apocalypse, many Christians believe that the final judgement will take place and those who believe in Christ, will be taken up into the clouds, to enjoy an eternal bliss in heaven. How anything eternal could remain blissful forever is beyond me, however, that is not the point to be addressed here. Non-believers, as opposed to believers, will not be so lucky come the catastrophes that await us all. They, according to both scripture and tradition, will be cast into the fiery pits of hell to suffer an eternal torment. Ah! So, if I want to come out of this impending doom in good shape, I should believe in Christ and submit to the Church, his body here on earth, for if I do not, I will be tortured by the all-loving and forgiving god, Yahweh, for an eternity without parole.

These warnings are a form of mind control, manipulating the audience via two common and semi-related fears; the fear of the unknown and the fear of death. By employing these fears in conjunction with one another, in the warning, the creators and administrators of these myths have had a high level of success in not only maintaining their flocks, but gaining new converts, who, like Paschal, do not wish to gamble against such confident claims. It comes down to a simple carrot and stick incentive scheme. Join and follow us, believe as we believe and you will live forever in bliss. Refuse to submit to both us and our god, and you will die horribly and suffer an eternity of torment. Thus, the function of the warning in Christianity is to gain and maintain converts, it is that simple. The only problem is that Islam, Hinduism, Zoroastrianism, and various other religions carry the very same Apocalyptic warning, leaving the open-minded and uncertain thinker, scratching their head and wondering whether or not, they should just join them all to cover their bases, or pay their manipulation no mind. The trouble is, is that there are so many hells and so little time to pack for the right one!

Charter Myths: Myths that Justify

The Christian myth contains quite a few charter myths, or tales that justify many of the ecclesiastic (church) rituals, along with many western social institutions as well. The Eucharist is one such rite, which derives its legitimacy from traditional interpretations of the Christian myth found in the Gospels.

The Eucharist is the symbolic cannibalism and vampirism, of eating of the flesh and drinking the blood of Jesus Christ, the incarnated god-man. It derives its legitimacy from both the Gospels and the Epistles of Paul, but in truth, pre-dates even these sources and the Christian religion itself.

One of the most popular religions of the Roman Empire, which preceded Christianity was a religion known as Mithraism. This religion worshiped a demiurge (divine intercessor/god-man) called Mithras. Mithras was a sun-god,[35] whose headquarters, are buried directly beneath the very location where the Vatican sits today.[36] Long before the myth of the Lord's Supper was invented by the mythographers of the Christian myth, this pagan religion was already practicing its own Eucharistic rite. Initiates into this religion would eat the body of their earthly incarnated god-man, in the form of bread, and drink his blood, symbolised by wine.[37]

In the Gospel of John, Jesus is alleged to have said:

Verily, verily, I say unto you, Except ye eat the flesh of the Son of man, and drink his blood, ye have no life in you. Whoso eateth my flesh, and drinketh my blood, hath eternal life; and I will raise him

---

[35]Roger Beck. The Religion of the Mithras Cult in the Roman Empire: Mysteries of the Unconquered Sun. Oxford University Press. (2006). p. 5.

[36]http://www.world-archaeology.com/travel/vatican-cults-christianity-and-the-vatican/ ; http://www.italymag.co.uk/italy/roma/romes-underground-treasures-show ; http://freethoughtpedia.com/wiki/Jesus_and_Mithra

[37]J.M. Robertson. Pagan Christs: Studies in Comparative Hierology. Watts and Co. (1911). p. 318; Paul J. Achtemeier. Harper-Collins *Bible* Dictionary. Harper Collins (1996). p. 723; Guy de la Bedoyere. The Romans for Dummies. John Wiley and Sons Ltd. (2006). p. 159.

up at the last day. For my flesh is meat indeed, and my blood is drink indeed.

~John 6:53-55

The Eucharist or "Lord's Supper," is echoed in the earlier Gospels of Mark, Matthew and Luke. (see Mark 14:22-25, Luke 22:14-22 & Matthew 26:26-28) and also supported by Paul's letter to the Corinthians (see Corinthians 11:23-26).

From these various passages within these ancient texts can be found the justification for the Eucharist as a ceremony, demonstrating how charter myths form the constitution of certain rites and practices within a religion.

The next charter myth contained within the Christian texts worthy of mention, is the story of Christ declaring the sanctity of the institution of marriage, between a man and a woman (see Matthew 19:3-12, Mark 10:2-12, for example). This declaration has permeated not only the religion of Christianity, but western society and its laws. Such laws we are assured by other laws, underscore a legal and political system which is separate from the superstitious reach of the Church. So how is it then that the Church's laws, which derive from its various charter myths, have become the rule for those who may neither believe in this particular myth, nor its teachings?

When I first moved to the *Bible* thumping state of Tasmania (a state of Australia) in the 1990's, homosexuality was still a crime. It was illegal for a man or a woman, to have sexual relations with another person of the same sex, the consequence of which was imprisonment. It is absurd when we consider that this law was built upon a myth, not exclusively Christian, for we also find its origins within the myths of the *Old Testament*, as well (Leviticus 20:13). As ridiculous as this situation is, the foundation of most societies' laws and customs are built upon myth, to some degree at least. There are still many states in the USA that do not recognize gay marriage and other Christian and Islamic countries still have not been able to surpass the tremendous pressure of myth-based tradition, to allow consenting adults to formalize their love for one another in marriage.

The final charter myth of the Judeo-Christian religion, I wish to briefly mention, relates to the laws prohibiting murder; thou shalt not kill. Now, this particular law is one of my favourites and helps balance our argument a little, that is to say, some laws and customs derived from ancient myths are useful to humanity, but even this one is quite nuanced, not only today, but when it was first written, if the myth contain any historical truth.

We are told that as soon as Moses returned from the top of Mt. Sinai, he explained The Ten Commandments (there were actually quite a few more than ten, and they changed the second time Moses went up to re-write them) to the Israelites, one of which was; do not kill (see Exodus 20:13). This charter myth has been incorporated into the west via Christianity, being a religion partly founded upon Judaism and it is certainly not unique to Judeo-Christian countries. This law's somewhat pragmatic application reflects the tenuous nature of its application in the original charter myth of the Hebrews, as we find in both, the original story and its modern application, many exclusion clauses. Shortly after Moses exhorted "God's" rule not to kill, he commanded:

Thus saith the LORD God of Israel, Put every man his sword by his side, and go in and out from gate to gate throughout the camp, and slay every man his brother, and every man his companion, and every man his neighbour. And the children of Levi did according to the word of Moses: and there fell of the people that day about three thousand men.

~Exodus 32:27-28

Just as the case is today, with capital punishment, laws of self-defence and provocation, military laws, laws governing police conduct, etc., the rule against killing is not so much an immutable principle established to preserve the sanctity of life in all circumstances, but rather, a pragmatic one, intended to protect the ruler's power and his religion (means of control), or ideology (means of control), as the case may be.

Myths that Instruct

Even though many of the instructive aspects of the Christian myth are geared toward persuading people to suspend their rational faculties, switch off their minds and believe without evidence, I thought I might balance this essay with a positive instructive myth from the Gospels.

86

The author of the Gospel of Luke, or their source, constructed a dialogue between Jesus and the Jewish authorities, regarding the idea of loving one's neighbour, which, according to the somewhat xenophobic Jews, was a concept generally limited to one's immediate family, tribe and or, nation. Jesus, however, extends this definition ("neighbour") by way of a parable, which is quite often his platonic means of instruction, to humanly include anyone in need. When asked by a certain Jewish leader; what exactly is a neighbour, Jesus replies with the following parable:

A man was going down from Jerusalem to Jericho, and fell into the hands of robbers, who stripped him, beat him, and went away, leaving him half dead. Now by chance a priest was going down that road; and when he saw him, he passed by on the other side. So likewise a Levite, when he came to the place and saw him, passed by on the other side. But a Samaritan while travelling came near him; and when he saw him, he was moved with pity. He went to him and bandaged his wounds, having poured oil and wine on them. Then he put him on his own animal, brought him to an inn, and took care of him. The next day he took out two denarii, gave them to the innkeeper, and said, "Take care of him; and when I come back, I will repay you whatever more you spend." Which of these three, do you think, was a neighbour to the man who fell into the hands of the robbers?" He said, "The one who showed him mercy." Jesus said to him, "Go and do likewise."

~Luke 10:30-37

This is a beautiful instructive parable, teaching the audience, whose ears are more often in attention at the times when promises are made for their own salvation, to help the poor and the needy, to show mercy to those in need and to assist even strangers. Of course, there are other beautiful parables and messages in the Gospels, yet unfortunately, they have often been ignored, rationalized, re-interpreted and perverted by power-mongers, to the detriment of their true instructive beauty. Also, we must recognize here that such sentiments and teachings found within the Christian Scripture are not original to Christianity and in fact, date many centuries before, amongst the Platonists, and other so called, pagans of antiquity. Nevertheless, this instructive myth is one of my favourites within the corpus of the Christian Canon.

6. MYTHS AND THE SUPERNATURAL

On this final element in professor Vandiver's definition of myth, she says:

Myths, very frequently involve gods and the supernatural. They do not have to involve gods and the supernatural, but they very frequently do.[38]

Unfortunately, Professor Vandiver hasn't given us a definition of the term, "supernatural", possibly because it seems to be a word commonly understood by most people; however, for the sake of prudence, we should begin by defining what exactly the word means, and how such a definition might impact upon our understanding of the nature of a myth and ultimately, whether or not the Gospels therefore fit that category.

One online dictionary defines the word "supernatural" in the following manner:

1. of, pertaining to, or being above or beyond what is natural; unexplainable by natural law or phenomena; abnormal.
2. of, pertaining to, characteristic of, or attributed to God or a deity.
3. of a superlative degree; preternatural: a missile of supernatural speed.
4. of, pertaining to, or attributed to ghosts, goblins, or other unearthly beings; eerie; occult (hidden).[39]

And the Collins World English Dictionary defines it as:

1. Of or relating to things that cannot be explained according to natural laws
2. Characteristic of or caused by or as if by a god; miraculous
3. Of, involving, or ascribed to occult beings
4. Exceeding the ordinary; abnormal[40]

---

[38]Professor Elizabeth Vandiver. Classical Mythology. Lecture 2: What is Myth? The Teaching Company. (2002).
[39]http://dictionary.reference.com/browse/supernatural
[40]Ibid.

I think given most people's familiarity with what we might all agree, constitutes a supernatural event, state, or being, I should draw upon the bolded aspects of the definitions above to give us a working definition for the purpose of this investigation.

The word "supernatural" relates to something: above and beyond nature and the natural; generally, but not exclusively, related to a god, which cannot be explained by natural laws; that exceeds the ordinary and is miraculous.

If we define the word in this way, we find many supernatural aspects in the Gospel tales, the Epistles of Paul and the Book of Revelation.

I think no one, at least no one in their right mind, will see the impregnation of a virgin by a ghost, or angels visiting people in their sleep, or a star which breaks its regular orbit to travel east to Jerusalem, stopping there for a while, then going on to Bethlehem, to signify the birth of a god-human hybrid child, as natural. They might also be hard-pressed to find a natural explanation for this god-son walking on water and stopping a storm with his words, let alone, instantly turning water into wine, a trick which we might assume, many liquor companies would have seized upon, if natural. The bringing to life of a dead person, and many dead people, the death and resurrection of this god-man himself and his ascension into the clouds, etc..

I think it is pretty safe to say that the stories in the Gospels contain many supernatural tales, and even safer to say that most people reading this essay would be familiar with this fact.

What many people may not be familiar with is the fact that many of the supernatural tales from the Gospels are simply re-scripted myths, taken from earlier pagan myths. The divine announcement of the saviour's birth was a common motif attached to the story of Alexander the Great's birth and Pythagoras, for example. The virgin-born earthly incarnated god-man, was also a common motif employed by much earlier Hellenistic mythographers, among others, along with the death and resurrection of the god-man, first recorded amongst the ancient Egyptian texts regarding Osiris, the bringing of the dead back to life, utilized by the creators of the Hercules myth, a thousand plus years earlier, the healing of the sick, commonly associated with the healing god Aesclepius, the turning of water into wine, written into the Osiris-Dionysius myth many centuries before "Jesus Christ," and on and on it goes until we are left with virtually nothing original in the supernatural accounts of Christ.

In the second volume of the three volume series I have authored, entitled, *I Am Christ*, I list these similarities with primary and ancient sources, along with the leading scholarship in the field of mythology and comparative mythology, to demonstrate the probability that the stories of Christ written in the Gospels are not merely myth, but second-hand myth.

In the words of the second century church father, Justin Martyr:

And when we say also that the Word, who is the first-birth of God, was produced without sexual union, and that He, Jesus Christ, our Teacher, was crucified and died, and rose again, and ascended into heaven, we propound nothing different from what you believe regarding those whom you esteem sons of Jupiter…And if we even affirm that He was born of a virgin, accept this in common with what you accept of Perseus. And in that we say that He made whole the lame, the paralytic, and those born blind, we seem to say what is very similar to the deeds said to have been done by Aesculapius.[41]

So what do we, or should we, make of these second-hand miraculous events, which defy the laws of nature and were hidden in obscurity and remoteness from the majority of people of that day and everyone living today?

I think Thomas Paine put it best, when he said:

All the tales of miracles with which the Old and New Testament are filled, are fit only for impostors to preach and fools to believe.

CONCLUSION

In this essay I have attempted to apply one of the best working definitions of myth to the narratives which underscore the Christian religion. In so doing, I hope I have demonstrated that the stories of Jesus Christ are just that, stories, which were set in the remote past and in a

---

[41]The Apostolic Fathers with Justin Martyr and Irenaeus. Justin Martyr. (trans. Philip Schaff.) First Apology. Chapter 21: Analogies of Christ. pp.170–171.

remote location and that these remote accounts changed over time. They were and still are, believed by Christians to represent true historical facts, to varying degrees and the tales serve the four primary functions of myth, set out by Professor Vandiver. Finally, they are built upon a supernatural theme and contain many accounts of miraculous and unnatural phenomena. The only reasonable conclusion one can draw from such evidence is that; the Christian religion was built upon myth, propagated by lies and believed by fools.

◆

THE TRUTH ABOUT THE DEVIL – THE GREATEST TRICK!

The ancient Persians had a significant impact upon the mythologies of both the Jews and the Christians. Among other things, Judeo-Christianity owes thanks to the Persian priests of Zoroaster, for the light versus darkness motif, the apocalypse and the idea of the coming of a messiah, among other mythical motifs. But above all, both Jews and Christians should thank Persia for the devil himself. For if they did not adopt this character from the Persians they might not have succeeded in persuading and maintaining their frightened and superstitious flocks over the millennia.

The religion of Zoroaster, or Zarathustra, received its name from a Magian Priest by the name of Zoroaster (Greek)/Zarathustra (Persian), who was a loyal servant of the "one true" Persian God, Ahura Mazda or Ormuzd. Ormuzd was commonly referred to as the "The Holy Spirit" in the pre-Christian portions of the Avesta.[42] This religion began to flourish toward the end of the second and beginning of the first millennium bce and its primary corpus of Holy Scriptures are known as the *Zend Avesta*.[43] These ancient scriptures contain

---

[42]Joseph McCabe. The Sources of the Morality of the Gospels. Watts & Co. (1914). p. 60.
[43]Peter Clark. Zoroastrianism: An Introduction to An Ancient Faith. Sussex Academic Press. (1998). p. 19. Within the Zend Avesta library are numerous books. Some of which are as follows; The Gathas, Yasna, Visperad Vendidad. Khordeh Avesta, which contains the Yashts and the Siroza. The rest of the materials from the Avesta are called "Avestan fragments." Also, later redacted material includes; the Denkard, Bundahishn, Menog-i Khrad, Selections of Zadspram, Jamasp Namag, Epistles of Manucher, Rivayats, Dadestan-i-Denig, and Arda Viraf Namag.

numerous similarities to Judaism and Christianity. Such parallels have led the learned Rabbis responsible for compiling the *Jewish Encyclopaedia* to make mention of the closeness of the two later Abrahamic religions, saying:

Most scholars, Jewish as well as non-Jewish, are of the opinion that Judaism was strongly influenced by Zoroastrianism in views relating to angelology and demonology, and probably also in the doctrine of the resurrection, as well as in eschatological ideas in general, and also that the monotheistic conception of Yhwh may have been quickened and strengthened by being opposed to the dualism or quasi-monotheism of the Persians.[44]

Furthermore, the *Harper-Collins Bible Dictionary* is in agreement with the scholarly consensus on this issue, teaching us that it is only from the late postexilic period (after 200 bce) that Satan becomes the evil counterpart to God, as he is depicted in the *New Testament*. The dictionary attributes this transformation to the influence of Persian's dualistic religion over the Hebrew religion. As the Hebrews already believed in a heavenly court of angels presided over by a good God, it wasn't hard for them to adopt the reverse concept from the Persians, but they had not yet developed a devil of their own.[45]

Prior to the Persian invasion of Babylon, the religion of Judaism believed that their chief God(s) was responsible for all that happened in the universe. Both good and evil were the manifestations of their God(s).

This is reflected in the book of Isaiah, in which the author writes:

I form the light, and create darkness: I make peace, and create evil: I the LORD do all these things.

~Isaiah 45:7

Isaiah probably wrote the passage cited above as a warning to the Hebrews not to fall into the Persian heresy of believing in an evil supernatural counterpart to Yahweh/Elohim.[46] Thus, the author of the book of Isaiah has Yahweh taking direct responsibility for both good

---

[44]http://www.jewishencyclopedia.com/articles/15283-zoroastrianism
[45]Paul. J. Achtemeier. Harper-Collins *Bible* Dictionary Revised Edition. Harper Collins, (1989). p. 975.
[46]http://www.jewishvirtuallibrary.org/jsource/judaica/ejud_0002_0006_0_05429.html

and evil, leaving no room for the existence of a devil or evil entity, unlike the ancient Persian religion, which was dualistic, meaning, there was a positive God and an evil one, living in constant opposition to one another. In the sixth century bce, Cyrus the Great of Persia invaded Babylon whilst the Israelites were living in exile amongst the Babylonians.[47] The story goes, that Cyrus the Great freed the Hebrews from their Babylonian captors and sponsored the building of the Second Temple at Jerusalem (See Ezra 1-5), although a number of historians question this biblical version of history due to a lack of extra-biblical evidence, where such evidence should exist.

In Paolo Sacchi's *The History of the Second Temple Period*, he discusses Cyrus' role as the great liberator and is sceptical of the historical value of the *Bible*'s version of this event. Sacchi points out that the depiction of Cyrus as the liberator is probably Persian propaganda; propaganda for which the arguments from the silence of credible historical sources bring into question. Regarding Cyrus' edict and his role as liberator, Sacchi produces as evidence, both a list of liberated peoples known as the "Cylinder of Cyrus" in which there is no mention of the Jews being among these liberated peoples and Jewish tradition itself, which holds that the first return of exiles only came about with the rise of the later Persian ruler, Darius I in 521 bce.[48]

Despite the historical problems associated with the biblical narrative of Cyrus' liberation of the Jews, this alleged event has been used to mark the beginning of what is known in Jewish history as the Second Temple Era, which lasted until the war with Rome in 70CE.[49] It was during this era that the Hebrew religion split into various sects as a result of the foreign influence involved in the construction of the temple at Jerusalem, which many Israelites saw as nullifying its legitimacy and due to the various political struggles between the former

---

[47]Oded Lipschitz & Joseph Blenkinsopp. Judah and the Judeans in the Neo-Babylonian Period. Eisenbrauns. (2003). p. 271; John Barton and John Muddiman. The Oxford *Bible* Commentary. Oxford University Press. (2001). p. 309.
[48]Paolo Sacchi. The History of the Second Temple Period. T&T Clark International. (2000). Pp. 58–59
[49]Ibid. p. 302.

rulers of Judea, who were usurped when Persia took control.[50] From this point on we see deep divisions between the Pharisees and the Sadducees and we also see the emergence of Jewish sects such as; the Messianic Jews, the Theraputae, the Essenes, the Ebionites and many others. Amongst all of this theological chaos, more and more Persian beliefs crept their way into the very core of the previously Egyptian and Mesopotamian inspired mythology of the Jews. The biggest alteration to their religion was the appearance of the Persian style devil, known in the Persian religion as "Ahriman".

The *Harper-Collins Bible Dictionary* supports this idea, stating that Satan only appears three times throughout the *Old Testament* (See Job 1-2; Zech. 3:1-2; and 1 Chron. 21:1) and that all of these references are post-exilic (sixth century BCE).[51]

The devil has never managed to achieve a unique character and identity within the Hebrew religion and has been known by many names and occupied many forms, none of which represent a single definable character. The Hebrew word, *ha satan* (הַשָּׂטָן) or Satan, as it is translated in English, was not originally a name/proper noun, but a verb, meaning "to accuse", or "to oppose" and was used in its common noun form by "David" in 2 Samuel 19:22, in which he was alleged to have described the sons of Zeruiah as "satans" (adversaries) unto him. It also appears in verb form in various other places throughout the *Old Testament* (See Numbers 22:22, 1 Samuel 29:4 and Psalms 109:6). Satan was a word which pre-existed the devil in the Hebrew Scriptures, however, when he was introduced into the religion it was chosen as one of the most appropriate epithets to apply to his Zoroastrian character.

Another name for the devil is "Lucifer" and it means "light bearer".[52] Astronomically, it has been said to represent the planet Venus, as Venus is the brightest star in the morning before the sun

---

[50]Ibid. p. 211; Jeff S. Anderson. The Internal Diversification of Second Temple Judaism: An Introduction to Second Temple Judaism. University Press of America. (2002). pp. 23–34

[51]Paul. J. Achtemeier. Harper-Collins *Bible* Dictionary Revised Edition. Harper Collins, (1989). p. 974.

[52]Ibid. p. 628.

has fully risen and obliterated it from the sky.[53] In a misinterpreted passage from chapter fourteen of the book of Isaiah, describing the King of Babylon, the name "Lucifer", which derives its current form from the Latin "Lucem/Lux Ferer", was incorrectly applied to the devil.

Some of the confusion surrounding the misinterpreted passages from Isaiah arose due to the King of Babylon being described as having "falling from heaven" and many theologians misunderstood the use of the word "heaven" to mean the "literal" heaven, rather than its obvious figurative application. The king of Babylon enjoyed success on a grand scale, success which brought with it pleasure, wealth, dominion, abundance and as a result, became arrogant and so the heaven we was said to be falling from was his luxurious lifestyle. Much like the way we use the term heaven to describe a taste or a feeling or a state of being.

To refute any apology to the contrary, the Lucifer of Isaiah was described as having been:

the king of Babylon (Isaiah 14:4),

who ruled nations with aggression (Isaiah 14:6), as the king of one of the largest empires did, also ;

who other defeated kings will say; "you have become weak like us," (Isaiah 14:10), and;

who would not let his captives (the exiled Jews) go home (Isaiah 14:17), but most importantly,

was said to have been a man (Isaiah 14:16).

It is obvious that this Lucifer ("shining one") was the king of Babylon, but beliefs require a minimal amount of fuel and a maximum amount of propagation to catch on and spread, as has been the case in this instance.

Modern apologists have twisted these passages in every conceivable manner to try and claim that it is a double entendre for both the devil and the king of Babylon, however as seen above, the term was only referring to the man himself. The association between Lucifer and Satan was made by Christians who errantly interpreted Luke

---

[53]Ibid.

10:18 (*I saw Satan fall from heaven like lightning*), to be a reference to Isaiah's Lucifer.[54]

The epithet Lucifer is translated from the Hebrew *Helel* (ללי‎ה) "shining one" or *Ben Shachar* ("Day Star", "Bringer of Light" or "Sun of the Morning").[55] It is very interesting to note that Jesus was also called Lucifer in (2 Peter 1:19 and Rev. 22:16). So if Lucifer is the devil's name, then one would have to admit that Jesus is the devil. It does make sense, ironically speaking, as more people have killed and been killed in Jesus' name, than almost any other name in history.

Another name for the devil within the Judeo-Christian belief system is "Beelzebub". The word, Beelzebub, stems from the Hebrew *Ba'al-Zebub* (זככעל‎). In English, *Ba'al-Zebub* means "Lord of the Flies",[56] and it is the first part of this name which is of interest to scholars of comparative mythology. The name *Ba'al*, which may well descend from the ancient Babylonian Sun-god *Bel*, yet in its present form, represents the later Phoenician and Canaanite God, *Ba'al*, who guest stars in the Hebrew Scriptures on many occasions (See Numbers 22:41, Judges 2:13: the husband of the goddess Asherah[57], 6:25, 28, 30-32, 1Kings 16:31 etc.) This epithet, "Ba'al", seems to have been incorporated into the Hebrew language and came to have a variety of meanings, including; "Lord", "Master", "Husband" and "Possessor".[58]

---

[54]Ibid.

[55]J.P. Douglas, Merrill C. Tenney & Moises Silva. Zondervan Illustrated *Bible* Dictionary. Zondervan. (2011). p. 863; http://www.etymonline.com/index.php?term=lucifer

[56]John Barton and John Muddiman. The Oxford *Bible* Commentary. Oxford University Press. (2001). p. 248; Paul. J. Achtemeier. Harper-Collins *Bible* Dictionary Revised Edition. Harper Collins, (1989). p. 94

[57]The Canaanite god Ba'al was described in Judges 2:19 as the "husband" of the goddess Asherah. This is significant as Zeev Herzog, Ze'ev Meshel and other archaeologists have discovered that the ancient Israelite's primary god Yahweh, was commonly worshipped alongside his consort, the Canaanite goddess Asherah, both being seen as the father and mother of heaven ruling equally together. This fact is evidenced by various eighth century B.C.E relicfs, statuets and inscriptions that depict and describe YHVH and ASHERAH as being a couple. (see discovery at Kuntillet Ajrud and Khirbet el-Kom). This fact further explains why Yahweh is directly referred to as a Ba'al at Isaiah 54:5: For your maker (Yahweh) is your Ba'al (Lord/Master).

[58]Paul. J. Achtemeier. Harper-Collins *Bible* Dictionary Revised Edition. Harper Collins, (1989). p. 94.

The conflicting characterizations attributed to the devil within the Hebrew Scriptures, along with the contradictory verse found within Isaiah 45:7 (*God alone is responsible for good and evil*), seems to indicate that the devil himself had been a more recent interpolation by Jewish mythographers, who grafted him into the existing scriptures, thereby creating a situation in which the devil has multiple names and titles. Further, the very form or being of the devil has been the subject of much confusion. Many Christians and Jews try to suggest that the serpent in the Garden of Eden was the devil, but the description of the serpent contradicts this notion.

Once again, the *Harper-Collins Bible Dictionary* informs us that the serpent in the Garden of Eden is "never" identified in the *Old Testament* as Satan.[59]

The serpent is described as being one of the *beasts of the field* and after tempting Eve to eat the forbidden fruit from the tree of Knowledge of Good and Evil, the serpent is punished by God in the following manner:

And the LORD God said unto the serpent, Because thou hast done this, thou art cursed above all cattle, and above every beast of the field; upon thy belly shalt thou go, and dust shalt thou eat all the days of thy life. And I will put enmity between thee and the woman, and between thy seed and her seed; it shall bruise thy head, and thou shalt bruise his heel.

~Genesis 3:14-15

One does not need to be a theologian to understand what the author was talking about in the passage above. The serpent was a cunning beast of the field who, prior to his indiscretion, had legs and spoke. This alleged description of the devil as being a beast of the field contradicts the description of him given in the book of Job, in which he (Satan) is counted amongst the sons of God (See Job 1:6).

Regarding Satan's role in the book of Job, the *Harper-Collins Bible Dictionary* further informs us that in the first two instances in the *Bible* (See Job 1-2; Zechariah 3:1-2), Satan plays a kind of henchman role in God's divine court. It was his job to accuse human beings on behalf of

---

[59]Ibid. p. 975.

God, which demonstrates that in the beginning he was not considered an enemy of God, as he later came to be depicted.[60]

The motif of the serpent tempting the female of the first primordial couple existed within Persian mythology, long before this Hebrew account was written. T.W. Doane, in his great work, *Bible Myths and their Parallels,* draws from the work of Bishop Colenso and in so doing, informs us that within Persian mythology, the idea of the first couple of innocent human beings living in purity existed prior to the composition of the Hebrew tales found within the book of Genesis. Further, Doane enlightens us as to the ancient Persian myths which told the story of those first two innocent humans being tempted by a demon in serpent form, who encouraged them to eat fruit from a *wonderful tree*, resulting in their fall. Interestingly, these two humans, having eaten the forbidden fruit, went straight away to kill beasts and clothe themselves with their skins, as was later written into the Hebrew myths.[61]

In addition, Sunderland supports the Persian origin of the devil, saying:

Even if we admit that the serpent in the Genesis paradise story ought to be identified with Satan, we have here no exception, for it should be borne in mind that the Book of Genesis was probably not completed before about the beginning of the fifth century before Christ, a century after the Captivity closed. Satan appears in the Books of Job, Zechariah, and Chronicles; but these are all late writings. Belief in the existence of such a bad being the foe of God, the accuser of the good, the tempter of men to evil seems to have come into Judaism from the religion of the Persians, through contact with that people during or after the Exile.[62]

In support of the above proposition, Sunderland goes on to point out the discrepancy between the accounts of David being tempted to take a census, given in both the books of 2 Samuel and 1 Chronicles.

---

[60]Ibid.

[61]T.W Doane. *Bible* Myths and Their Parallels in Other Religions. The Commonwealth Company. (1882). p. 8.

[62]Jabez Thomas Sunderland. The Origin and Character of the *Bible* and its place among sacred books. The Beacon Press, (1924). pp. 246–247.

Within both books David is tempted to take a census of his people, the only difference is that in 2 Samuel it is God who tempts him to do so and in the book of 1 Chronicles, it is Satan.

On this issue Sunderland points out that in the older book, Samuel, it is God who tempts David to take the census, but in the updated and revised version of this myth found in the book of Chronicles, it is Satan. The reason for this discrepancy, according to Sunderland and a number of other scholars, is that prior to the composition of the book of Chronicles, Satan did not exist within the mythology of the Hebrews, so this temptation was re-scripted in Satan's name when the mythological foundation of the religion of the Hebrews shifted.[63]

This contradiction is irreconcilable until one realizes that the Hebrews probably adopted their devil from the Persians and so, evil acts which were once attributed to Yahweh, were now being rewritten and passed off as the devil's handiwork.

If we also keep in mind Isaiah 45:7, this divergence in theology becomes explainable and the contradiction is exposed for what it probably is; a shift in the theology of the Hebrews, influenced by the dualistic Persian religion at the time of the Persian's conquest of Babylon in around 539 bce. Thus, it is a near certainty that Judaism inherited the devil from the Persian Zoroastrians and the Christians in turn, inherited their devil from the Jews and other pagan religions.

Finally, there was a related concept that the Christians seemed to have directly inherited from the Persians and this was the concept of the anti-Christ. The Anti-Christ as described in the Zoroastrian texts, is literally called, the Anti-Mithras, keeping in mind that Mithras was the Sun God and son of the supreme God of the Persians, Ahura-Mazda.

From the ancient Zoroastrian Scriptures we read:

Backward flies the arrow which the anti-Mithras shoots on account of the wealth of bad unpoetic thoughts which the anti-Mithras performs. Even when he shoots it well, even when it reaches the body, even then it does not harm him on account of the wealth of bad unpoetic thoughts which the anti-Mithras performs.

~Yasht 10:20-21

---

[63]Ibid'. p. 247.

CONCLUSION

So what is the truth about the devil, other than he doesn't exist and has been used as a kind of stick to enforce compliance, by way of fear-manipulation? The truth is, he is a re-scripted mythical character, adopted by the Hebrews, passed onto Christians and fed into young and trusting minds, as a boogey man that will torture you if you don't submit to the religion of Christianity. I would like to conclude with a passage from Thomas Paine's great work, *The Age of Reason:*

The Christian Mythologists, after having confined Satan in a pit, were obliged to let him out again to bring on the sequel of the fable. He is then introduced into the Garden of Eden, in the shape of a snake or a serpent, and in that shape he enters into familiar conversation with Eve, who is no way surprised to hear a snake talk; and the issue of this tete-a-tete is that he persuades her to eat an apple, and the eating of that apple damns all mankind. After giving Satan this triumph over the whole creation, one would have supposed that the Church Mythologists would have been kind enough to send him back again to the pit; or, if they had not done this, that they would have put a mountain upon him (for they say that their faith can remove a mountain), or have put him under a mountain, as the former mythologists had done, to prevent his getting again among the women and doing more mischief. But instead of this they leave him at large, without even obliging him to give his parole- the secret of which is, that they could not do without him...[64]

WAS THE PROPHET MUHAMMAD A PAEDOPHILE?

The word "Paedophile" is defined in the dictionary as:
    *An adult who is sexually attracted to young children.[65]
    The popular Psychology Website, *Psychology Today* says of Paedophilia:
    Paedophilia is considered a paraphilia, an "abnormal or unnatural attraction." Paedophilia is defined as the fantasy or act of sexual activity

---

[64]Philip S. Foner, PhD. The Complete Writings of Thomas Paine. The Citadel Press. (1945). p. 470.
[65]http://dictionary.reference.com/browse/paedophile?s=t

with prepubescent children. Paedophiles are usually men, and can be attracted to either or both sexes. How well they relate to adults of the opposite sex varies. Perpetrators often delude themselves into viewing their actions as helpful to children. They might tell themselves they are contributing to a child's development…[66]

Now, my Muslim brothers and sisters, please do not be alarmed or feel persecuted by the question this article poses, for it is a fair question given the evidence.

I have recently begun my research into Islam and I should first explain my methodology. As I have done with other religions and mythologies, I began by buying three notebooks. One for the central texts, which I read and write out, verse for verse, with my own personal commentary on verses that grab my attention; another notebook for commentaries on both the central and peripheral texts, along with traditions arising from these texts, by members of that religion/mythology, (if available); and the third notebook for critical and impartial commentary. I work on all three notebooks at the same time, allotting portions of each day, for each of the three aspects of my research. On my third day, working with the materials I have at present, (anxiously awaiting the arrival much more) I came across this little curiosity. You see, when I start looking at the commentaries, I read through the contents of the commentaries, and begin where I find something that grabs my attention. I feel that combining both chronological and random methods of research works well for me and keeps me inspired.

Here is what I found that garnered my attention and led me to look a little deeper into the issue. You see, in the peripheral Islamic body of texts, known as the *Hadith*, (specifically within the *Sahih Bukhari; Sahih* meaning "reliable and *Bukhari*, being the name of the Imam, Muhammad bin Ismail al-Bukhari [810-870 CE], who compiled these particular *Hadith*), I discovered something quite disturbing about the Prophet Muhammad and his favourite wife, Aishah. Perhaps I should let Aishah tell the story herself, as there is nothing better than letting the subjects of an investigation speak for themselves, if we can in fact, trust these alleged "holy texts":

---

[66]http://www.psychologytoday.com/conditions/pedophilia

My marriage (wedding) contract with the Prophet was written when I was a girl of six (years). My mother, Umm Ruman, came to me while I was playing in a swing with some of my girl friends. She called me, and I went to her, not knowing what she wanted to do to me. She caught me by the hand and made me stand at the door of the house. I was breathless then, and when my breathing became normal, she took some water and rubbed my face and head with it. Then she took me into the house. There in the house I saw some Ansari [recent Muslim converts] women who said, "Best wishes and Allah's Blessing and a good luck." Then she entrusted me to them and they prepared me (for the marriage). Unexpectedly Allah's Messenger came to me in the forenoon and my mother handed me over to him, and at that time I was a girl of nine years of age.[67]

Ok, so how old was Muhammad when he took his prepubescent bride? He was just over fifty years of age.[68] And how old was Aishah, when he had sexual intercourse with her? She was nine years old.[69]

In her revealing book, *Sexual Ethics & Islam: Feminist Reflections on Qur'an, Hadith and Jurisprudence,* Professor of Religion, Kecia Ali teaches us that the *Sahih Bukhari* is seen by Sunni Muslims as the most authentic compilation of *hadith*. Professor Ali then points out the agreement between the *Sahih Bukhari* and the *Sahih Muslim*, both of which report that Aishah was nine years old when Muhammad consummated his marriage with her.[70]

This is what the "reliable", or *Sahih Hadith* says. Now, add to this the definition of the word, "paedophile", furnished above and we have perfectly reasonable grounds for asking the question; was the prophet Muhammad a paedophile?

If not, then how do we explain the following law from the "perfect and complete" *Qur'an*, which prescribes a three month waiting period

---

[67]Sahih Bukhari, Volume 1. Book 6. No. 304. Cited in: Robert Spencer. Islam Unveiled. Encounter Books. (2002). p. 47.
[68]Sahih Bukhari. Volume 7. Book 67. No. 5196. Ibid.
[69]Sahih Bukhari. Book of Marriage. No. 64, 65, 88. Cited in: Kecia Ali. Sexual Ethics & Islam: Feminist Reflections on *Qur'an*, Hadith and Jurisprudence. Oneworld Publications Oxford (2006). p. 135.
[70]Ibid.

before divorcing women who have commenced menstruation (reached puberty) and:

The same shall apply to those who have not yet menstruated.

~ Surah 65:4

Further, if Muhammad did not set this precedent, then why in Muslim countries like Iran, which are under Sharia (Islamic) Law, for example, is the legal age for marriage (for girls) set at the age of nine?[71]

The answer of whether or not this possibly fictitious historical character, Muhammad, was or was not a paedophile, is a question which is less significant, in my opinion, than the belief that he was. For with this belief, children have been molested and raped, young girls have been forced into unnatural wedlock and exploited by the male members of this religion and the practice of taking child brides has become so firmly fixed by tradition, that it seems almost sacrilegious to the participants of this tradition to uproot it and move toward a more egalitarian and healthy way of living and thinking.

◆

THE BOOK OF GENESIS UNVEILED

THE FIVE BOOKS OF "MOSES"

Genesis is the first book of the *Bible* and is subsequently, the first book of "Pentateuch" or "Torah" or "The Five Books of Moses." According to both Christian and Jewish tradition, Moses wrote the first five books of what Christians refer to as the *Old Testament*. Those books are Genesis, Exodus, Numbers, Leviticus and Deuteronomy. There are a number of serious problems with the belief in the mosaic authorship of the Pentateuch. First and foremost, nowhere in these books does it say that Moses was the author. Further, Moses never mentioned the account of creation written in Genesis, nor did Samuel, Elijah, Elisha, Amos, Hosea, Isaiah, Micah, and Nahum, for that matter. One would expect these prophets to have at least mentioned the most significant event and work of their creator. Their silence on this issue

---

[71]Lisa Beyer, "The Women of Islam," Time, 25 November, 2001.

implies that they did not know of it, which in turn raises the possibility that the accounts of creation located in Genesis were composed after any of these characters were written about. The first prophet to refer to the Pentateuch was Jeremiah, who said:

How can you say, "We are wise, and the Torah of the Lord is with us," when, in fact, the false pen of scribes has made it into a lie?

~Jeremiah 8:8

What Jeremiah was saying is that the entire Torah, the "First Five Books of the *Bible*", had been corrupted by lying scribes. Thus, according to Judeo-Christianity's very own prophet Jeremiah, the scriptures upon which these two religions have built their foundations are untrustworthy.

One would be forgiven for asking how Moses was able to give an account of the creation of the universe, Adam and Eve, the Garden of Eden and the Flood, when all of these incidents occurred before he was born. One may wish to appeal to the idea that historians also write about things in the past, yet, if you read the account of creation, for example, events are recorded, to which no human witness was privy. We are being asked to believe quite a lot here. But Christians and Jews say that Yahweh revealed all these things to Moses, yet nowhere in the *Bible* does it say that he (Yahweh) told Moses any of it.

Writing in the early twentieth century, the brilliant lawyer and independent religious scholar, Joseph Wheless, addressed the absurdity of Moses writing about events which occurred well before and after his time, saying:

According to the Bible chronology, Moses lived some 1500 years before Christ; the date of his Exodus out of Egypt with the Israelites is laid down as the year 1491 Before Christ, or some 2500 years after the Biblical creation of the world.' So, if Moses wrote the account of the creation, the fall of man, the flood, and other notable historical events recorded in Genesis, he wrote of things happening, if ever they happened, 2500 years more or less before his earthly time, and some of them before even man was created on earth; things which Moses of course could not personally have known....But the Book of Genesis, and all the "five Books of Moses," contain many matters of "revealed" fact which occurred, if ever at all, many hundreds of years after the death of Moses. Moses is not technically "numbered among the Prophets," and he does not claim for himself to have been inspired both backwards and forwards, so as to write both past history and future history. It is evident therefore by every internal and human criterion, that these "five Books of Moses," containing not only the past events referred to, but many future events narrated not in form of prophecy of what would be, but as actual occurrences and "faits accomplis" (established fact) could not have been written by Moses...[72]

We are expected to simply believe that Moses wrote these five books. Further, within the first five books, events are described during the life of Moses, to which he could not have been privy, as they occurred outside of his geographic and conscious proximity. In other words, he wasn't there to have witnessed and recorded events that happened in other countries; he was in Egypt. Again the Jews and Christians say he was made privy to these events by their God, Yahweh, but we should expect to be furnished with some evidence concerning this extraordinary proposition, for in the words of Carl Sagan; *extraordinary claims require extraordinary evidence* yet, we are told by these faith-peddlers that it is not our right to ask for it.

As further testimony against the proposition that Moses wrote these books, he is written about in the third person past tense (*"Moses was"*), as opposed to the first person present tense ("I am") or even first person past tense (*"I was"*). One example of this, which seems to demonstrate that the account was written as a reflection from an author looking back, comes from the book of Exodus in which the anonymous author says:

Moreover, the man Moses was very great in the land of Egypt.

~Exodus 11:3

The most perplexing issue of all is how Moses wrote concerning events that occurred after his death. Tradition dictates that Moses wrote the following words with his own post-mortem hand:

And Moses was an hundred and twenty years old when he died: his eye was not dim, nor his natural force abated.

---

[72]Joseph Wheless. Is it God's Word? Alfred A. Knopf. (1926). pp. 29–30

And the children of Israel wept for Moses in the plains of Moab thirty days: so the days of weeping and mourning for Moses were ended.

And Joshua the son of Nun was full of the spirit of wisdom; for Moses had laid his hands upon him: and the children of Israel hearkened unto him, and did as the LORD commanded Moses.

And there arose not a prophet SINCE in Israel like unto Moses, whom the LORD knew face to face…

~Deuteronomy 7-10

As you may have guessed, Jews and Christians have an apology for this illogicality. Their argument boils down to a single word; "oops." That portion of Deuteronomy wasn't supposed to be in that book, but later redactors accidently placed it there, instead of where it truly belongs, which is in the next book, the book of Joshua. Notwithstanding this unsubstantiated apology, one which bodes against the notion of omniscient construction, we must consider the probability that if Moses was indeed an historical figure, he did not write regarding events that occurred before and after his existence and on those things outside of his proximity, or any human's for that matter. To believe otherwise is to offend our most sacred cognitive institution, reason.

Addressing the claim that Moses wrote the first five books of the Tanakh, Judge Parish. B. Ladd commented:

In some of the minor details there is quite a diversity of opinion, some maintaining that the five books were written in whole and taken from tradition at the Babylonian captivity; while others assert that Moses and the early Hebrews left the substance of these books in different manuscripts; and still others assert that they were made up partly from fragmentary writings and traditions. But all of these authors agree that at least the first four books of the Pentateuch, and probably the fifth, in their present form, were first made known and published in the world by Ezra and Nehemiah, about 445 B.C, nearly 1,000 years after Moses.[73]

---

[73]Judge Parish B. Ladd. Commentaries on Hebrew and Christian Mythology. The Truth Seeker Company, (1896). pp. 53–54.

Finally, biblical scholar and professor of Jewish studies at the University Georgia, Richard Elliot Friedman, enunciated the problem of believing in the Mosaic authorship of the Torah, saying:

...early Jewish and Christian tradition held that Moses himself wrote them (Pentateuch), though nowhere in the Five Books of Moses themselves does the text say that he was the author. But the tradition that one person, Moses, alone wrote these books presented problems. People observed contradictions in the text. It would report events in a particular order, and later it would say that those same events happened in a different order. It would say that there were two of something, and elsewhere it would say that there were fourteen of that same thing. It would say that the Moabites did something, and later it would say that it was the Midianites who did it. It would describe Moses as going to a Tabernacle in a chapter before Moses builds the Tabernacle.

People also noticed that the Five Books of Moses included things that Moses could not have known or was not likely to have said. The text, after all, gave an account of Moses' death. It also said that Moses was the humblest man on earth; and normally one would not expect the humblest man on earth to point out that he is the humblest man on earth.[74]

RE-DATING THE BOOK OF GENESIS

As mentioned, Christian tradition dates the composition of the book of Genesis somewhere between 1500-1200bce, at around the time of the Israelite's alleged exodus from Egypt.[75] This tradition has now been proven to be nothing less than erroneous and unsubstantiated belief. According to the overwhelming amount of archaeological, textual and extra-biblical evidence, the book of Genesis was probably written or finally redacted in large part, sometime during the sixth to the fifth centuries bce, either during or after the Israelites were exiled in Babylon, also known as the exilic and post-exilic

---

[74]Richard Elliot Friedman. Who Wrote the *Bible*? Harper-San Francisco. (1997). pp. 17–18.
[75]http://www.theology.edu/faq01.htm

periods. At this point the reader may be wondering why this fact is significant. It is important because the Chaldeans, Sumerians and Babylonians, all had near identical myths from the creation of heaven and earth, the Fall of Man, the Great Flood, the Tower of Babel, the Ten Commandments and even a Garden of Eden. All of these ancient Babylonian myths pre-date the Hebrew Scriptures by at least a thousand years or more.

There have been a number of recent discoveries made in the fields of philology, archaeology, history and textual criticism that have led scholars to re-date the book of Genesis to the exilic and even post-exilic periods. The following are just a few of those discoveries.

THE HEBREW LANGUAGE

The first and foremost reason for considering a much later date for the composition for the book of Genesis than is held by the Judeo-Christian tradition, is the fact that the Hebrew language was not yet in existence during the period in which the book was allegedly written (second millennium bce). There are two major forms of Hebrew script, the *Ketav Ivri*, which is derived from the Phoenician (ancient Lebanese) language and the *Ketav Ashuri*, rooted in the Acadian or Babylonian language. Neither Hebraic Scripts originate with the actual Hebrews themselves; they are borrowed languages from people who worshiped other gods. This begs the question; in what language would Yahweh have spoken to the Hebrews, if the language of Hebrew itself did not exist at the time he allegedly spoke to them? And why did the "one true God" fail to directly bestow a language upon his chosen people, leaving them to plunder the languages of much more advanced civilizations, which the Hebrew Scriptures themselves, tells us he despised? Whether the original manuscripts of Genesis were penned in the Babylonian Hebrew or the Phoenician Hebrew, one thing is almost certain and that is, the earliest possible date that the Hebrew book of Genesis could have been written is no earlier than 1000bce.

With regards to the late development of the Hebrew language the *Cambridge Encyclopaedia of the World's Ancient Languages* relates that no extant inscriptions that can be identified as Hebrew antedate the tenth century bce, and that Hebrew inscriptions do not begin to appear widespread until the eighth century bce.[76]

Such a fact appears to be difficult to reconcile in the face of such a xenophobic God, who loved "his people" and no one else. Why wouldn't he have given them their own language? Why, if these stories were written in the second millennium bce, don't we find any evidence of the existence of Hebrew at that time and why, if he instructed Moses to pen the Ten Commandments, wouldn't he have done so in his chosen people's own language?

THE PHILISTINES AND THE CITY OF GERAR

Another piece of evidence indicating that the book of Genesis, as it has come down to us today, could not have been written any earlier than around the eighth century bce, relates to the mention of the Philistines and the Philistine city of Gerar. Based on the archaeological evidence, the Philistines did not arrive in Canaan until around 1200bce. What's more, the Philistine city Gerar, mentioned at Genesis 26:1, did not become a city until sometime between the eighth and seventh centuries bce, which pushes back the composition or alteration of the book of Genesis to sometime between the eighth and seventh centuries bce, around 800 years later than the traditionally accepted date of its authorship.

In their book, *The Bible Unearthed,* professor of archaeology at Tel Aviv University in Israel, Prof. Israel Finkelstein, and historian, Neil Asher Silberman, discuss this piece of evidence in the following words:

Then there is the issue of the Philistines. We hear of them in connection with Isaac's encounter with "Abimelech, king of the Philistines," at the city of Gerar (Genesis 26:1). The Philistines, a group of migrants from the Aegean or eastern Mediterranean, had not established their settlements along the coastal plain of Canaan until sometime after 1200bce. Their cities prospered in the eleventh and tenth centuries and

---

[76]Roger D. Woodward. The Cambridge Encyclopaedia of the World's Ancient Languages: The Ancient Languages of Syria-Palestine and Arabia. Cambridge University Press. (2008). p. 36.

continued to dominate the area well into the Assyrian period. The mention of Gerar as a Philistine city in the narrative of Isaac and the mention of the city (without the Philistine attribution) in the stories of Abraham (Genesis 20:1) suggest that it had a special importance or at least was widely known at the time of the composition of the patriarchal narratives. Gerar is today identified with Tel Haror northwest of Beersheba, and excavations there have shown that in the Iron Age-the early phase of Philistine history-it was no more than a small quite insignificant village. But by the late eighth and seventh century bce, it had become a strong, heavily fortified Assyrian administrative stronghold in the south, an obvious landmark.[77]

CAMELS

The next reason for questioning the traditional date of Genesis is the presence of camels in the narrative. This issue is not as cut and dry as some of the other issues that demonstrate the late composition of the book of Genesis, but there is some evidence (in the negative form) to suggest that camels were not domesticated in the middle of the second millennium bce. According to Ladaj Saphir, an archaeo-zoologist working in the Archaeo-zoology Department of Tel Aviv University in Israel, camels were not domesticated, at least in Egypt, until after 1000bce. She says:

According to the archaeological evidence, the camel could not have been domesticated as a beast of burden before the first millennium B.C.[78]

You may be wondering why this issue is important.

In Genesis 12:16 Abraham is rewarded by the Pharaoh of Egypt for giving the Pharaoh his "sister," who was actually Abraham's wife/half-sister. For this gift of prostitution, the Pharaoh rewarded him with sheep, asses, slaves and a camel. There are numerous other

---

[77]Israel Finkelstein and Neil Asher Silberman. The *Bible* Unearthed: Archaeology's New Vision of Ancient Israel and the Origin of its Sacred Texts. Touchstone (2002). pp. 37–38

[78]Thierry Ragobert and Isy Morgenzstern. The *Bible* Unearthed. TV. Documentary Series. Part 2: The Exodus. (2005).

references to camels throughout the book of Genesis, as well (see Gen. 24:10-11, Gen. 29:43, Gen 31:17, Gen. 32:7, 32:15 and Gen. 37:25, for example).

However, camels were not domesticated until after 1000bce and this story is traditionally said to have taken place around 2000bce, that is, toward the end of the third and beginning of the second millennium bce. Therefore, the author of Genesis was living in a time when camels were domesticated, which according to both archaeological evidence and the scholarly consensus amongst modern archaeologists, couldn't have been before the first millennium bce (1000bce - 1bce). This pushes both the story of Abraham and the book of Genesis to after 1000bce, at least.

The *Harper Collins Bible Dictionary* corroborates the above point, whilst disagreeing slightly on the date of the introduction of the Camel to Canaan and Egypt. It informs us that there is no archaeological evidence for the domesticated camel in Egypt at the beginning of the second millennium bce, as the references in Genesis suggest and that the scholarly consensus on the issue says that such references to the camel in Genesis are anachronisms only.[79]

Further, volume 2 of *The Cambridge Ancient History*, states:

The attribution to Abraham (Gen. xii. 16; xxiv. 10) and Jacob (Gen. xxx. 43;xxxii) of camels as transport and riding animals may be looked upon as an anachronism. At the time assumed for these patriarchs, that is the first half of the second millennium B.C, there seem to have been no domesticated camels in Western Asia and Egypt.[80]

And professor of Archaeology at Boston University, Kathryn A. Bard says that the camel wasn't introduced into Egypt until late in the first millennium bce.[81]

Further, in her book, *Encyclopaedia of the Archaeology of Ancient Egypt*, Professor Bard reaffirms and elaborates upon her previous

---

[79]Paul. J. Achtemeier. Harper-Collins *Bible* Dictionary Revised Edition. Harper Collins, (1989). p. 165.
[80]I. E. S. Edwards. C. J. Gadd. N. G. L. Hammond E. Sollberger. The Cambridge Ancient History: Vol. 2. Part 1. Cambridge University Press. (1973). p. 24.
[81]Kathryn A. Bard. An Introduction to the Archaeology of Ancient Egypt. Blackwell Publishing (2007). p. 60.

findings, saying: *The few contested camelid figurines and the few bone finds suggest that dromedaries were known to the ancient Egyptians but not adopted. Later in the first millennium BC, dromedaries and perhaps camels were brought to the Delta and the Nile Valley.*[82]

In addition, two Jewish Rabbis, Messod and Roger Sabbah, discuss this point in their bestseller, *Secrets of the Exodus: The Egyptian Origins of the Hebrew People*, arguing that the appearance of camels within the narratives found in the Book of Genesis are tell-tale signs that the book was composed much later than previously believed:

Biblical researchers believed that the presence of camels in the story of the patriarchs was an error of the scribes. However, the scribes went into great detail, as if they wanted to pass on a message. "He caused the camels to kneel ..." (Genesis 24:11). "Rebecca looked up and alighted from the camel ..." (Genesis24:64). Presenting Biblical characters alighting from camels' backs is an anachronism that the scribes apparently wished to present.

By the sixth century bce, the camel, a symbol of wealth and power, had already been domesticated in Babylonia.

Had they forgotten that camels did not exist in ancient Egypt?

Couldn't they have presented and described Abraham's power and wealth without camels? The camels give a Mesopotamian twist to the story, which would have been pleasing to their captors.[83]

Further still, although differing with the above mentioned dates of the introduction of the domestic camel in ancient Egypt, Professor of Egyptology, Rosalie David, supports the findings of both Prof. Bard and the scholars at Cambridge University with regards to the absence of domestic camels prior to 1000bce, stating that the camel wasn't introduced into Egypt until the Greek period.[84]

Finally, professor of archaeology at Tel Aviv University in Israel, Professor Israel Finkelstein says that despite the book of Genesis' depictions

---

[82]Kathryn A. Bard. Encyclopaedia of the Archaeology of Ancient Egypt. Routledge (1999). p. 363.

[83]Messod and Roger Sabbah. The secrets of the Exodus: The Egyptian roots of the Hebrew People. Allworth Press (2004) p. 90.

[84]Rosalie David. Handbook to Life in Ancient Egypt. Facts on File Inc. (2003). pp. 303–304.

of camel caravans, we know that the camel wasn't domesticated until the first millennium bce and that at Tell Jemmeh in the southern coastal plain of Israel, excavations revealed the increase in camel bones (a tell-tale sign of domestication), as late as the seventh century.[85]

CHALDEA

The book of Genesis describes Abraham's birthplace as being in Ur in Chaldea, which as mentioned, is more popularly known today as Babylon. At Genesis 11:28, 31 and 15:7, the Hebrew word *Kasdim* (Eng. Chaldee) is used to describe the ancient region of Babylonia. The problem with the use of *Kasdim* is that it was not used to describe ancient Babylonia until the sixth century bce, which is known as the Neo-Babylonian Period. Before this it was known as *Sumer,* yet the account given in Genesis refers to this region as *Chaldea.* This fact provides further evidence that the book of Genesis was more than likely written or at least redacted, sometime during or after the sixth century bce. According to Messod and Roger Sabbah, the story of Abraham was a sixth century composition constructed to pander to the Jew's Babylonian captors and masters. They tell us that although the city of Ur existed in Sumeria, the name "Chaldea" was not applied until the sixth century bce; that the authors of Genesis made the story compatible with sixth centurybce Babylon and that the story, as it has come down to us, is unhistorical.[86]

Moreover, if you read through the entire *Old Testament,* you will only find four references to Ur being mentioned as the home of Abraham (See Genesis 11:28, 31; 15:17; Nehemiah 9:7) and in each of these instances the Hebrew phrase *Ur Kasdim* is used. *Kasdim* is the Hebrew of the English transliterated word,"'Chaldeans'" The trouble is, as mentioned above, that the name Chaldea didn't exist in the second millennium bce and only began to be used in the Neo-Babylonian period.[87]

---

[85]Israel Finkelstein & Amihai Mazar. The Quest for the Historical Israel: Debating Archeology and the History of Early Israel. Brill (2007). p. 46.

[86]Ibid. p. 91.

[87]Paul. J. Achtemeier. Harper-Collins *Bible* Dictionary Revised Edition. Harper Collins, (1989). p. 1187.

Further still, the President of the Biblical Archaeology Society of New York, Gary Greenberg said in his book, *101 Myths of the Bible*:

These references to Ur of the Chesdim, Chesed, and Aram obviously stem from a time when:

1. Aramea and Chaldea had come into existence;
2. The Hebrews started to adopt Aramaic terminology;
3. Chaldea had become a major force in Mesopotamia;
4. The collective memory of Chaldean and Aramaic origins had receded into myth; and
5. The Hebrews would use the Aramaic pronunciation rather than the native dialect for the Chaldean name.

This suggests a timeframe well after the Babylonian conquest of Judah and almost certainly into the Persian or Hellenistic period (fifth century bceor later.)[88]

It appears that many, if not all of the accounts of Abraham's birth and travels, were created no earlier than the sixth century bce, which seems to indicate that the writer(s) was either in Babylon during the exilic period or had already returned to Israel. Either way, the authors of the Hebrew Scriptures had ample opportunity to copy and re-script the mythologies of the ancient Babylonians to suit their own social and theological needs.

KINGS IN ISRAEL

Genesis 36:31 says;

And these are the kings that reigned in the land of Edom, before there reigned any king over the children of Israel.

The obvious implication of this statement is that at the time the author was writing this passage, there had been numerous kings who had reigned in Israel, as evidenced by the phrase, *any king over the children of Israel*.

---

[88]Gary Greenberg. 101 Myths of the *Bible*: How Ancient Scribes Invented Biblical History. Sourcebooks Inc. (2000). p. 116.

The very first king of Israel was Saul and his reign has been dated from 1020bce-1000bce.[89] Thus, the author must have been writing the account in Genesis following this period. There may well be good reason to suggest it was long after this period, due to the fact that the author says; *before there reigned any king over the children of Israel.* Use of the phrase, *any king* implies that he was aware of more than one king. If only one king had reigned it would have made more sense for the author to name that king or if there were two, to use the phrase "either king" or "both kings", or use their names, but it seems as if there had been many kings which preceded the account. This indicator coupled with the textual and archaeological evidence showing that Saul was the first king of Israel in the tenth century bce, seems to indicate that the account in Genesis was written well after this date.

BOZRAH IN EDOM

The next clue to the late composition of the book of Genesis can be found within the reference to an Edomite king by the name of Jobab ruling in place of King Bela, who was reported to have died. Jobab's father was Zarah, a king from Bozrah (see Genesis 36:33).

Recently, the ancient city of Bozrah was excavated by archaeologists, who discovered that it came into being no earlier than the eighth century bce.

Bennett, the archaeologist responsible for excavating Bozrah, said that there is no archaeological evidence to support the story of the king of Edom refusing passage to Moses, or for a powerful kingdom of Edom in the time of David and his son Solomon. He further informs us that archaeology teaches us that the biblical traditions enunciated at Genesis 36:31 (kings of Edom) and Numbers 20:14 (Edomite king blocking the passage of Moses) reflect eighth to sixth century bce conditions.[90]

---

[89]Bruce Metzger and Herbert G. May. The New Oxford Annotated *Bible* With Apocrypha. (1977). p.1548.

[90]Crystal M. Bennett. "Excavations at Buseirah (Biblical Bozrah)." John F. A. Sawyer & David J. A. Clines, editors. Midian, Moab and Edom; The History and Archaeology of the Late Bronze and Iron Age Jordan and North-west Arabia. 1983. Journal for the Study of the *Old Testament*. Supplement 24. Sheffield, England. pp. 16–17.

The *Harper Collins Bible Dictionary* supports this conclusion by highlighting the archaeological excavations performed by Crystal-M. Bennett, which show quite clearly that Bozrah, as with the other Edomite sites, didn't flourish until the seventh and even as late as the sixth centuries bce. *Harper Collins Bible Dictionary* raises this issue in relation to the historical accuracy of the Edomite king list mentioned at both Genesis 36:33 and 1 Chronicles 1:44, which is now deemed by most scholars to be spurious.[91]

In providing evidence contrary to the alleged conquest of Canaan by Joshua, the *Oxford Handbook of Biblical Studies* discounts the existence of Bozrah prior to the traditional date of Joshua's alleged conquest. As well as debunking the Bronze Age existence of the cities of Jericho, Ai, Heshbon, and Arad, the learned compilers of the handbook report that the kingdom of Edom didn't exist when the traditional tale of Moses being blocked by the king of Edom (Numbers 20:14), was supposed to have transpired.[92]

Further to this point, Finkelstein informs us that Edom did not exist as a political entity until a relatively late period. He points to the various Assyrian historical and archaeological sources we have, which clearly show that Edom did not become a fully developed state until the late eighth century. To this point, Finkelstein says:

The archaeological evidence is clear: the first large-scale wave of settlement in Edom accompanied by the establishment of significantly large settlements and fortresses may have started in the late-eighth century bce, but reached its peak only in the seventh and early-sixth centuries bce Before then, the area was sparsely populated. Excavations at Bosrah (Buseirah), the capital of late-Iron II Edom, revealed that it grew to become a large city only in the Assyrian period.[93]

Another clue which seems to suggest that the passage in question was written in the post-exilic period, is that the author, if living within

---

[91]Paul. J. Achtemeier. Harper-Collins *Bible* Dictionary Revised Edition. Harper Collins, (1989). p. 153.
[92]J.W. Rogerson. Judith. M. Lieu. The Oxford Handbook of Biblical Studies. Oxford University Press, (2006). p. 63.
[93]Israel Finkelstein & Amihai Mazar. The Quest for the Historical Israel: Debating Archeology and the History of Early Israel. Brill (2007) pp.47–48.

the seventh century would have known that contrary to the account given in Genesis (36:31), there were kings in Israel before there were kings in Edom and not vice versa, as was asserted by the author of Genesis (see Genesis 36:31). Quite a lot of time would have to elapse before this fact would be forgotten by the people of Israel and the authors of Genesis. As a result of this historical inaccuracy, it may not be unreasonable to suggest that the book of Genesis as we know it today could have possibly been written as late as, or even later than, the sixth or even fifth centuries bce.

NINEVEH

Yet another piece of evidence which seems to show that Genesis was written in either the exilic or post-exilic period is the primary reference to Nineveh, listed first and foremost amongst the cities of Babylonia (Gen. 10:11-12). During the period in which Genesis was traditionally believed to have been written, the capital city of Babylon was Asshur, yet there is no mention of this city, instead we see three major cities listed; Nineveh, Rehoboth and Calah.

Genesis 10:11-12 lists the cities of Babylonia as follows;

…Nineveh and the city Rehoboth and Calah.

And Resen between Nineveh and Calah: the same is a great city.

The fact that Nineveh is the first mentioned city is of great importance from a literary point of view. It seems to indicate that it was the most significant city, probably the capital. Moreover, in verse twelve it is once again given first place over the city of Calah. The issue here is that it did not become the capital city until the seventh century bce.

We may once again turn to the *Harper Collins Bible Dictionary* for confirmation that the city of Nineveh did not become the capital until Sennacherib's ascension to the throne, which took place in the eighth century bce, and that it finally lost this title in the fifth century bce.[94]

---

[94]Paul. J. Achtemeier. Harper-Collins *Bible* Dictionary Revised Edition. Harper Collins, (1989). p.759.

There is little doubt that the author of this passage in Genesis, saw Nineveh as the chief city of Babylon, leading him to give it pride of place as the first city mentioned and that in so doing betrayed the fact that he belonged to a period later than the sixth century bce.

LUD/LYDIA

The final piece of evidence I will provide to show a late date for the composition of the book of Genesis relates to the mention of a town yet unfamiliar to the fifteenth century bce inhabitants of the region, a town called Lud or Lydia in English. In Genesis 10:22 the town of Lud (Lydia) is mentioned, however it was unheard of before the seventh century bce, according to Ashurbanipal, the king of the Babylonian Empire. According to Ashurbanipal, Lud was unheard of by his fathers and so it is unlikely that an Israelite author writing in the fifteenth century bce would have heard of it.[95] Ashurbanipal was the head of a great empire that had conquered almost all of the surrounding nations, their exploits spanned across many countries and yet his fathers had not heard of this place known as Lud. What are the chances of an author hearing about this place before the kings of a mighty empire? However, if the author of Genesis was writing the account after Ashurbanipal's testimony, then he would have had the opportunity to learn of such a place and include it in his record. This seems to be the most probable scenario and would place the author sometime after Ashurbanipal's reign in the seventh century bce.[96]

In Knight's comprehensive work entitled *Ancient Civilizations,* we learn that Lydia did not emerge as a civilization until the Mermnad dynasty, around 685 bce, which uses the ancient historian Herodotus as its source[97]

Finally, with regards to the late composition of the book of Genesis, referring to the *Oxford Handbook of Biblical Studies*, we are able to

---

[95]George Smith. History of Ashurbanipal. Williams and Norgate. (1871). pp. 64, 73.
[96]J.B. Bury, M.A, F.B.A., S.A. Cook, Litt.D., F.E. Adcock, M.A. The Cambridge Ancient History. Vol. 1: Egypt and Babylonia to 1580 B.C. Cambridge University Press. (1928). p. 149.
[97]Judson Knight, Stacy A McConnell & Lawrence W. Baker. Ancient Civilizations Almanac. Vol. 1. A.X.L An Imprint of the Gale Group. (2000). p. 145.

establish the probable truth that the book of Genesis was written no earlier than the seventh century bce:

Attempts to identify Abraham's family migration with a supposed westward Amorite migration at the collapse of the Early Bronze Age c.2100–1800 bce, or to explain personal names, marriage customs, or laws of property by reference to fifteenth century Nuzi or Mari documents have failed to convince. Abraham's life-style is no longer seen as reflecting Intermediate Early Bronze/Middle Bronze bedouin, or donkey caravaneers trading between Mesopotamia and Egypt, or tent-dwellers living alongside Middle Bronze Age cities in Canaan; rather, with its references to Philistines and Aramaeans, Ammonites, Moabites, and Edomites, Ishmael and his descendants Kedar, Nebaioth, and Tema, Assyria and its cities of Nineveh and Calah, camel caravans and spices, Genesis reflects the first millennium world of the Assyrian empire. With its emphasis on the southern centres of Hebron and (Jeru)salem (Gen. 14: 18) and the northern centres of Bethel and Shechem, the Abraham story reveals knowledge of the kingdoms of Israel and Judah (cf. Gen. 49: 8–12, 22–6), in its present form probably deriving from Judah's Floruit in the seventh century bce.[98]

Finally, let us learn from the professor of theology at the University of Hull, Lester G. Grabbe, who, in his book, An Introduction to Second Temple Judaism: History and Religion of the Jews in the Time of Nehemiah, the Maccabees, Hillel and Jesus, says that the Pentateuch was likely composed late in the Persian period (sixth to fourth centuries bce) and that we have no way of knowing who the authors of these works were.[99]

All of the available evidence, of which I have canvassed a small sample, suggests that Moses was not the author of the first five books of the *Bible* and that the authors (of at least a majority portion) of the book of Genesis, probably lived some time during or after the sixth century bce. This places them in the exilic or post-exilic period, thus

[98]J.W. Rogerson. Judith. M. Lieu. The Oxford Handbook of Biblical Studies. Oxford University Press, (2006). p. 61.

[99]Lester G. Grabbe. An Introduction to Second Temple Judaism: History and Religion of the Jews in the Time of Nehemiah, the Maccabees, Hillel and Jesus. T&T Clark. (2010). p. 4.

affording them opportunity to copy the myths of their former hosts, the Babylonians.

◆

ARMAGEDDON – THE SELF-FULFILLING PROPHECY

I decided to write this article to point out the danger of the Armageddon, not as a prophecy which will come to fruition as a result of divine forces, but rather, one which has the potential to unfold due to certain social and psychological factors, associated with the belief in an impeding Armageddon.

The origins of the Christian Armageddon enunciated in the book of Revelation (Rev. 16:16), which is rooted in earlier apocalyptic and proto-apocalyptic traditions found in the earlier works contained in both the *New Testament* and the Old, are dubious to say the least. The book of Revelation itself has been steeped in controversy with regards to its authorship,[100] from the protests of the third century Christian scholar from Alexandria, Dionysius, to the objections of the fourth century Church historian, Eusebius, to the complaints of the founder of the Protestant Church in the sixteenth century, Martin Luther.

The term "Armageddon", used exclusively in the book of Revelation, describes the final battle here on earth between the cosmic forces of good and evil that will allegedly herald the apocalypse of an alleged God.[101] The author of the book of Revelation, who calls himself John, (Rev. 1:1), employed the term Armageddon, claiming it to be of Hebrew origin (Rev 16:16), yet nowhere in the Hebrew Scriptures, from which this author allegedly sourced this word, or in any other book from the *New Testament*, had the term Armageddon been used.[102] The term has been translated in various manuscripts of the *New*

---

[100]The author gives his name as, John, but most contend this is not the alleged John who allegedly authored the pseudonymous Gospel of "John."

[101]Margaret M. Mitchell & Frances M. Young. The Cambridge History of Christianity – Origins to Constantine. Cambridge University Press (2008). p. 107, 170 & 298; Apocalypse: Anc. Greek: *'apokalypsis;'* meaning to "uncover, reveal or disclose."

[102]Paul. J. Achtemeier. Harper-Collins *Bible* Dictionary Revised Edition. Harper Collins, (1989). p. 71.

Testament in a number of ways. Some manuscripts translate this Greek transliteration of the alleged Hebrew term to mean; "Mount Megiddo," "city of Megiddo," "land of Megiddo," "mount of assembly," "city of desire," and "His fruitful mountain."[103] However, as mentioned, nowhere throughout the entire corpus of the Hebrew *Bible* (*Old Testament*) does this term make an appearance. It seems to have been a word which was unique to the author of that hallucination filled book, Revelation, and him alone.

Here we must pause for a moment and make a brief distinction between two semi-related, yet conflated and confused eschatological terms.[104] Armageddon, as mentioned, refers to the questionable Greek transliteration of the alleged Hebrew term Mount Megiddo, or any one of its other possible renderings, used by the author of Revelation to describe the final battle prevalent in many apocalyptic myths, whilst the word "apocalypse", pertains to the final revelation of "God's" word, logos, or presence on earth and the mysteries associated therewith."[105]

The concept of an apocalypse can be found in the Hebrew Scriptures, in particular within the books of Daniel, Ezekiel, Zechariah and Isaiah, and outside of the official Hebrew Canon, in books like 2 Baruch, 3 Baruch, Ezra, Enoch, *The Apocalypse of Abraham and the book of the Jubilees*. Further, we find apocalypses within the official Gospels (see Mark 13, Matthew 24 and Luke 21) and also within the epistles of Paul (see 2 Corinthians and 1 Thessalonians). There are also apocryphal Christian texts which speak of the apocalypse, such as the Apocalypse of Paul, the Apocalypse of Peter and a number of other apocryphal Christian works.

Christianity took the Hebrew, or Second Temple Era Jewish apocalyptic tradition, which the Hebrews had themselves adopted from their liberators, the more ancient Persians,[106] and applied it to the

---

[103]Ibid.

[104]The term eschatology comes from the Greek *'eschatos'* meaning 'things,' and refers to beliefs associated with the so-called end times and a future aeon or time.

[105]Fred Skolnik & Michael Berenbaum. *Encyclopaedia Judaica* 2nd *Ed. Vol. 2.* Thompson Gale. (2007). pp. 256–257.

[106]J.W. Rogerson. Judith. M. Lieu. The Oxford Handbook of Biblical Studies. Oxford University Press, (2006). p. 405.

second coming of Christ, which, according to Christian mythology, would be preceded by John's Armageddon, or final battle, asserted to act as the brutal and bloody gateway for the earthly return of the all-loving God.

Enunciating the pre-Christian and even pre-Judean belief in the apocalypse, or "final revealing", found amongst the more ancient Persians, Dr Paul Carus informs us that:

The most characteristic features of the Persian religion after the lifetime of Zoroaster consist in the teaching that a great crisis is near at hand, which will lead to the renovation of the world called 'frashokereti' in the Avesta, and 'frashakart' in Pahlavi. Saviours will come, born of the seed of Zoroaster, and in the end the great Saviour who will bring about the resurrection of the dead. He will be the "son of a virgin " and the "All-conquering." His name shall be the Victorious….Righteousness-incarnate…., and the Saviour…... Then the living shall become immortal, yet their bodies will be transfigured so that they will cast no shadows, and the dead shall rise, "within their lifeless bodies incorporate life shall be restored." (Fr. 4. 3.)[107]

Further, George Cox, in volume two of his series, *Aryan Mythology,* says:

The Apocalypse exhibits Satan with the physical attributes of Ahriman (the devil of the more ancient Persian myth): he is called the dragon, the old serpent, who fights against God and his angels. The Vedic myth, transformed and exaggerated in the Iranian books, finds its way through this channel into Christianity.[108]

Finally, quoting the scholars responsible for compiling the online Jewish Encyclopaedia, we learn:

Most scholars, Jewish as well as non-Jewish, are of the opinion that Judaism was strongly influenced by Zoroastrianism in views relating to angelology and demonology, and probably also in the doctrine of the resurrection, as well as in eschatological ideas in general…[109]

---

[107]Paul Carus, *The History Of The Devil And The Idea Of Evil* (New York: Gramercy Books, 1996) p. 58.
[108]George. W. Cox. M.A. Aryan Mythology. Vol. 2. Longman's, Green and Co. (1870). p. 357.
[109]http://www.jewishencyclopedia.com/articles/15283-zoroastrianism

As mentioned above, many scholars, Jewish, Christian and secular, have noted the profound impact that the Persian religion had on both Judaism and Christianity, particularly with the good god versus the evil god motif, found in both Second Temple Judaism, which later made its way into the Christian religion, and with regards to the various eschatological traditions within these two and even three religions, including Islam, which has its own borrowed version.

Returning now to our discussion on the term Armageddon, the town from which the term derives part of its etymological root, Megiddo, is a real place located in the north of Israel and was recorded in the *Old Testament* as the location of many ancient battles (see Judges 5:19, 2 Kings 9:27, 2 Kings 23:29), of which, the archaeological evidence, to a degree at least, seems to support. So it may be that the second century author of the book of Revelation was symbolically locating his final mythological battle between the forces of good and evil at Megiddo, due to the fact that renowned biblical battles were recorded as taking place there centuries ago.

Whether the author of Revelation located his final battle in Megiddo for symbolic reasons or not, one thing is certain, the final battle as described by the author of Revelation, has not taken place yet. This does not mean that countless people throughout history haven't claimed that the end was imminent, for barely a year has passed without some heralder of doom, screaming at the top of his lungs, "the end is nigh," causing believers to fall to their knees in prayer and nonbelievers to fall on their faces with laughter.

Just to give you an idea of how many times Christians have predicted the end of the world and been wrong, I will provide the following list which is neither comprehensive, nor exhaustive.

- 70-100 ce – Gospels and Pauls Epistles (*New Testament*) predicted that the end of days and Jesus' second coming would occur in the lifetime of the first century Christians.
- 90 CE: Saint Clement 1 predicted that the world would end during his lifetime.
- Second Century ce: Members of the Montanist movement predicted that Jesus would return during their lifetime and

establish the New Jerusalem in the city of Pepuza in Asia Minor.

- 365ce: Hilary of Poitiers, announced that the end would come about in 365 ce.
- 375 to 400 ce: Saint Martin of Tours predicted that the end would happen sometime before 400 ce.
- 500 ce: Hippolytus and the Christian academic Sextus Julius Africanus predicted the end of the world in 500 ce.
- 968 ce: An eclipse was interpreted as a prelude to the end of the world by the army of the German emperor Otto III.
- 1000-JAN-1: Many Christians in Europe predicted the end of the world in 1000 ce.
- 1000-MAY: The body of Charlemagne was disinterred on Pentecost. A legend had arisen that an emperor would rise from his sleep to fight the Antichrist.
- 1005-1006: A famine throughout Europe was seen as a sign of the end of the world and Jesus' second coming.
- 1147: Gerard of Poehlde believed that the millennium had actually started in 306 ce during Constantine's reign. Thus, the world end was expected in 1306 ce.
- 1179: John of Toledo predicted the end of the world during 1186.
- 1205: Joachim of Fiore predicted in 1190 that the Antichrist was already in the world, and that King Richard of England would defeat him.
- 1346 and later: The black plague spread across Europe, killing one third of the population. This was seen as the prelude to an immediate end of the world.
- 1496: This was approximately 1500 years after the birth of Jesus. Some mystics in the 15th century predicted that the millennium would begin during this year.
- 1524: Many astrologers predicted the imminent end of the world due to a world-wide flood.
- 1533: Melchior Hoffman predicted that Jesus' return would happen a millennium and a half after the nominal date of his execution, in 1533.

- 1669: The Old Believers in Russia believed that the end of the world would occur in this year. Twenty thousand burned themselves to death between 1669 and 1690 to protect themselves from the Antichrist.
- 1689: Benjamin Keach, a 17th century Baptist, predicted the end of the world for this year.
- 1736: British theologian and mathematician William Whitson predicted a great flood similar to Noah's for October 13th of this year.
- 1783: On June 8th, a volcanic eruption in southern Iceland started. It pumped massive amounts of toxic dust, sulphur dioxide and fluorine into the atmosphere. Cattle died, crops failed, and about one quarter of the island's population died of starvation. Many predicted that the end of the world was imminent.
- 1794: Charles Wesley, one of the founders of Methodism, thought that Doomsday would occur in this year.
- 1830: Margaret McDonald, a Christian prophetess, predicted that Robert Owen would be the Antichrist. Owen helped found New Harmony, Indiana.
- 1832: Joseph Smith was the founder of the Mormon Church and predicted the end of the world in this year.[110]

More recently, although there have been plenty of other failed prophecies both before and after, in the 1970s, Christian theologian Hal Lindsey, prophesied the end of the world and the coming apocalypse. He asserted that the world would end sometime before 1988, based on his interpretation of a parable allegedly spoken by Jesus, in the Gospel of Matthew. The parable is as follows:

From the fig tree learn this parable. When its branch becomes tender and it puts forth its leaves, you know that summer is near. So also you, when you see all these things you know that he [the Son of Man] is near, at the very gates. Truly I tell you, this generation will not pass away before all these things take place.

~Matthew 24:32-34

---

[110]http://en.wikipedia.org/wiki/List_of_dates_predicted_for_apocalyptic_events

The dazzling footwork Lindsey needed to perform in order to make this obscure parable foretell the end of the world in 1988 would impress even the most professional dancer, for in forming this failed prophecy, he had no date, no specific details, nothing at all to work with, but a sincere belief in the inerrancy of the *Bible* and a very active, rationalizing imagination.

His "reasoning" serves to illustrate one of the means by which these erroneous eschatological beliefs are held together by cognitions that are compelled to keep tenuous beliefs intact.

Lindsey, in his bestseller, *The Late Great Planet Earth,* argued that the "fig tree", spoken of in the parable, was an analogy for the nation of Israel and by *putting forth its branches*, the author of the parable had intended it to mean when Israel again became a nation, which, as you probably know, was in 1948, after the second World War. So how did he arrive at the end date 1988? The parable goes onto say: *Truly I tell you, this generation will not pass away before all these things take place.* Lindsey, and most of the other credulous believers in the 1970s and early 1980s, took this to mean that a generation after the fig tree put forth its branches, the end would come; so, with the *Bible* suggesting that forty years is a generation, *Bible*a forty-year countdown began once Israel became a nation in 1948, thus leading to 1988 as the date for the end of the world. As you are reading this little article now, decades later, I think we can safely conclude that Lindsey's errant interpretation of this alleged prophecy was wrong.

These eschatological beliefs rely on vague and ambiguous language, as a kind of passive component for survival, whilst they are combined with the active component, belief, or more accurately, the rationalizations, adaptational strategies and distorted cognitive processes, which accompany belief in order to protect it. With these active and passive components combined, such eschatological beliefs are real in the mind of the believer; at least until they fail and even then, some believers will not be deterred by the obvious failure of a believed prophecy.[111]

---

[111]Festinger, L., Riecken, H. W., & Schachter, S. When Prophecy fails. University of Minnesota Press. (1956). p. 3.

To further illustrate the vague and ambiguous nature of these alleged prophecies of doom, we turn to the warning of Christian apologist, Dave Hunt.

In his book, An Urgent Call to a Serious Faith, he asserts:

Current events seem to be heading in that direction and leading to Armageddon. That horrible war will bring the intervention of Jesus Christ from heaven to rescue Israel and to destroy Antichrist and his world government. All indications today are that we are indeed heading toward a world government. The Bible declares that Antichrist will control all banking and commerce in the entire world with a number, a remarkable prophecy anticipating modern computer technology.[112]

Ok, what are these "events" that "seem" to be heading in the direction of Armageddon?

If we are to conflate, blend and mix the eschatological warnings and signs from both the pseudonymous authors of the Gospels, the Epistles of Paul and that profoundly delusional, yet poetic prelate and author of the book of Revelation, we may establish the rough and general theological ingredients that go into bringing about this violent and final episode, but for the sake of preserving both space and time, Matthew's gospel gives us a good idea of the primary ingredients for the end of the world:

Wars and rumours of wars (24:6)

Famines (24:7)

Pestilences/diseases (24:7)

Earthquakes in diverse places (24:7)

There are a few other minor pre-requisites for the apocalypse, but these are the main signs of the impending doom and they serve us well in illustrating the vagaries with which these prophecies have been cleverly constructed.

If one carefully reads the excerpt from Dave Hunt's "urgent" book, cited above, it becomes clear that Hunt, and those like him are searching for meaning in words and events that are altogether barren. To reiterate, he says; *current events seem to be heading in that direction and*

---

[112]David Hunt. An Urgent Call to Serious Faith. Berean Call. (2006).

leading to Armageddon! Now that the reader is familiar with what those events are alleged to be, we are in a position to ask a very pertinent question. Weren't they also heading in that direction during the collapse of the Roman Empire with the brutal strife between the Goths and the Vanguards; couldn't those living during the great plagues of Europe during the first few Christian centuries have also seen that the world was in its death throes? Take for example, the Antonine Plague which wiped out over ten million people across Europe and the Near East, surely with the wars that were occurring simultaneously, these times would have seemed like the world was heading for Armageddon. Wouldn't the witnesses of the furious eruption of Mt. Vesuvius (79CE) been justified in applying these eschatological prophecies to their own time? What about at the outbreak of World War 1? Ahh! The end is nigh! Or even the second World War? Ah! The world is on the brink of Armageddon! How about the outbreak of the Sars Virus or any of the thousands of times throughout our history where times have seemed to have fit the vague description of the End of Days enunciated within the texts of the *New Testament*?

Curiously, or suspiciously, we might say, every apocalyptic religion claims to possess the exclusive antidote to the horrors which will ensue during this terrifying time and each of these apocalyptic religions have promoted the end of the world, it would certainly seem, in order to scare people into submission. I see it to be a lot like the "hurry in, stocks won't last" sales strategy, in which frightened people are psychologically manipulated and hastened to get saved before the end comes, by such an "urgent call to faith." Once these newly converted believers make a psychological commitment, one induced through fear, their minds commit to the belief/belief-system and it becomes imbedded and entrenched in their psyche like a psychological virus. From this point on, as far as the newly converted believer is concerned, it makes little difference whether the promised prophecy comes to fruition or not. Here is where we arrive at the possible danger of such eschatological beliefs.

There is a danger that an Armageddon can be brought about, not by "God," but rather, by man himself. This could happen as a result of what psychologists call a "self-fulfilling Prophecy".

Before discussing self-fulfilling prophecies, we should first canvass some of the background components that give these self-fulfilling prophecies their power to manipulate the possessor to achieve the
prophesized outcome.

For a prophecy to gain power over a person's cognitive faculties,
they must believe it. It is little use trying to sell a vaguely worded and
superstitious prophecy to a sceptical non-believer, but to a believer,
someone prone to accepting information without intelligent inquiry
and solid evidence, the prophecy has the ability to dictate the very
parameters of the believer's worldview. So then, it would seem that
belief is a primary criteria for prophecy acceptance, but what is belief
and how does it work in the mind? The answers to these questions
may furnish us with an understanding of how dangerous beliefs can
be readily adopted by well-meaning human beings. I will avoid a
long drawn out discussion on the epistemological nature of belief versus knowledge and instead offer a brief dictionary definition which
should be suitable for our purposes.

Belief: noun

1. Something believed; an opinion or conviction: a belief that the
   earth is flat.
2. Confidence in the truth or existence of something not immediately susceptible to rigorous proof: a statement unworthy of
   belief.
3. Confidence; faith; trust: a child's belief in his parents.
4. A religious tenet or tenets; religious creed or faith: the Christian belief.[113]

These beliefs, according to neuroscientific studies, are located in both
the Ventromedial and the Anterior Cingulate Prefrontal Cortex regions of the brain, which are the very regions responsible for governing feelings of self-relevance, self-worth, self-esteem and most
importantly for the purposes of this investigation, emotion.[114]

---

[113]http://dictionary.reference.com/browse/belief
[114]http://www.sciencedaily.com/releases/2009/10/091005092302.htm

Thus, it appears that neuroscience, a relatively recent science, has come to support the long held theories of psychology, which hold that beliefs are located in the ego and that the ego has certain defence mechanisms, which come into play automatically and as a result of emotional stress. Such stress is the result of what social-psychologists refer to as cognitive dissonance. Cognitive dissonance describes the simultaneous possession of two conflicting ideas or beliefs, or the clash of one's behaviour with one's beliefs. The sufferer, being in a state of mental and emotional distress attempts to resolve this clash or dissonance in varying ways. Some of the most common solutions to resolving dissonances are to be found within confirmation biases (preferring information that supports your beliefs) and disconfirmation biases (ignoring information that conflicts with your beliefs). As many tests have concluded, primacy is one of the most significant factors regulating the resolution of a perceived challenge to the ego-housed beliefs.[115] Primacy refers to the significance we place on the earliest or primary beliefs we hold, generally speaking, as opposed to those we come into contact with later.

So what does all this have to do with the dangers of a self-fulfilling eschatological prophecy?

Before we answer that question, let us hear a final word from so-cial-psychologist, Leon Festinger, the father of cognitive dissonance theory:

A man with a conviction is a hard man to change. Tell him you disagree and he turns away. Show him facts or figures and he questions your sources. Appeal to logic and he fails to see your point. We have all experienced the futility of trying to change a strong conviction, especially if the convinced person has some investment in his belief. We are familiar with the variety of ingenious defences with which people protect their convictions, managing to keep them unscathed through the most devastating attacks. But man's resourcefulness goes beyond simply protecting a belief. Suppose an individual

---

[115]Lord, Charles G.; Lee Ross, Mark R. Lepper (1979). "Biased assimilation and attitude polarization: The effects of prior theories on subsequently considered evidence". Journal of Personality and Social Psychology (American Psychological Association 2098–2109.)

believes something with his whole heart; suppose further that he has a commitment to this belief, that he has taken irrevocable actions because of it; finally, suppose that he is presented with evidence, unequivocal and undeniable evidence, that his belief is wrong: what will happen? The individual will frequently emerge, not only unshaken, but even more convinced of the truth of his beliefs than ever before. Indeed, he may even show a new fervour about convincing and converting other people to his view.[116]

THE END IS NIGH!

I guess I have showered you with the necessary background and held you in suspense for long enough, so what is a self-fulfilling prophecy?

Self-fulfilling prophecies relate to expectations regarding the anticipated occurrence of a future event, behaviour or outcome, which acts to foster and fuel the likelihood of the future occurrence of that event, behaviour or outcome. Put simply, your beliefs and expectations can cause you to unwittingly bring about a future that begets your expectations. [117]

The term, self-fulfilling prophecy was first coined in 1948 by Robert Merton and as mentioned above, it describes:: ... *a false definition of the situation evoking a new behaviour which makes the originally false conception come true.*[118]

In the *Oxford Handbook of Analytical Sociology*, Michael Biggs breaks down the explanation of how and why self-fulfilling prophecies occur in a two-step explanatory framework. First, he addresses why X forms a false and arbitrary belief and behaves accordingly? Second, Biggs looks at why X's behaviour subsequently fulfils those beliefs? [119]

---

[116]Ibid. Pg. 3.
[117]Robert S. Feldman. Understanding Psychology. 10th Ed. McGraw Hill (2011). p. 598
[118](Merton 1968: 477) cited in; Michael Biggs, Peter Bearman and Peter Hedström The Oxford Handbook of Analytical Sociology. Oxford University Press. (2009). Chapter 13, p.1.
[119]Ibid. p. 13.

One of the explanations offered by Biggs regarding the first limb, relevant to the subject matter of this article is as follows (with my own bracketed additions):

One explanation is that X (i.e., Christian eschatological belief) has power over Y or that Y accepts X's (e.g. Hal Lindsay's) expertise. X then has considerable latitude in forming beliefs about Y, whether or not they are justified by evidence. Y cannot challenge false or arbitrary beliefs due to this power imbalance, or—more insidiously—Y accepts those beliefs as true.[120]

Biggs addresses the second limb (fulfilment of prophecy), with my bracketed additions, as follows:

One type of explanation depends on Y(The Christian) believing in the validity of X's(The Christian Religion's Eschatological Beliefs) expectations. In some circumstances, this invidious belief could simply have its effect by means of altering Y's (The Christian's) perceived payoffs. A student accepting the teacher's low opinion of his ability would rationally choose to reduce the time spent on study or practice. A more intriguing explanation is "response expectancy," originally proposed to explain placebo response. Here Y's belief has its effect beneath the actor's consciousness. Believing that you have been given morphine leads to pain relief, but you are not aware of the causal connection. Researchers on pain have actually discovered a chemical substance that enhances placebo response, by interacting with the brain's endogenous opioid system (Colloca and Benedetti 2005). This substance has no inherent physical powers to relieve pain—demonstrated by the fact it has no effect when administered covertly. It simply amplifies the effect of belief.[121]

Elaborating on this brief sociological explanation, *The Concise Corsini Encyclopaedia of Psychology*, describes a Self-fulfilling Prophecy in the following words:

The "self-fulfilling prophecy" is another interesting phenomenon in which an expectation about what will happen influences one's behaviour. Archibald has reviewed possible interpretations of such

---

[120]Ibid. p. 15.
[121]Ibid. p. 18.

effects. An expectation of failure may arouse anxiety so that a person tries to alleviate such feelings, or the aroused state may produce inappropriate effort (trying too hard or paying attention to the wrong cues). Alternatively, an expectation of a favourable outcome may simply increase effort and thereby facilitate performance. A person highly involved in a task may be oriented primarily to preserve self-esteem or some important value. Therefore, the task or goal may be redefined to avoid disconfirmation of the expectation.[122]

How is this eschatological self-fulfilling prophecy a danger to anyone who isn't a complete idiot? Well, let us turn to some recent statistics of one of the world's largest military powers, the U.S.

According to a Gallup poll taken in 2012, 77% of the American population identify themselves as Christian.[123] Also, approximately 55% of the population believe in angels and only 39% believe in evolution.[124] Furthermore, according to an article in the *Washington Times* (September 12, 2013):

A new finding from a research firm that focuses on faith issues says that two-fifths of Americans believe we're at the end times, living out Revelation biblical principles.

An estimated 41 percent of respondents in the Barna Group poll who were at least age 18 agreed that "the world is currently living in the 'end times' as described by prophesies in the Bible.[125]

These are the constituents, but what about the members of congress, those whose fingers are closest to the button, so to speak?

Well, according to figures taken in 2013, approximately 85% of the Senate are Christian,[126] which, according to the doctrines of their faith, means that they too believe in the looming doomsday allegedly awaiting us all on the horizon.

---

[122]The Concise Corsini Encyclopaedia of Psychology and Behavioral Science. 3rd Ed. W. Edward Craighead & Charles B. Nemeroff. John Wiley & Sons Inc. (2004). p. 477.
[123]http://www.gallup.com/poll/159548/identify-christian.aspx
[124]http://www.economist.com/blogs/democracyinamerica/2009/12/statistics_of_the_day
[125]http://www.washingtontimes.com/news/2013/sep/12/4-in10-american-adults-were-living-end-times/
[126]http://www.pewforum.org/files/2012/11/113-congress-relig-affil.pdf

Despite the multitude of failed doomsday prophecies that did not bring about a self-fulfilled Armageddon, a fact which may reasonably put the reader's mind at ease, we should, in my opinion, guard against the possibility, given that the world's most formidable military force belongs to a nation in which the majority of its citizens hold eschatological beliefs and that for a politician to succeed to the presidency or any position of influence, they must believe in God (the God of Abraham), and that such beliefs or prophecies can be self-fulfilling, meaning; the believer or group of believers can unconsciously and even consciously bring about circumstances that foment the believed prophecy. I think you may agree that when dangerous religious beliefs are mixed with the psychological defects of a species prone to egocentrism and belief-affirmation, a species prone to rationalizing the irrational, we need to take stock of our minds and vaccinate them against the superstitions of a credulous past, in order that we might enjoy a brighter future, or a future at all.

A QUICK THANK YOU TO THE RELIGION OF CHRISTIANITY.

Dear Christianity,

We the citizens of earth would just like to take a moment to thank you for the following:

The deliberate and dishonest rewriting of history by the Church Father Eusebius (fourth Century); As well as many of his successors throughout the ages.

The fining and imprisoning of non-Christians and non-orthodox Christians, by Constantine and the Church. (mid-fourth Century)

The mass slaughter of non-Christians by the Christian Emperor Theodosius the Great (Late fourth Century)

The destruction of non-Christian literature by the Christian Emperor Theodosius the Great (Late fourth early 5th centuries).

The mass murder in a church of Pope Damasus' rivals to the papacy (fourth Century)

The brutal molestation and murder of the female philosopher Hypatia (5th Century)

The murder of the followers of his rival to the papacy, by Pope Symmachus (6th Century)

The heartless abduction of Jewish infants from their parents in Spain (7th Century)

The beheading of 4,500 Saxons in a single day for not converting to Christianity, by Charlemagne (8th Century)

The forging of the *Donation of Constantine* a document which gave temporal authority to the Church. (8th Century)

The invasion of Ireland and outright slaughter of the Druids, ordered by Pope Adrian IV. (12th Century)

The burning to death of the deist, Matthew Hamont, by the Anglican Church (16th Century)

Calvin's brutal murdering of Michael Servetus (16th Century)

Saint Francis Xavier's drowning of thousands of Indian infants in Goa, in forced baptisms (16th Century)

Saint Francis Xavier's brutal Inquisition in Goa, India, and murders of thousands of Hindus (16th Century)

The wholesale slaughter of the Anabaptists, by Martin Luther and the Catholic Church (16th Century)

The Slaughter, disenfranchisement and persecution of Jews by both the Catholics and Martin Luther's own fierce exhortations to "Slaughter the Jew where you find him."

The imprisonment of Galileo by the Catholic Church (17th Century)

The burning alive of the brilliant martyr for free thought and science, Giordano Bruno (17th Century)

The reduction of the Tahitian population by 200,000 or so, by the London Missionary Society. (Late 18th early 19th Century)

The traumatic abduction of Australian Aboriginal infants from their parents (20th century)

As well as, but not limited to;

Your zealous protests against smallpox vaccinations and valuable scientific and medical progresses in general, including, your unhelpful protests against stem-cell research.

Your exhaustive oppression of women

The racism and slavery created and fostered by your hard work

Your tireless discrimination against same-sex couples

Your concerted efforts in molesting and abusing our children, along with your ingenious modes of covering those crimes up.

And all of the other wonderful things your beneficent religion has bestowed upon our species.

Now, I understand that I have not even scratched the surface of the 10,000 wonderful things, for which we should thank you, but I hope this sincere note and its meagre contents are enough to show our appreciation for all your hard work.

Yours Sincerely
The Human Race.
P.S. Loved your work in the Dark Ages!

DEAR ISLAM,

I would like to sincerely apologize for stating that the *Qur'an* might be less harmful if used as toilet paper. I did not intend in any way to imply that the *Qur'an* should actually be used as toilet paper, although I understand that toilet paper has been used as a *Qur'an*. It was a tongue in cheek suggestion. The intention of my expression was to strip the *Qur'an* of reverence, as I have attempted to do with the *Bible* in the past, and highlight its plagiarised, dubious and destructive nature. It seems that this suggestion has offended some of my more "liberal" brothers and sisters, who found my lack of reverence for this religious text, blasphemous and uncouth. I now understand why such a suggestion is offensive and unnecessary.

Having read a little more of the Qur'an and investigated the laws and many of the cases in the purely Islamic country of Saudi Arabia, from a non-western point of view, I now see how wrong I was to question the wisdom of this beautiful recitation we call, the *Qur'an*.

In my ignorance, I thought it wrong to beat one's wife,[127] but failed to understand that this beating is not only for her own good and protection, but that the beating is much more tempered and loving than the one delivered to one's slave-girl.[128] In my ignorance, I thought it

---

[127]*Qur'an* 4:34; Sahih Muslim Book 4: 2127
[128]Sahih Bukhari Volume 8; Book 73. No. 68

repulsive and contrary to nature, to bed children of nine years[129] and if they refuse, employ the divine and lofty wisdom of the one and only true God, Allah, and beat that child until she submits. I thought it unfair that sisters inherit only half of what their brothers inherit,[130] and that a woman/girl should be a virtual slave to her male partner.[131] My strange, yet misguided sense of justice, perceived it as unfair that the majority of hell's inhabitants should be women[132] and that due to the imperfection of this profane sex, Allah must construct perfect virgins in heaven for the Jihadist to enjoy in pious orgies,[133] as a reward for their gruesome service toward his beautiful ends.

A Jinn, I assume, had possessed my mind, leading me to see as insane, the beheading of an individual in Saudi Arabia, Allah's earthly bastille, who in desperation employed superstitious "witchcraft" to reunite his divorced parents,[134] not realizing how truly powerful and threatening to Allah, (all-powerful and most wise), this black magic really is. I ridiculed Allah who, I now understand has good reason to predetermine who will be a believer and who will not,[135] and to deliberately lead astray, into the fiery pits of hell, those he chooses so to do.[136] In my darkness, I failed to see how Allah, the universal and wise father, could utter words to an illiterate nomad of the Quraysh tribe in Mecca, which made it acceptable to kill those who chose to think, rather than merely follow and believe,[137] no matter how seemingly insane and severe the herd may appear to behave. In my utter stupidity, I could not for a moment fathom, the seeming hypocrisy of a God

---

[129]Sahih Bukhari, Volume 1. Book 6. No. 304; Sahih Bukhari. Volume 7. Book 67. No. 5196; Sahih Bukhari. Book of Marriage. No. 64, 65, 88.
[130]Qur'an – Surah 4:11
[131]Qur'an – AnNisa Surah 4:34; Surah 223; Sahih Muslim Book 4:1982; Sahih Bukhari 7:19; Sahih Muslim Book 8: Marriage; etc..
[132]Sahih Bukhari, The book of Belief, Volume 1, Book 2, Number 28; Sahih Bukhari, The book of Eclipses, Volume 2, Book 18, Number 161
[133]Qur'an Surah 37:40-4, 44:51-55, 52:17-20, 55:54-59, 55:70-77, 56:37-40, 78:31-34
[134]http://www.dailymail.co.uk/news/article-2055636/Sudanese-man-beheaded-Saudi-Arabia-car-park-sorcerer.html; http://article.wn.com/view/2011/10/31/Sudanese_man_beheaded_in_Saudi_Arabia_car_park_for_being_a_s/
[135]Qur'an Surah 1:6-7.
[136]Qur'an Surah 14:4.
[137]Qur'an Surah 2:191-193, 3:56, 4:89, 5:33, 8:12, 8:15, 8:59-60, 9:5 etc…

who encourages, nay decrees, mutilation in return for the theft of property,[138] yet who at the same time, built his earthly kingdom (Islam) on such theft.[139]

I would also like to offer my solemn apology, for having the nerve to question the theocracy of Allah's greatest and most wonderful Kingdom of Saudi Arabia. I believed that a ruler should not govern his people with a religious constitution,[140] a compilation of documents written by people who heard voices in their heads, and saw what I then understood to be hallucinations in the sky. I ignorantly questioned the Jurisprudence of a society built on such insanity, but, as I now understand, it is established on the sturdy foundation of the one and only true religion from God/Allah, Islam. How blatantly dimwitted I was to think that the Mutaween (religious police) sent by Allah himself to patrol his most holiest of holy lands, were nothing but mere robots of the powerful Islamic oligarchs, whose only job is the patrolling of the streets and peering in of windows, to ensure the prevention of vice and liberty, amongst a people exposed to the sublime inspiration of the *Qur'an*, on an hourly basis, yet who still, find themselves cornered by and caged by Jinn and wickedness. These wise and noble Mutaween, who protect the King's, (Allah's divinely appointed ruler) regime, lest it be undermined, and the king left embarrassed in front of the unrighteous and profane infidels, who watch on and unjustly scorn this great monarch of heaven and earth.

I was outraged by the imprisoning of professor Sa'id Bin Zu'air, who lost his liberty on the trumped-up charge of financially aiding terrorists, when in fact, his crime was much worse.[141] If he had supported those proud soldiers of Islam, the mighty hand of Allah himself, who seek to create a homogeneous Islamic paradise here on earth, with sword, gun and bomb, that would have been a thousand times more acceptable than what this apostate, this treasonous and venomous heretic, was attempting to do. His true crime was vastly

---

[138]*Qur'an* Surah 5:38.
[139]Karen Armstrong. Islam: A Short History. Modern Library. (2002) p.19.
[140]http://www.saudiembassy.net/about/country-information/laws/The_Basic_Law_Of_Governance.aspx
[141]http://www.state.gov/j/drl/rls/hrrpt/2010/nea/154472.htm

more depraved, more immoral and rancid than the killing of thousands of infidels, for he, in his arrogance and ungrateful passion, was attempting to criticise the human rights record of Saudi Arabia, and in the process, darken the name of Allah's most righteous and beautiful sword, king Abdullah bin Abdulaziz Al Saud, as well as the source of his authority, the beautiful and wise *Qur'an*.

I now see the light of Allah like a lamp at my feet and will do everything I can to convert the whole world to Islam, so that once and for all, we may all fear this fictitious and fallacious creation, spawned from the minds of depraved southern Arabian nomads of the seventh century. I solemnly swear that I will do all in my power to ensure that everyone trembles at both his imaginary feet and the real feet of his child marrying, wife beating, difference-fearing and egocentric earthly representatives. To this end, I am sending out this sincere apology. I am sorry.

♦

CHRISTIAN CHARITY AND THE BREAD OF SHAME – EXPLOITING THE NORM OF RECIPROCITY

Growing up as a child during the eighties in Sydney, many companies began placing free samples of their products in the mail, which my friends and I would go around collecting until we had bags full of "free stuff". The reason for this alleged charity was not apparent to me at that age. Having worked for large companies and studied some of their marketing strategies, the reason for this seemingly innocent charity is now clear. The "free sample" marketing strategy is one of the least expensive and most effective forms of marketing. It not only gets the brand and the company's name circulating in society in a positive manner, with recipients bragging to their friends and family about the free sample they got from such and such a company, but it establishes trust and a feeling of obligation in the recipients. This technique has ancient roots and is founded upon a principle popularized by the Jewish Kabbalah, known as the "bread of shame".

Cabbalists are ancient Jewish mystics who interpret the Jewish scriptures in a symbolic and allegorical manner. According to

Cabbalists, before the creation of the physical universe, all souls lived as part of the one creator and had a completely one sided relationship with him, in which they received his essence unconditionally without having to earn it. This situation would have continued forever, except for that aspect of the soul which feels shame in receiving something for nothing. For this reason the souls implored the creator to create the physical universe so that they may descend as less perfect beings and strive, suffer and toil, so that they might have a chance to share with each other and earn their place with the divine creator.

Torah scholar and the Dean and Co-coordinator of the Kabbalah Centre, Rav Berg, in his book *The Kabbalah Method,* illustrates the principle embodied within the concept of the "bread of shame" in the context of an old Jewish tale.

The story is a rich man who was having a dinner party with his friends. When the party was due to commence, the rich man noticed a poor man walking by. Overwhelmed with pity, he invited the poor man to join them and to his and his friend's surprise, the poor man refused. The rich man, taken aback by his refusal begged him to reconsider, but his prostrations were to no avail, for this poor man said that he was in no need of such charity. The rich man continued to implore the poor man to join them and finally after much begging and pleading, the poor man threw his hands up in helplessness and said, "ok, if it means that much to you, I will join you." Relieved by the poor man's compliance with the kind offer, the participants of the party began their festivities.[142]

Rav Berg explains that the key to this allegorical tale is balance. Once the poor man saw how he could give as well as receive, and only once he saw this, he consented to join the feast. It is all about reciprocity and balance.[143]

It is the understanding of this need for balance and the manipulation of the obligation of the receiver that underpinned and continues to underpin, the seemingly benevolent charity of the Christian religion in third world countries and impoverished communities in more developed nations.

---

[142]Rav Berg. The Kabbalah Method. Kabbalah Centre International (2005). Pg. 46.
[143]Ibid. Pg. 47.

The Roman Emperor Julian, who for a brief period created a problem for the up and coming religion of Christianity during his two and a half year reign in the fourth century, made reference to this Christian conversion strategy, saying:

For when it came about the poor were neglected and overlooked by the priests (of the Roman state religion), then I think the impious Galatians (Christians) observed this fact and devoted themselves to philanthropy. And they have gained ascendancy in the worst of their deeds through the credit they win for such practices.[144]

In modern psychological terms the principle embodied within the concept of the "bread of shame" is known as the "norm of reciprocity".

The norm of reciprocity is a universal feature of social life and dictates that people generally feel a deep seeded obligation to repay what others have given them.

Referring to the *Handbook of Psychology*, we learn that:

The social obligation that there be a give for every take is well-documented (DePaulo, Brittingham, & Kaiser, 1983; Eisenberger, Cotterell, & Marvel, 1987; Regan, 1971). Even when gifts and favours are unsolicited (or unwanted), the recipient feels compelled to provide something in return. The ability of uninvited gifts to produce feelings of obligation in the recipient is successfully exploited by many organizations, both charitable and commercial. People may not need personalized address labels, key rings, or hackneyed Christmas cards, but after they have been received, it is difficult not to respond to the organization's request...[145]

The manipulation of this principle lies in the fear of the receiver to refuse a request of the giver once this charity has been given. With regards to this point the *Handbook of Psychology* teaches us that non-reciprocation can damage the exchange relationship, or balance and may cause damage to the non-reciprocator's reputation. Cognisant of

---

[144]Daniel T. Reff. Plagues, Priests and Demons. Cambridge University Press (2005). Pg. 75.
[145]Irving B. Weiner, Theodore Millon & Melvin J. Lerner. Handbook of Psychology: Vol. 5; Personality and Social Psychology. John Wiley & Sons Inc. (2003). Pg. 393.

this fact, as observed by a number of psychological experiments, many of us fear non-reciprocation because of the implied threat to future transactions of exchange.[146]

In other words, how would it look if one were given charity and upon the simple and "harmless" request of the giver, like promising to convert to a religion or making a commitment to attend church, the receiver refused such a humble request? No one wants to look bad in front of their peers, or feel bad in the face of such benevolence and so the giver gains power over the receiver, who is now in a compromised position with relation to the giver.

In the case of the Christian converter, all he is asking in return for his material charity is a spiritual commitment; he is merely asking you to commit to Christ by accepting the doctrines of the Christian faith. It's all about the commitment. Once you commit to Christ, especially in front of witnesses, you will more than likely make a more personal and cognitive commitment to the belief as well, which, as we saw in Chapter one, will then effectively trap your mind within the prison of that belief.

Furthermore, Commitment, although not listed as a social norm, can influence behaviour to the same extent as reciprocity and other social rules and expectations. Generally speaking, when people commit themselves to an opinion or course of action, it is difficult for them to go back on their word or change their minds. The commitment works its magic by operating on a fundamental psychological principle of the human mind, namely, consistency. People generally act consistently with their beliefs and attempt, in most cases, to fulfil what they have promised, especially if they have made the commitment in front of witnesses.[147]

The minister or preacher may ask for "those who wished to be saved" to come to the front of the congregation and commit to Christ; or a newcomer may be personally asked, if he or she will be attending again next week. Once this commitment is made, especially in front of one or more witnesses, it establishes in the mind of the target, a psychological drive to fulfil the obligation.

---

[146]Ibid.
[147]Ibid.

It is the understanding of the above principles and the application of related techniques, coupled with a comprehensive knowledge of the target community's culture, which is proving successful for this new generation of mind manipulating Christian missionaries.

◆

CHRISTIANITY: TWELVE PAINFUL FACTS.

Fact 1: The earliest Gospel, Mark, was written over a generation (forty years) after the alleged death of Jesus and fails the historical test of contemporanity.[148]

Fact 2: Of the 662 verses in the Gospel of Matthew, 612 were plagiarised from the Gospel of Mark (or Mark's source).[149]

Fact 3: None of the Gospels were written by the alleged authors and two of which, John (See John 21:24) and Luke, (See Luke 1:1-4) specifically state that they were not eyewitnesses to Jesus.[150]

Fact 4: The Gospels contain forgeries, contradictions and errors.[151]

Fact 5: The four Gospels were not selected as Scripture until 180 ce (approx.).[152]

Fact 6: There are no first century witnesses outside of the corrupt and biased Gospels, that attest to the earthly existence of Jesus Christ, but for a forged passage in the work of the Jewish Historian Josephus (Testamonium Flavium) and a second reference in that work, which is also suspect and in no way represents a specific reference to the Jesus of the Gospels.[153]

---

[148]Paul. J. Achtemeier. Harper-Collins *Bible* Dictionary Revised Edition. Harper Collins, (1989). p. 653; John Barton and John Muddiman. The Oxford *Bible* Commentary. Oxford University Press. (2001). p. 886.

[149]Graham N. Stanton. The Gospels and Jesus. Oxford University Press (1989), pp.63–64.

[150]Bart D Ehrman. *Jesus Interrupted*. Harper Collins Publishers. (2005) p. 111.

[151]Re: Story of woman taken in adultery in "John's" Gospel; Paul. J. Achtemeier. Harper-Collins *Bible* Dictionary Revised Edition. Harper Collins, (1989). p. 535; Re: Final 12 verses of "Mark;" Bruce Metzger, *A Textual Commentary on the Greek New Testament* . Stuttgart, (1971). pp. 122–126. There are other examples.

[152]Bart D Ehrman. *Jesus Interrupted*. Harper Collins Publishers. (2005) p. 111.

[153]Re: No first century witnesses to earthly Jesus; Bart D Ehrman, Jesus Interrupted. HarperCollins. 2009. p. 158; Re: Josephus forgeries; John E Remsburg. *The Christ: A Critical Review and Analysis of the Evidences of His Existence*. The Truth Seeker Company. (1909) pp. 32–35.

Fact 7: Almost all of the myths and moral philosophies attributed to Jesus can be found in earlier mythologies, held by people that were proximate to the lands in which the Gospels first arose.[154]

Fact 8: Most of the earliest Christians believed that Jesus was either a phantom (non-human apparition) or a completely human Jewish rabbi.[155]

Fact 9: Christianity only rose to power due to its blatant disregard for its own Scripture, meaning, it aligned itself with a psychotic pagan emperor, Constantine, who boiled his wife in a hot tub, murdered his son and executed his co-emperor, and who, merely used Christianity to solidify his sole emperorship, evidenced by the fact that he continued to practice his pagan faith and mint his coins with Mithras (pagan sun-god), long after his alleged conversion.[156]

Fact 10: The sect of Christians that aligned themselves with Constantine became known as the Catholic (Universal) Church and their chief historian, Eusebius, re-wrote Christian history to present a false picture that favoured his sect and made it look like, his group's theology, found in our four Gospels, was always the dominant and original form, when the contrary is true.[157]

Fact 11: For the majority of its history (fourth Century ~ nineteenth Century), Christianity has been a violent religion, which, like a deadly virus, has taken over its hosts and killed in order to spread.[158]

---

[154]Joseph McCabe. Sources of Morality in the Gospels. Watts & Co. (1914). McCabe compiled many of the primary source pre-Christian references to the sources of Jesus' alleged revelations, so you can go to those works and read them for yourself.

[155]Bart Ehrman *Lost Christianities* Oxford University Press (2003); Earl Doherty. The Jesus Puzzle: Did Christianity Begin with a Mythical Christ? Challenging the Existence of an Historical Jesus. Age of Reason Publications (2005).

[156]Helen Ellebre, The Dark Side of Christian History. Morningstar Books (1995); Phillip Schaff. History of the Christian Church, Volume 5: The Middle Ages. A.D. 1049-1294. Christian Classics Ethereal Library. (1882). p. 322; J.N. Hillgarth, The Conversion of Western Europe Englewood Cliffs, NJ: Prentice Hall, (1969). p. 46; Frank Viola & George Barna. *Pagan Christianity.* Tyndale House Publishers. (2008).

[157]Bart Ehrman *Lost Christianities* Oxford University Press (2003); Joseph Wheless. *Forgery in Christianity.* .Psychiana. (1930); Bart D. Ehrman. *Jesus, Interrupted*(2009). New York: HarperCollins. P. 214.

[158]Helen Ellebre, The Dark Side of Christian History. Morningstar Books (1995); Rev. J.E. Riddle. *The History of the Papacy, to the Reformation (Multiple volume series);* Edward Gibbon. The Decline and Fall of the Roman Empire (multiple volume series).

Fact 12: The only reason we see more psychotic behaviour from religious nuts in Islamic countries today, versus Western countries, is because the West is increasingly more secular and has separated (at least to a greater degree), religion and politics.[159]

♦

CHRISTIANITY – A SYMPTOM OF A GREATER VIRUS

Christians often ask me, why I hate Christianity. To this charge, I usually respond by saying; I do not hate Christianity at all, just as a doctor does not hate a given symptom of a virus, or disease. The doctor merely attempts to treat it and if possible, cure the disease or virus which has caused it.

Christianity, as with Islam, Hinduism, Buddhism, Communism, Capitalism, Nationalism, etc., is not a virus in and of itself, but rather, it is a symptom of a greater illness. The disease which lies at the core of this symptom and ones like it is fear. Our fear of suffering spawns beliefs, established to appease the psychological pressure we experience as a result of such fear. Religious beliefs often have an inbuilt sedative for the human being's most primal fear, that being, mortality (see religious beliefs, re: afterlife, rebirth/reincarnation and immortality).

Yet, this is not the fear, with which I am primarily concerned. The fear I am attempting to address is the fear inspired by uncertainty, the fear of the unknown, which motivates an individual to produce and maintain a belief, in order to avoid uncertainty.

As it is with a virus, the victim of a religion is besieged by an invasion of externally derived qualities, qualities which our psychological antibodies, reason and logic, try to stave off lest the virus gain complete control over its host. When these antibodies strengthen, the believer experiences what is known as a "crisis of faith," but the truth is that this is not a crisis, but an epiphany. It is the mind's way of curing the illness that has taken over the psychological body of the human being and it works by creating cognitive dissonance in the mind to

---

[159]Compare Islamic Shariah regulated societies to western pre- secular and post secular ones and use your common sense.

provoke the virus to surface, so that it can be subjected to the healing light of reason and rational thought. When the virus wins a victory over these psychological antibodies, the believer's ego dictates his or her reality and their beliefs beget their experience, creating a living dream world in which the believer will often spend the entirety of their life. We may observe this phenomenon when we hear believers attributing events, the perceived beauty of nature or natural disasters, to their gods. They behold a beautiful mountain range and say that such a beautiful and awe inspiring sight must be the work of their creator. Or when a plane crashes, an earthquake strikes or some other natural disaster hits, they look past the multitude of victims to point to one or two survivors and exhort; "The Lord has spared them!" The Hindus see their gods in nature and daily life, the Christians see theirs, the Muslims experience Allah, the Jews, Yahweh, etc., all experience their own conflicting versions of reality and yet they all share a common symptom or trait, namely, fear-induced egocentrism.

Such a fact led the Indian Philosopher, Jiddu Krishnamurti, to ask and add:

> Why do you believe? And what difference does it make to what actually is whether you believe one thing or another? Facts are not influenced by belief or disbelief. So one has to ask why one believes at all in anything; what is the basis of belief? Is it fear, is it the uncertainty of life - the fear of the unknown the lack of security in this ever-changing world? Is it the insecurity of relationship, or is it that faced with the immensity of life, and not understanding it, one encloses oneself in the refuge of belief? So, if I may ask you, if you had no fear at all, would you have any belief?[160]

This false certainty has created and continues to create, more problems for both the individual and society as a whole, than the temporary relief it brings to the lazy and frightened believer. Some of the problems created by the ill-gotten certainty afforded by the belief include, but are not limited to:

---

[160]Jiddu Krishnamurti. The Urgency of Change. Harper and Row. (1977) pp. 98–99.

1. War (religious/political/ethnic/nationalistic
2. Genocide
3. Religious persecution
4. Bigotry
5. Racism
6. Social inequality
7. Gender inequality
8. Wilful ignorance
9. Mental illness (see; Neurosis, Paranoia, psychosis, xenophobia, egocentrism, and narcissism, for just a few examples)

To illustrate some of the chaos caused by belief induced certainty, in particular, religious certainty, I would like to quote from the work of neuroscientist and philosopher, Sam Harris, who, in his book The End of Faith, said:

> *Indeed, religion is as much a living spring of violence today as it was at any time in the past. The recent conflicts in Palestine (Jews v. Muslims), the Balkans (Orthodox Serbians v. Catholic Croatians; Orthodox Serbians v. Bosnian and Albanian Muslims), Northern Ireland (Protestants v. Catholics), Kashmir (Muslims v. Hindus), Sudan (Muslims v. Christians and animists), Nigeria (Muslims v. Christians), Ethiopia and Eritrea (Muslims v. Christians), Sri Lanka (Sinhalese Buddhists v. Tamil Hindus), Indonesia (Muslims v. Timorese Christians), and the Caucasus (Orthodox Russians v. Chechen Muslims; Muslim Azerbaijanis v. Catholic and Orthodox Armenians) are merely a few cases in point. In these places religion has been the explicit cause of literally millions of deaths in the last ten years. These events should strike us like psychological experiments run amok, for that is what they are.[161]*

Aside from the more tangible mayhem caused by this perverse psychological experiment, another casualty of this virus and its symptoms is intelligence. I am almost certain that the believer who reads the previous

---

[161]Sam Harris. The End of Faith. W.W. Norton. (2005). p. 26.

statement will scream, "hyperbole!" What about Isaac Newton, Coperni-cus, Galileo or any of the other brilliant men who were believers!? What you need to understand is that the mind is a multidimensional composi-tion of the brain and as such, even great minds can be held to ransom by ill-gotten and unsubstantiated beliefs. Think about it this way. When we believe something, we have arrived at a perceived truth and reached the conclusion of a given thought process, such that true unencumbered thought ceases. That is to say, if you believe you have an answer to some-thing, you will generally stop seeking and questioning, at least in the same tenacious manner you did before you caught this virus. Further-more, the belief, being a product and resident of the ego, is plagued with defence mechanisms that serve to distort reality to accommodate these beliefs, so believers often find it difficult to move beyond their beliefs because they carry with them, self-perpetuating qualities like confirma-tion biases, disconfirmation biases, rationalizations and adaptational strategies, all seeking to preserve the primary belief by sacrificing free thought and open minded growth.

Again, we see evidence of this when the science of geology debunked the young earth propagated by the Church's interpretation of the *Bible*'s chronology of the earth, enunciated primarily by Ussher's famed chro-nology. No longer did the facts support a 6,000 year old earth and so what was the result? Those who could not immediately reconcile such a dissonance producing scenario sought to reinterpret their scripture and we saw a proliferation of theories about what the book of Genesis actu-ally says. The Day Age theory, the Gap Theory and so on, all came about as a result of this virus' ability to cause the believer to distort, rationalize and adapt their beliefs in order to continue to host this pernicious virus and its symptom. Alternatively, many Christians simply ignored the overwhelming facts produced by the science of geology and to this day we have those who believe that the earth is only 6,000 years old. It is little wonder why the brilliant MIT scholar, Robert Anton Wilson said that belief was the death of intelligence,[162] for we see it, not just with re-gards to religion's obstinacy towards the facts produced by the various

---

[162]Robert Anton Wilson. Cosmic Trigger. Vol. 1: Final Secret of the Illuminati. New Falcon Publications. (1977). Pg. Preface ii.

sciences, or towards its stubbornness to foster a more intelligent egalitarian society with regards to gender equality and same-sex marriage, but we also now have a study that has roundly demonstrated it.[163]

Quoting from The Huffington Post:

Are religious people less intelligent than atheists?

That's the provocative conclusion of a new review of 63 studies of intelligence and religion that span the past century. The meta-analysis showed that in 53 of the studies, conducted between 1928 to 2012, there was an inverse relation between religiosity – having religious beliefs, or performing religious rituals – and intelligence. That is, on average, non-believers scored higher than religious people on intelligence tests.

What might explain the effect?

Scientists behind studies included in the review most often suggested that *"religious beliefs are irrational*, not anchored in science, not testable and, therefore, unappealing to intelligent people who 'know better.'"

But the researchers who conducted the new meta-analysis say the answer is a bit more complicated. They suspect intelligent people might have less of a "need" for religion.

"Intelligence may also lead to greater self-control ability, self-esteem, perceived control over life events, and supportive relationships, obviating some of the benefits that religion sometimes provides," study co-author Jordan Silberman, a graduate student of neuroeconomics at the University of Rochester, told The Huffington Post in an email."[164]

This stupidity comes about because the virus fools its host into believing that they know that which they do not, which effectively stops them seeking further information, particularly with regards to information that comes into conflict with their belief.

As mentioned, psychologists refer to the strategy employed by believers to avoid the disconfirmation of a belief, as "disconfirmation bias" and it is commonly employed in conjunction with "confirmation

---

[163]http://psr.sagepub.com/content/early/2013/08/02/1088868313497266
[164]http://www.huffingtonpost.com/2013/08/14/religious-people-less-intelligent-atheists_n_3750096.html

bias", which describes the motivation for individuals to place more weight and focus more attention on information that affords a reason to continue believing the things they believe. These forms of bias seem to be utilized by the believer to avoid or resolve the cognitive dissonance alluded to above, which is a kind of mental and emotional suffering, brought about by the holding of two contradictory beliefs and ideas simultaneously.[165]

When dissonance occurs in the mind of the believer, it is usually the pre-established belief that wins the day (further, see; confirmation bias and "primacy"), albeit by dubious means. The rationalization process, adaptational strategies and self-delusion that prevents a believer from growing past their beliefs, has underscored some of the most insane thinking and behaviour throughout human history, yet its most tragic consequence has been the protection of those who have gained power of the masses by relying on these psychological defects in those they control. All a leader need do to achieve a desired outcome from a non-thinking/believing public, is push the right emotional buttons and trigger a reaction that would be unavailable to them, if people would only stop believing so much and begin to think. This is where we get into the issue of dependency, or as the brilliant scientist, Wilhelm Reich called it, "chronic dependency." Our earthly masters who control us via religion, political sophistry, media manipulation, trend manufacturing and various other means, have achieved this control by making us dependent on the thoughts and beliefs of others and in this way the virus is transmitted and contracted.

It was this sad state of affairs that led the great thinker and philosopher, Immanuel Kant, to say:

> *Laziness and cowardice are the reasons why such a large proportion of men, even when nature has long emancipated them from alien*

---

[165]For a good survey of this subject see; Leon Festinger. Theory of Cognitive Dissonance. Stanford University Press (1957); Festinger, L., Riecken, H. W., & Schachter, S. When Prophecy fails. University of Minnesota Press. (1956); Lorne L. Dawson. When Prophecy Fails and Faith Persists: A theoretical Overview. University of California Press. (1999); and Adam Kowol. The Theory of Cognitive Dissonance. http://works.adamkowol.info

guidance, nevertheless gladly remain immature for life. For the same reasons, it is all too easy for others to set themselves up as their guardians. It is so convenient to be immature! If I have a book to have understanding in place of me, a spiritual adviser to have a conscience for me, a doctor to judge my diet for me, and so on, I need not make any efforts at all. I need not think, so long as I can pay; others will soon enough take the tiresome job over for me. The guardians who have kindly taken upon themselves the work of supervision will soon see to it that by far the largest part of mankind should consider the step forward to maturity not only as difficult but also as highly dangerous. Having first infatuated their domesticated animals, and carefully prevented the docile creatures from daring to take a single step without the leading-strings to which they are tied, they next show them the danger which threatens them if they try to walk unaided. Now this danger is not in fact so very great, for they would certainly learn to walk eventually after a few falls. But an example of this kind is intimidating, and usually frightens them off from further attempts.[166]

So, when I attack the religion of Christianity or any other religion for that matter, please do not take it personally, for Christianity, as with the others, is merely the symptom of a greater virus.

FROM SOPHISTS TO SERMONIZERS – RHETORICAL RELIGION

There is nothing so easy as by sheer volubility to deceive a common crowd or an uneducated congregation.[167]

~St. Jerome (5th Century)

In ancient Greece there arose a class of highly literate and skilful orators, known as Sophists. These men would go about Athens and

---

[166]Immanuel Kant: An Answer to the Question: What is Enlightenment? Konigsberg in Prussia, 30th September, (1784). pp. 1–2.
[167]Father Jerome's Epistle to Nepotian. Cited in: Philip Schaff. Nicene and Post Nicene Fathers: Series 2, Volume 6. Christian Classics Ethereal Library. (2009). p. 250.

other main cities in Greece, speaking to paying audiences about such things as, religion, philosophy and politics. Their gift was not that of true knowledge, but of the ability to persuade. They used rhetoric, as modern preachers and politicians do, to persuade their patrons of the truth of their opinions, on facts that they often knew very little about. They were well respected by the masses of ill-informed citizens, but from the true thinkers and philosophers, they received nothing less than utter contempt. As democracy increased in Athens, the ability to persuade the masses became paramount to the success or failure of any given politician. Thus, the sophists became highly sought after and their powers of persuasion made them very wealthy. According to Philostratus, a writer of late antiquity, Gorgias was the father of Sophism.[168]

Plato's student, Aristotle, described Gorgias in the following words:

> Like other sophists, he travelled from city to city offering his services for money. He did not claim to teach virtue but specialized in teaching rhetoric (cf. 95c1–4), and his own oratorical skills were both innovative and widely admired.[169]

Aristotle was contemptuous of Gorgias' art, and derided it in the following words:

> Now for some people it is better worthwhile to seem to be wise, than to be wise without seeming to be (for the art of the sophist is the semblance of wisdom without the reality, and the sophist is one who makes money from an apparent but unreal wisdom); for them, then, it is clearly necessary to seem to accomplish the task of a wise man rather than to accomplish it without seeming to do so.[170]

---

[168]Robert Wardy. The Birth of Rhetoric. Plato, Aristotle and their Successors. Routledge 1996. p. 6.
[169]Dominic Scott. Plato's Meno. Cambridge Studies in the Dialogues of Plato. Cambridge University Press. 2005. Chapter 1: The Opening. p. 12.
[170]Jonathan Barnes. The Complete Works of Aristotle. Sophistical Refutations Princeton University Press, Princeton, N.J. 1991. p. 3.

As established above, Aristotle viewed the sophists as charlatans, passing off rhetoric as truth and wonderful words, as wisdom. They were nothing more than clever speakers, who knew how to engage their audiences, draw them in and hypnotize them with the clever use of linguistics.

Aristotle was not alone in accusing sophists of misleading the masses. His esteemed teacher, Plato, who was in turn Socrates' pupil, condemned these early pagan preachers as being nothing more than clever speaking fools. In a series of lectures on Platonism, delivered at Princeton University in 1917, Paul Elmer More, said the following:

> If there is any truth in Plato s account of the debates between Socrates and such masters of the craft as Gorgias and Protagoras, it is clear that the sophists directed their instruction chiefly to the acquisition of skill in manipulating individual men and popular assemblies. I do not mean to say, following an ancient accusation, that the sophists set out deliberately to instruct men in the art of making the better cause appear the worse, in the sense that they had any vicious or anti-social end in view; but rather that they had in view no end at all, except the end of success. Their concern was very much with practical cleverness and very little with moral consequences, very much with current opinion and very little with truth for its own sake; hence the supreme place of rhetoric in their curriculum, as the art of persuasion.[171]

It seems that in their day the sophists were the preachers, who like Billy Graham, could persuade, mislead and hypnotize listeners, with the skilful use of rhetoric that brought them both acclaim from the profane masses and condemnation from those in search of the truth.

According to *The New Schaff-Herzog Encyclopaedia of Religious Knowledge*, it was Origen who, in the third century, introduced the sermon in the form of the homily, as a fixed ecclesiastical (church) custom.[172] It appears that it is Origen we have to thank for the sophists

---

[171]Paul Elmer More. Platonism. Princeton University Press. Princeton 1917. Pg. 20.
[172]Phillip Schaff. The New Schaff-Herzog Encyclopaedia of Religious Knowledge, Vol. IX: Petri – Reuchlin. Grand Rapids: Christian Classics Ethereal Library. Pg. 361.

of the Christian churches today, for Billy Grahams, the Joel Osteens, the televangelists and above all, we have Origen to thank for Christianity's lure in an age where they can no longer force us to believe in their superstitions. We would be mistaken however, for assuming that rhetoric made its way into Christianity as late as the third century, or that it was only Origen who influenced the proliferation of sophistry within the religion of Christianity, for in the book of Acts we find it, within the works of Augustine it's persuasive pull may be glanced and in the credulous works of John Chrysostom it can be clearly seen.[173] All these masters of superstitious sophistry have the Hellenes to thank, because had it not been for the hard work of sophists like Gorgias and his Grecian predecessors and inheritors, Christianity would have to rely on facts and facts alone, which, we may justifiable conclude, would ruin it.

From the start, Christianity was a blend of its father religion, Judaism, and paganism too. Being that such is the case, not only does the Christ myth itself and the gospel narratives contain many pagan symbols, motifs and stories, but the practices also, have from a relatively early stage, been incorporated into the religion of Christianity. From the fourth century, the Church was fully institutionalized and as part of that process, although not beginning this late, the Church employed the sophistry of paganism, brought into the religion by former pagans, many of who became renowned Church fathers. The concept of the trained professional speaker was and continues to be, a vital aspect of the worship service and we can trace its origins to ancient Greece.

In their book, Pagan Christianity, Frank Viola and George Barna say:

> *If you compare a third-century pagan sermon with a sermon given by one of the church fathers, you will find both the structure and the phraseology to be quite similar.*

[173]Marsha E. Ackermann Michael J. Schroeder Janice J. Terry Jiu-Hwa Lo Upshur Mark F. Whitters. Encyclopaedia of World History: Vol. 1. Facts on File. Infobase publishing (2008). Pg., 174.

So a new style of communication was being birthed in the Christian church—a style that emphasized polished rhetoric, sophisticated grammar, flowery eloquence, and monologue. It was a style that was designed to entertain and show off the speaker's oratorical skills. It was Greco-Roman rhetoric. And only those who were trained in it were allowed to address the assembly![174]

Viola and Barna go on to conclude:

> *Summing up the origin of the contemporary sermon, we can say the following: Christianity had taken Greco-Roman rhetoric and adapted it for its own purposes, baptized it, and wrapped it in swaddling clothes. The Greek homily made its way into the Christian church around the second century. It reached its height in the pulpit orators of the fourth century—namely Chrysostom and Augustine.*[175]

It has been said that the influence of the spoken and written word is profound. It has the power to free and it also possesses the ability to enslave. Herein lies the true power of sophistry and rhetoric and there is little doubt that sophistry and rhetoric have been synonymous with the Christian church service.

Sophistry is the heart and soul of the Christian religion, without which, the religion, I dare say, would not be so persuasive and attractive to the profane masses. Subtract the entertainment of emotion-invoking homilies and the dramatic appeals of the talented rhetoricians of the Church, all that would remain would be the claims they make, which, absent the bells and whistles of flowery rhetoric, would be subjected to a more rational analysis.

◆

ISLAM: 10 PAINFUL TRUTHS

Truth 1: The word "Islam" doesn't stem from the Arabic word, "Al Salaam" (Peace), but from the word, "Al-Silim" (Surrender/Submission)

---

[174]Frank Viola, George Barna. Pagan Christianity. Tyndale House Publishers. (2008). Pg. 126–127.
[175]Ibid. Pg. 131.

and Arabic words have only one single root, meaning, Islam cannot mean both. This is also further evidenced by the multiple verses throughout the *Qur'an*, which encourage actual physical violence. Surah 2:191, 193, 218, 3:151, 4:89 and on and on.

Truth 2: Muhammad's tribe (Quraysh Tribe) first funded Islam by way of armed robbery (ghazawāt), therefore, the earthly/fiscal origins of Islam are criminal and corrupt.

Truth 3: The original authors of the *Qur'an*, whoever they were, plagiarised large portions of the *Bible* and Jewish and Christian theology, to establish their religion and in so doing, made mistakes with regards to Biblical chronology, like, naming Moses' brother Aaron, as Mary's brother too (about 1400 years off according to Biblical chronology). Surah 19:27-28

Truth 4: Jihad does not mean "spiritual war"/"inner struggle", but actual violent holy war. This is evidenced by the fact that the elderly and the young are spared from partaking in Jihad. Surah 4:19

Truth 5: Both the Islamic god, Allah (pre-Islamic lunar deity) and the Kabbah (focal place of Islamic worship in Mecca) were stolen from pre-Islamic Southern Arabian pagan religions.

Truth 6: Shi'ite Muslims interpret Surah 4:24 of the *Qur'an* to allow for temporary marriage (Mut'ah), which, depending on the stamina of the man, can be as short as half an hour and involves the act of sex for a fee (prostitution).

Truth 7: The *Qur'an* permits and even encourages men to own female sex slaves. Surah 33:50, 23:5-6, 70:29-30, 4:24, for example.

Truth 8: Both the *Qur'an* and the most reliable Hadiths (peripheral holy Islamic texts) permit and even encourage paedophilia, by a) setting a waiting period for the divorce of girls who have not yet began their menstrual cycles (Surah 65:4) and b) by way of Muhammad's example of marrying the six year old Aisha and sleeping with her when she turned nine. Sahih Bukhari Vol. 5: 234, Vol. 7: 65, Sahih Muslim Vol. 2: 3309, for example. Further, there are approximately ninety-one verses throughout the *Qur'an* that encourage Muslims to follow Muhammad's example.

Truth 9: The *Qur'an* encourages men to beat their wives. Surah 4:34

Truth 10: Angels probably do not exist and therefore, the story of Muhammad receiving the *Qur'an* from the Jewish angel, Gabriel, is either a complete myth or a lie told by Muhammad, if he even existed as an historical person, for which we have no independent evidence outside of the corrupt and biased accounts of religious fanatics.

◆

JESUS - ACCORDING TO THE JEWS

Christian apologists, in a desperate attempt to locate Jesus in history, often turn to the references to Jesus within the vast tomes of Jewish rabbinical writings. The purpose of this essay is to assess the validity of those references, by examining their content and their historical value.

Before we begin to assess the Jewish opinion of this possibly mythical or at least, legendary Character, it is necessary to provide context with regards to this huge body of work known as the *Talmud*, in order that the reader be given a chance to fully understand the relevance or irrelevance of any reference to Jesus within these texts. The *Talmud* constitutes a library of Jewish texts pertaining to rabbinic discussions regarding the Torah (the first five books of the *Bible*), and its application of the laws of Judaism. The word "*Talmud*" is translated in English as; "Instruction or Learning." Thus, it forms the central body of work within the religion of Judaism and records thousands upon thousands of discussions between rabbis and documents their rulings on day to day issues pertaining to the practical interpretation of the laws laid out in the Jewish Torah. For the reader who may know something about our current legal system, the best way to explain the relationship between the Torah and the *Talmud*, would be to describe the Torah as analogous to Statute Law, or those laws enacted by the government and the *Talmud*, as comprising the record of case law, which interprets those statutes, or written laws.

There are two versions, or additions of the *Talmud*, the earliest being the *Jerusalem Talmud*, written sometime around the third to fourth centuries ce and it's later counterpart, the *Babylonian Talmud*, compiled sometime between the fifth to seventh centuries ce. As their names suggest, the Jerusalem *Talmud* was compiled in Jerusalem, although some scholars argue that it may have originally been composed in Galilee. The Babylonian *Talmud*, on the other hand, was put together by Rabbis living in Babylon (modern day Iraq), just beyond the reach of the then powerful and ruthless Christian Empire. Ironically, it was in the very land that had once persecuted and held the Jews captive that later afforded them refuge from the brutal persecution and harassment they suffered at the hands of the Christian Church, a church which controlled the very powerful Roman Christian Empire. In Babylon, the Jewish rabbis put together this massive library from more ancient texts and other early oral traditions (Mishnah) that appear to date back in time to possibly around the second century ce, as will be seen shortly. The more astute reader may have already grasped the problem with using any reference to Jesus found within these relatively late works. They lack any real contemporanity, that is, they were written long after any first, second, or even twentieth hand accounts regarding historically valuable testimony of events and people living in the first century of the Christian era. Yet, not only do these texts lack any real contemporanity, but they are also unreliable with regards to their contents, as will also be demonstrated. So let us now look at two of the first recorded references to Jesus in the Jerusalem *Talmud* and assess their historical value.

JESUS IN THE JERUSALEM TALMUD - JESUS THE SON OF PANDERA

There are a few different references to a Jesus ben (son of) Pandera in the Jerusalem *Talmud*, the following are two examples:

Jacob ... came in the name of Jesus Pandera to heal him
~Book of Shabboth 14:4

Someone ... whispered to him in the name of Jesus son of Pandera
~Book of Abodah Zarah 2:2

These are two of the main references to Jesus in the Jerusalem *Talmud*. There is a fundamental discrepancy between the Christian's Jesus and the one mentioned above. Jesus, according to the Christians, was the son (foster-son) of Joseph (*Yeshua* Ben-Yoseph). In the Gospels, the Jews expressly identify Jesus as the son of Joseph (see Luke 3:23, 4:22 & John 1:45), so why, if the Jews knew the Christian's messiah to be the son of Joseph, would they refer to him as the son of Pandera? This is obviously not the Jesus of the Gospels. Or is it? If not, then who is this son of Pandera alleged to have been? And what, if anything, does he have to do with Jesus of Christianity? To adequately answer the questions above, we must investigate the earliest references to this son of Pandera, who was called Jesus.

JESUS SON OF PANDERA IN THE TOSEFTA

When we examine the possible textual source of the reference to Jesus the son of Pandera, found in the *Talmud*, we discover that it seems to have been taken from another rabbinical text known as the *Tosefta*, which Christian apologists also use as evidence for the historicity of their Jesus. The *Tosefta*, as its name in Hebrew implies, is a "supplement" to the study of the Mishnah. It was compiled around the third century ce and contains a little more information regarding our Jesus the son of Pandera.[176]

It once happened that R. Elazar ben Damah was bitten by a snake and Ya'akov of the village Sechania came to heal him in the name of Yeshu ben Pandira, but R. Yishmael did not allow him.

~*Tosefta*: Book of Chullin 2:23

This is all we have with regards to evidence that Jesus Christ was mentioned in both the Jerusalem *Talmud* (third to fourth centuries ce) and the *Tosefta* (third century ce), the two earliest rabbinical sources which many Christians hold up as evidence for the historical nature of their saviour.

However, the character referred to in these texts does not seem to correspond with the Jesus of the Gospels, for even the Gospels admit that Jesus was known to the Jews as the son of Joseph and not the son of Pandera/Pandira.

Travelling back in time from the date of the composition of the Jerusalem *Talmud* has been virtually useless in trying to establish the identity of this Jesus, so perhaps we should travel forward in time, remembering that the later we travel, the less reliable, generally speaking, our historical source will be.

---

[176]Fred Skolnik & Michael Berenbaum. Encyclopaedia Judaica 2nd Ed. Vol. 14. Thompson Gale. (2007). p. 202.

THE BABYLONIAN TALMUD

Turning to the Babylonian *Talmud* we find references to persons named Jesus, one of whom does seem like a rather loose match for the Jesus of the Gospels. Before examining these references, we need to consider the context with which such references were rooted. As mentioned, the Babylonian *Talmud* was written sometime between the fifth to the seventh centuries ce, a time when Christians had control of the Roman Empire and were by decree, the only permitted religion. The persecution of non-Christians, especially Jews, was commonplace throughout the Roman Empire, an empire which spanned from Turkey to Egypt and beyond. Jews were often slaughtered, or at the very least disenfranchised, robbed, and dislocated by Christian church officials and Roman Christian Emperors, who saw the Jews as their worst enemies, for it was the Jews, Christians believed, who were the "killers of Christ" and the "sons of Satan!" Let us now hear from the third century Church father Commodanius, to gain some understanding of how, many early Christians viewed the Jews. In so doing, we may gain a little more insight into the background and motivations upon which the *Talmud*ic tales of Jesus were based. In speaking against the Jews, Commodanius said:

There is not an unbelieving people such as yours. O evil men! In so many places, and so oft en rebuked by the law of those who cry aloud. And the loft y One despises your Sabbaths, and altogether rejects your universal monthly feasts according to law, that ye should not make to Him the commanded sacrifices; who told you to throw a stone for your offence. If any should not believe that He had perished by an unjust death, and that those who were beloved were saved by other laws, thence that life was suspended on the tree, and believe not on Him. God Himself is the life; He Himself was suspended for us. But ye with indurate heart insult Him.[177]

Such was the anti-Jewish sentiment echoed throughout much of Christendom and things only became worse after the fourth Century, when Emperor Constantine made Christianity the one and

---

[177]Philip Schaff . Ante-Nicene Fathers of the Third Century: Tertullian Part Fourth; Minucius Felix; Commodian; Origen Parts First and Second. Grand Rapids. Christian Ethereal Library. (1885). p. 385.

only official religion of the Roman Empire. Following Constantine's persecutions of all those who were not Christian, came perhaps one of the most zealous and fanatical Christian Emperors to walk the face of the earth. His name was Theodosius "the Great," and in 380 ce he enacted the following decree throughout the entire Roman Empire:

We shall believe in the single Deity of the Father, the Son, and the Holy Spirit, under the concept of equal majesty and of the Holy Trinity. We command that those persons who follow this rule shall embrace the name of Catholic Christians. The rest, however, whom we adjudge demented and insane, shall sustain the infamy of heretical dogmas, their meeting places shall not receive the name of churches, and they shall be smitten first by divine vengeance and secondly by the retribution of our own initiative, which we shall assume in accordance with the divine judgment.[178]

Needless to say, such conditions were not conducive to Jewish life and thus, many rabbinical scholars having moved outside of the immediate grasp these ruthless Christian zealots, seem to have felt at ease in retaliating against the persecution they had suffered, by composing works that were highly offensive to Christianity.[179] Let us now take a look at some of the *Talmudic* references to Jesus used by apologists to claim that Jesus was in fact, a real life hero and while we are at it, perhaps we may gain further understanding as to who this Pandera character was. The first reference we will examine is located in the Book of the Sanhedrin and is as follows:

On the eve of Passover Yeshu was hanged. For forty days before the execution took place, a herald went forth and cried, "He is going forth to be stoned because he has practiced sorcery and enticed Israel to apostasy. Anyone who can say anything in his favour, let him come forward and plead on his behalf." But since nothing was brought forward in his favour he was hanged on the eve of the Passover! - Ulla retorted: Do you suppose that he was one for whom a defence could be made? Was he not a Mesith [enticer], concerning him Scripture

---

[178]J.N. Hillgarth, The Conversion of Western Europe Englewood Cliff s, NJ: Prentice Hall, (1969) p. 46.
[179]Catherine M. Murphy, PhD. The Historical Jesus For Dummies. Wiley Publishing Inc. (2008). p. 269.

says, Neither shalt though spare, neither shalt thou conceal him? With Yeshu however it was different, for he was connected with the government for royalty [i.e., influential]. Our Rabbis taught: Yeshu had five disciples, Matthai, Nakai, Nezer, Buni, and Todah.

~Book of the Sanhedrin 43a

Aside from some resemblances, like having the name Jesus (a very common name), being viewed as a sorcerer, leading Israel "astray" and being descended from royalty, reading this sixth century work carefully, we see that this Jesus was stoned and hung, not crucified, and done so by the Jews, rather than by the Romans as the Gospels report. Further, we note that the number and identity of his disciples does not conform to the Gospel's account, they were not twelve, but five and were different people, but for, Matthai (Matthew) which was and still is a very common Hebrew name. One may have even noticed that unlike the Gospels, Jesus was given forty days to allow for witnesses to come forth and defend him, as opposed to the Gospel accounts in which he was given less than 24 hours (Matthew 26-27, Mark 14-15, Luke 22-23, John 18-19). The date of his execution does concur with John's Gospel (eve of Passover) (John 19:14), but contradicts the three Synoptic Gospels, as they allege that Jesus was crucified on the following day, during the Passover.(Mark 14-15, Matthew 26:18~27:1-50, Luke 22:7~23:46)

One of the possible reasons which may have led the author of John's Gospel to assert that Jesus was crucified on the eve of Passover was that he may have been attempting to make a theological point. In John's Gospel and only in John's Gospel, Jesus was given the epithet, the "Lamb of God," whose sacrifice takes away the sins of the world, (see John 1:29) thus, he was slaughtered on the eve of Passover, or as it was known to the Jews, "the day of preparation", a day when the Passover lambs were slaughtered for the following day's festivities.[180] With regards to the coincidental and rather convenient timing of Jesus' execution, being the eve of Passover, or day of preparation, John Remsburg, says:

---

[180]Bart D Ehrman. Jesus Interrupted. Harper Collins Publishers. (2005). pp. 28; http://www.jewishencyclopedia.com/articles/11934-passover-sacrifice; Exodus 12:1-20.

Referring to the Lord's Supper, as recorded in John, the Bible for Learners says: It was not the Paschal meal. The Passover did not begin until the following evening; for he himself who was the true Paschal Lamb, and as such made an end of all sacrifices, must be put to death at the very day and hour ordained for the slaughter of the lamb—not twenty-four hours later as the Synoptic Gospels say" (Vol. in, p. 684). Admitting the discrepancy, but without determining which is correct, Smith's "Bible Dictionary" says: "The crowning application of the Paschal rites to the truths of which they were the shadowy promises appears to be that which is afforded by the fact that our Lord's death occurred during the festival. According to the Divine purpose, the true Lamb of God was slain at nearly the same time as 'the Lord's Passover, in obedience to the letter of the law." It was not "according to the Divine purpose" that Jesus was slain at the Passover, but it was according to a human invention that he is declared to have been slain at this time. These attempts to connect the crucifixion with the Passover afford the strongest proof that it is a myth.[181]

As with the huge discrepancies found between the four Gospels themselves, the inconsistencies which exist between the Jesus mentioned in the Babylonian *Talmud* and the Jesus of the Gospels weakens and brings into question, the validity of this rabbinical reference to the historical Jesus. It constitutes neither proof, nor even good evidence for Jesus' earthly existence. The next reference Christians use from the Babylonian *Talmud* is as follows:

It is taught: R. Eliezer told the sages: Did not Ben Stada bring witchcraft with him from Egypt in a cut that was on his skin? They said to him: He was a fool and you cannot bring proof from a fool. Ben Stada is Ben Pandira. R. Chisda said: The husband was Stada and the lover was Pandira. [No,] the husband was Pappos Ben Yehudah and the mother was Stada. [No,] the mother was Miriam (Mary) the women's hairdresser [and was called Stada]. As we say in Pumbedita: She has turned away [Heb. Stat Da] from her husband.

~Book of the Sanhedrin 67a

---

[181]John E Remsburg. The Christ: A Critical Review and Analysis of the Evidences of His Existence. The Truth Seeker Company. (1909). pp. 286–287.

The above reference is very interesting for a number of reasons. First, the name Jesus does not appear in this reference, but we do have a further lead on Pandira/Pandera. It is alleged that Eliezer told the sages that Ben (son of) Stada brought witchcraft with him from Egypt in a cut that was on his skin and that this "son of Stada" (Sta-Da, being a Hebrew verb describing his mother Mary, for she "turned away" from her husband to seek adulteress pleasures with Pandira) was also the son of Pandera. Now, Pandera being a common Roman name, (Eng. Panther) makes it impossible to nail down exactly whether this reference corresponds to the reference found in both the Jerusalem *Talmud* and the *Tosefta*. Second, one can see here that this son of Pandira, not only practiced sorcery or witchcraft, which he was alleged to have contracted in Egypt, but that his mother's name was Miriam (Eng. Mary) who, it was said, was an adulteress. One could argue that the above reference relates to Jesus Christ, as he was a "sorcerer," or a "miracle worker," his mother's name was Miriam (Mary), he travelled to Egypt, but only as an infant and only in Matthew's Gospel in contradiction to Luke's. (See Matthew 2:13-15 vs. Luke 2:22-52) Further, if one did not believe that a ghost impregnated Mary, which would not be an overly sceptical opinion to hold, then she would have been viewed as an adulteress, if anyone knew about her extra-marital pregnancy that is. Having said all of this, we need to acknowledge the problems with this *Talmud*ic reference.

According to the author of Matthew's Gospel, no one knew that Mary was impregnated by anyone other than Joseph, as Joseph did not tell anyone about Mary's extra-marital pregnancy (see Matthew 1:18-20), thus the only way the Jews could have known that Jesus was not Joseph's true son, was if they had read the Gospels, which incidentally, had been in circulation throughout Asia Minor, the Middle East and Egypt, for hundreds of years prior to the creation of this *Talmud*ic reference. Further, the name Jesus does not appear in the above passage, making it impossible to tell if this passage is referring to the *Yeshu* ben Pandira mentioned in the Jerusalem *Talmud*, let alone Jesus of the Gospels. Additionally, the Gospels clearly say that the Jews knew Jesus' father was Joseph of the House of David and not Pappos Ben Yahuda, as stated above. Finally, the Gospels make no mention of any person

associated with Jesus, let alone a biological father by the name of Pandira. Thus, if we wish to compare this Son of Stada/Pandira to the Jesus
of the Gospels, we can only speculate on very vague similarities. Even
if the passage in question was referring to Jesus of the Gospels, which
has certainly not been established, it comes from a source which was
compiled centuries after Jesus was said to have walked the earth and
thus fails the historical test of contemporanity.

Thus far we have not been able to establish that the Jewish rabbinical texts made any mention of Jesus Christ and we have travelled
from the third century ce to around the seventh century. But perhaps
if we travel a little further in time to around the ninth century, well
beyond the scope of historical reliability, we may find more pieces to
the puzzle, at least with regards to whom this elusive *Yeshu* ben Pan-
dira/Pandera character was believed to have been.

THE TOLEDOTH YESHU (THE BIOGRAPHY OF JESUS)

In the ninth century, a piece of Jewish literature, in many forms and
versions, came to the attention of Agobard, the archbishop of Lyon
(France), which appeared to describe his saviour Jesus, as being the
bastard son of a menstruate adulteress. This Jewish biography of
Jesus provides further insight into the character known as Jesus ben
Pandera, found within the books of *Talmud* and the *Tosefta*. The
highly dangerous and controversial details contained within the
pages of the *Toledoth Yeshu*, would eventually spark a frenzy of anti-
Semitic sentiment amongst middle, to early modern age Christians,
that would see thousands of Jews slaughtered, dislocated and
robbed blind by a Church that wasn't about to be undermined or
criticized by its theological forbears. This shocking piece of literature was called, the *Toledoth Yeshu*, or "Biography of Jesus" and
seems to have been written as a Jewish polemic against the very
anti-Jewish Christian religion. The picture it paints of the Christian's
messiah is extremely unflattering, which on its face, appears to indicate that it was written for the purpose of "getting a rise" out of
Christians. There are, however, some intriguing curiosities surrounding certain details related in this Jewish literary work, details

that require further investigation. Before we begin this investigation, let us note that the consensus amongst Christian scholars is that the *Toledoth Yeshu* was originally composed sometime during the ninth century and was based upon traditions that arose no earlier than the sixth century.

As will be demonstrated, there is strong evidence to suggest that some of the stories related in the *Toledoth* may have existed as early as the second century CE. Although this date is still too late to establish reliable historical evidence for the Jesus of the Gospels, it does push the date of the stories of Jesus contained within the *Toledoth Yeshu*, back much further than previously estimated by many Christian scholars, which, as will be discussed, raises a very interesting possibility. There are many versions of the *Toledoth Yeshu*, however, for both the sake of brevity and of this investigation, I will deal with the most popular version known as the *Wagenseil Version*, adding information from other versions where necessary.

THE WAGENSEIL TOLEDOTH YESHU

The *Wagenseil Version* of the *Toledoth Yeshu* was translated from Hebrew by the fanatical 17th Century Christian and outspoken anti-Semite, Professor Johann Christian Wagenseil. It provides the following account of the information contained within a few versions of the *Toledoth Yeshu* and begins as follows:

In the year of the world 4671, in the days of King Jannaeus, a great misfortune befell Israel. There arose at that tune a scape-grace, a wastrel and worthless fellow, of the fallen race of Judah, named Joseph Pandira. He was a well-built man, strong and handsome, but he spent his time in robbery and violence. His dwelling was at Bethlehem, in Judah. And there lived near him a widow with her daughter, whose name was Miriam; and this is the same Miriam who dressed and curled women's hair, who is mentioned several times in the Talmud.[182]

These were the events which shortly preceded the conception and birth of Jesus ben Pandera. From the outset, we see a number of

---

[182]Rev. S. Baring Gould. *'The Lost and Hostile Gospels*. Williams and Norgate. (1874) p. 76.

parallels to the Gospel's accounts of Jesus; his father being a man named Joseph from the tribe of Judah, his residence in Bethlehem, in accordance with Matthew's Gospel, yet in contradiction to Luke's, (See Matthew 1 vs. Luke 2:4) and his mother being Miriam, or Mary. There is a striking peculiarity with this account, namely, the period in which Jesus' birth was supposed to have taken place. Leaving aside the ignorance of Wagenseil, who mistakenly ascribed the events to the year 4671 ("4671 years after the creation of the universe," or 910 bce, in secular terms), in accordance with the later Christian dating system, a system not used by the Jews until well after this manuscript was written, we are given a clue which does appear to correspond with other versions of the *Toledoth* and the *Talmud*. This, of course is the reference to King Alexander Jannaeus, of whom records show, ruled Judea from 106bce-79bce.

The *Toledoth Yeshu* places the birth of Jesus within this period, almost a century earlier than the Gospels claim their Jesus was born. We might also observe that the details match the description of ben Pandira given in the Book of the Sanhedrin in the Babylonian *Talmud*. Note, the mother was Miriam, a hairdresser/curler of women's hair (which may be an idiom describing an adulteress)[183] and her lover was Joseph Pandira. This later tradition not only appears to be somehow connected with the earlier *Talmud*ic one, but it also leads to yet another interesting curiosity. The term, "curler of women's hair" (hairdresser), was, as briefly mentioned, probably a Hebrew idiom applied to adulteress women. Looking into the matter further, we discover that the exact phrase "Mary the curler of women's hair", transliterated in English, reads, "Miriam Magdella Nashaia", Magdella, being the etymological root of the name, Magdalene.[184] Could these two Marys, Jesus' mother and his female disciple, have been originally one single historical character that were eventually split into two separate characters, in a bid to spare his later followers the embarrassment of having their saviour's mother remembered as a

---

[183]R. Travers Herford. *'Christianity in Talmud and Midrash.'* Williams and Norgate. (1903). p.4
[184]Ibid.

"prostitute," or "curler of women's hair"? We do not know, however it is food for thought. The story of Jesus ben Pandera follows:

The widow Miriam was engaged to an amiable, God-fearing youth, named Jochanan (John), a disciple of the Rabbi Simeon, son of Shetach; but he went away to Babylon, and she became the mother of Yeshu (Yeshu/Joshua/Jesus) by Joseph Pandira. The child was named Joshua, after his uncle, and was given to the Rabbi Elchanan to be instructed in the Law. One day Yeshu, when a boy, passed before the Rabbi Simeon Ben Shetach and other members of the Sanhedrin without uncovering his head and bowing his knee. The elders were indignant. Three hundred trumpets were blown, and Yeshu was excommunicated and cast out of the Temple. Then he went away to Galilee, and spent there several years.[185]

Let us stop the narrative here and examine some of the details. In this version, Mary was engaged to a god fearing Torah scholar by the name of Jochanan (John) whom she betrayed with Joseph Pandera, the biological father of Jesus. So we have the three names that appear in the Gospel account of Jesus, those being, Joseph, Mary and Jesus. Further we see that Mary's spouse John, does not want to cause a scene, or make a public example of Mary, deciding instead to go quietly to Babylon. This is rather similar to the story of Joseph in the Gospel of Matthew, who upon discovering that Mary was pregnant with someone else's child, seeks to avoid making a public example of her, wishing rather to quietly divorce her (see Matthew 1:18-20). As within the Gospels, we also find in this story, hostility between Jesus and the Jewish authorities, a hostility that resulted in a young Jesus ben Pandera, moving to Galilee, the home of the Gospel's Jesus.

The *Wagenseil version of the Toledoth Yeshu* continues by claiming that Jesus snuck into the Temple at Jerusalem and acquired the secret name of God, which granted the possessor magical powers, powers that Jesus used, with which to perform miracles like raising the dead and healing the sick. This is in contradiction to other versions of the *Toledoth Yeshu*, such as the Huldrich Version, which claims that Jesus

---

[185]Rev. S. Baring Gould. The Lost and Hostile Gospels. Williams and Norgate. (1874). p. 77.

acquired his magical powers in Egypt, thereupon returning to Israel in order that he might use his powers to seduce and lead astray, many trusting Israelites. This aspect of the Huldrich Version corresponds to the *Talmud* cited above, in which it was alleged that Jesus had acquired his magic in Egypt. Following the acquisition of these miraculous powers, in the *Wagenseil Version*, Jesus returned to Galilee and told many people that he was the prophesized ruler spoken of by the prophet Isaiah at 7:14 of the book of Isaiah, who would be "born of a virgin." This is a rather curious claim to be written within the Jewish tradition, for the Jews have always known that Isaiah did not refer to a virgin (*betullah*), who would come at some distant time in the future, but rather to a young women (*almah*), who was to be born in the days of King Ahaz, centuries before the Christian era. Such curiosities have led some Jewish scholars to assert that the *Toledoth Yeshu* was originally written by zealous Christians for the purpose of stirring up anti-Jewish sentiment however, the evidence for such a proposition, as likely as it may appear, is merely speculative and circumstantial.

Continuing on with the story, upon hearing of the miracles performed by Jesus, the priests accuse him of sorcery, again following the tradition laid down in the Babylonian *Talmud*, at which time Jesus left Galilee and entered Jerusalem upon the back of an ass, in likeness to the Gospels depiction of him entering Jerusalem in accordance with the *Old Testament* prophecy regarding the King entering Jerusalem upon the back of an ass. The priests then bring Jesus before King Jannaeus' wife, Queen Helena, whereupon Jesus brought a dead person back to life and healed a leper, convincing the Queen that he was in fact the son of God and thereupon she let him go free. The priests, knowing that Jesus had achieved these powers by sorcery from stealing the name of God from the temple, set forth one of their most admired scholars, Judas Iscarioti, to take also the name of God and battle Jesus. Prior to their battle, Judas questions Jesus before the queen, asking him:

If thy brother, the son of thy mother, or thy son, or thy daughter, or the wife of thy bosom, or thy friend, which is as thine own soul, entice thee secretly, saying. Let us go and serve other gods, which thou hast not known, thou, nor thy fathers; "Namely, of the gods of the people which are round about you, nigh unto thee, or far off from thee, from the one end of the earth even unto the other end of the earth; Thou shalt not consent unto him, nor hearken unto him; neither shall thine eye pity him, neither shalt thou spare, neither shalt thou conceal him; But thou shalt surely kill him; thine hand shall be first upon him to put him to death, and afterwards the hand of all the people.[186]

This line of questioning is interesting because it reflects the *Talmudic* passage examined above, in which Ulla says:

Do you suppose that he was one for whom a defence could be made? Was he not a Mesith [enticer], concerning him Scripture says, Neither shalt though spare, neither shalt thou conceal him?

According to this version of the *Toledoth Yeshu*, after Judas and Jesus finish their battle of wits, they fly through the air engaged in a comic book style aerial battle, during which, Judas defeats Jesus, leaving him helpless and at the mercy of the Jewish authorities. Jesus' followers help him escape to the Jordan river wherein he washes himself and regains his magical powers only to return and be defeated for the final time by Judas. The *Toledoth Yeshu* continues:

Then they led Yeshu forth before the greater and the lesser Sanhedrin, and he was sentenced to be stoned, and then to be hung on a tree. And it was the eve of the Passover and of the Sabbath. And they led him forth to the place where the punishment of stoning was want to be executed, and they stoned him there till he was dead. And after that, the wise men hung him on the tree.[187]

Here we may observe another similarity with both the *Talmudic* reference and the Gospel of John, in that Jesus was said to have been killed on the eve of Passover. The method of his death is contrary to the Gospels, which claim that Jesus was crucified by the Romans, a form of capital punishment that was somewhat unique to the Romans. Yet, in both this account and the *Talmud*, Jesus is hung from a tree. There is evidence within the canonized scriptures of the *New Testament* that many first century Christians believed that Jesus was not

---

[186]Ibid. pp. 82–83.
[187]Ibid.

crucified, but rather hung from a tree, in likeness to the accounts found within both the *Talmud* and *Toledoth Yeshu*:

Christ hath redeemed us from the curse of the law, being made a curse for us: for it is written, Cursed is every one that hangeth on a tree.

~Galatians 3:13

Who his own self bare our sins in his own body on the tree…

~1 Peter 2:24

And when they had fulfilled all that was written of him, they took him down from the tree, and laid him in a sepulchre.

~Acts 13:29

The God of our fathers raised up Jesus, whom ye slew and hanged on a tree.

~Acts 5:30

And we are witnesses of all things which he did both in the land of the Jews, and in Jerusalem; whom they slew and hanged on a tree.

~Acts 10:39

In the verse cited directly above, it may also been seen that the author of Acts asserted in likeness to the authors of both the *Talmud* and the *Toledoth*, that Jesus was hung on a tree by the Jews in contradiction to the Gospels, which claim that Jesus was crucified by the Romans. This conformity with the Jewish tradition may become a little more significant in a short while, when we look a little deeper into the matter. Following Jesus' death, the *Toledoth Yeshu* reports that the Jews buried Jesus in a grave and later, to their surprise, when they sought to dig him up and show the queen his dead body, it was gone and his disciples became elated, saying that he had been resurrected and thereupon ascended to heaven as he promised he would. The story continues:

Now there was amongst them an elder whose name was Tanchuma; and he went forth in sore distress, and wandered in the fields, and he saw Judas sitting in his garden eating. Then Tanchuma drew near to him, and said to him. What doest thou, Judas, that thou eatest meat, when all the Jews fast and are in grievous distress? Then Judas was astonished, and asked the occasion of the fast. And the Rabbi Tanchuma answered him, Yeshu the Fatherless is the occasion, for he was hung up and buried on the spot where he was stoned; but now is he taken away, and we know not where he is gone. And his worthless disciples cry out that he is ascended into heaven. Now the Queen has condemned us Israelites to death unless we find him. Judas asked. And if the Fatherless One were found, would it be the salvation of Israel? The Rabbi Tanchuma answered that it would be even so.

Then spake Judas, Come, and I will show you the man whom ye seek; for it was I who took the Fatherless from his grave. For I feared lest his disciples should steal him away, and I have hidden him in my garden and led a water-brook over the place. Then the Rabbi Tanchuma hasted to the elders of Israel, and told them all. And they came together, and drew him forth, attached to the tail of a horse, and brought him before the Queen, and said, See! This is the man who, they say, has ascended into heaven! Now when the Queen saw this, she was filled with shame, and answered not a word. Now it fell out, that in dragging the body to the place, the hair was torn off the head; and this is the reason why monks shave their heads. It is done in remembrance of what befell Yeshu. And after this, in consequence thereof, there grew to be strife between the Nazarenes and the Jews, so that they parted asunder; and when a Nazarene saw a Jew he slew him. And from day to day the distress grew greater, during thirty years. And the Nazarenes assembled in thousands and tens of thousands, and hindered the Israelites from going up to the festivals at Jerusalem. And then there was great distress, such as when the golden calf was set up, so that they knew not what to do. "And the belief of the opposition grew more and more, and spread on all sides. Also twelve godless run agates separated and traversed the twelve realms, and everywhere in the assemblies of the people uttered false prophecies.[188]

In summing up the context in which *Bible* scholar S. Baring Gould perceived the birth of the anti-Christian traditions found within the *Wagenseil Version* of the *Toledoth Yeshu*, he said:

That the Wagenseil Toledoth Yeshu was written in the eleventh, twelfth, or thirteenth century appears probable from the fact stated, that it was in these centuries that the Jews were more subjected to persecution, spoliation, and massacre than in any other; and the

---

[188]Ibid. pp. 88–89.

Toledoth Yeshu is the cry of rage of a tortured people,—a curse hurled at the Founder of that religion which oppressed them. In the eleventh century the Jews in the great Rhine cities were massacred by the ferocious hosts of Crusaders under Ernico, Count of Leiningen, and the priests Folkmar and Goteschalk. At the voice of their leaders (ad 1096), the furious multitude of red-crossed pilgrims spread through the cities of the Rhine and the Moselle, massacring pitilessly all the Jews that they met with in their passage. In their despair, a great number preferred being their own destroyers to awaiting certain death at the hands of their enemies. Several shut themselves up in their houses, and perished amidst flames their own hands had kindled; some attached heavy stones to their garments, and precipitated themselves and their treasures into the Rhine or Moselle. Mothers stifled their children at the breast, saying that they preferred sending them to the bosom of Abraham to seeing them torn away to be nurtured in a religion which bred tigers.[189]

The Jewish traditions related in both the *Talmud* and the *Toledoth Yeshu* seem, in connection with one another, to provide us with the Jewish perspective of the birth of Christianity and in so doing, challenge almost every article of faith held by Christians. The miraculous conception of Jesus, his virgin birth, his divine son-ship and his resurrection and ascension, are all brought into question by this Jewish tradition found in both the *Talmud* and the *Toledoth Yeshu*. It is for this reason that many Christian scholars deride this Jewish account of Jesus, as being nothing more than a middle-age forgery with neither truth nor antiquity at its backing. In Professor Catherine Murphy's book *The Historical Jesus for Dummies,* she says of the *Talmud*ic traditions of Jesus:

Jewish traditions about Jesus in the Babylonian Talmud were compiled sometime in the seventh century ce in a region that wasn't under Christian control at the time. Free of the constraints of Christian imperial religion, the Babylonian rabbis could afford to be more open in their assessments of Jesus and his followers. The Talmud preserves several separate traditions:

---

[189]Ibid. p. 96.

— Jesus' mother was an adulteress who had an affair with a Roman soldier.
— Jesus fled to Egypt and picked up magic there.
— Jesus was a rabbinic student who went astray or a rabbi who led his students astray.
— Jesus was tried fairly for blasphemy and idolatry, but no one came to his defence.

Each of these traditions confronts a gospel claim: that Jesus was the son of God and son of David, that he was a legitimate healer and teacher, and that he was arrested and tried hastily and illegally on trumped-up charges. While these are all late traditions and don't tell us much about the historical Jesus, they do tell us a tremendous amount about later historical debates between Jews and Christians in a region where the playing field was relatively level.[190]

Regarding the reliability, or lack thereof, pertaining to the *Talmudic* accounts of the "historical Jesus," *Bible* scholar and theologian Maurice Goguel adds:

The Talmud contains nothing about Jesus which does not come from Christian tradition.[191]

Further, with regards to the stories found in both the *Talmud* and the *Toledoth Yeshu*, Rev. S. Baring Gould protested:

That he was said by Christians to have been born of a Virgin, driven into Egypt by King Herod—that he wrought miracles, gathered disciples, died on the cross and rose again—they heard from the Christians; and these facts they made use of to pervert them into fantastic fables, to colour them with malignant inventions.[192]

If the opinions above contain merit, then there is no escaping the fact that the Jewish rabbinical sources for an historical Jesus are rendered void and cannot be used to testify to an historical Jesus. They are "perversions" based solely upon Christian traditions, leaving us with

---

[190]Catherine M. Murphy, PhD. The Historical Jesus For Dummies. Wiley Publishing Inc. (2008). p. 270.
[191]Maurice Goguel. Jesus the Nazarene: Myth or History? D Appleton and Company. (1926). p. 21.
[192]Rev. S. Baring Gould. The Lost and Hostile Gospels. Williams and Norgate. (1874)

nowhere else to turn, but back to that place where we came from in the previous chapter, the falsely named, forgery laced, mistake laden and error ridden Gospels, of which we have already established with some degree of certainty, do not and cannot, be counted upon as reliable historical testimony for a character who defies logic and reason, such as Jesus the Christ. However, let us reserve our judgment for the moment and look a little deeper into the matter as there is another way of looking at this quandary. A manner of investigation which might allow us to avoid the tenuous certainties occasioned by both belief and disbelief, a style of examination that may just provide a somewhat fresh perspective of the Christian's "Jesus of history." What if, and we must admit that we are about to go on a rather circumstantial and speculative journey, one based upon the highly contradictory and suspect testimonies of both the *Toledoth Yeshu* and the *Talmud*, which on some instances place the birth of Jesus at both the time of King Jannaeus (100 bce) and Herod the Great (6-4 bce) simultaneously, which also in some manuscripts ascribe the building of the Jewish temple to David, rather than to Solomon and in which can be found, as we have seen, a strong motive to spread malign rumours about their persecutors, the Christians. But, what if the Jesus of the Gospels is based upon a real mortal character from Jewish history, a Jesus who lived some 100 years or so earlier than the fictional Jesus of the Christian Gospels? What if the real-life character of whom the mythology of "Jesus Christ" was bestowed, was merely a charismatic rebel that managed to gain a following amongst the Jewish lower-classes of the first century bce and was, as they report, born illegitimately from a promiscuous mother, and who was eventually tried, stoned to death and hung from a tree as a heretic?

And what if, as absurd as it may sound, he did not rise from the dead like some Greco-Egyptian God, a divine zombie if you will, but instead, had his body taken away and hidden, either by his disciples or a devout Jew, seeking to circumvent a fraudulent claim of his heavenly ascension. Following which, it was later revealed that Jesus had actually died and that his disciples could not come to grips with the fact of his downfall, so they, like the members of the UFO cult discussed in chapter one, employed disconfirmation bias to rationalize, or otherwise completely ignore his demise. Given the fact that no one has ever truly been able to pinpoint Jesus' birthday, it may have been possible that he lived some 100 years earlier. This Jesus was not the son of the Jewish God, Yahweh, nor was he, as the Jews reported, a magical sorcerer who could fly through the air and raise the dead, he was simply a rebel born in painful circumstances, circumstances which led him to despise his own people, for the persecution that he had suffered growing up as an illegitimate bastard son of a menstruate adulteress, named Mary. This proposition will be the focus of the remainder of this chapter, so for those who would prefer to get off here, by all means feel free to end your journey at your own leisure.

THE JESUS OF HISTORY: A FRESH PERSPECTIVE

Above I made a promise to the reader that I would provide evidence that both the *Talmud*ic and *Toledoth Yeshu* traditions spanned as far back as the second century ce. It needs to be acknowledged, that by this time, the Gospels were already in circulation, or at least the oral traditions that formed the various Gospels were wide-spread and such timing does not take us beyond the influence the Gospels. Thus, such traditions constitute neither solid evidence for the aforementioned proposition, nor adequate historical evidence for the Jesus of the Gospels. Yet it may be somewhat enlightening to expand our previously narrow horizons and contemplate new possibilities, for we have neither the truth, nor even the semblance of it in the Gospels or any other Christian testimony relating to the historicity of Jesus. Instead, all we have are the testimonies of liars, deceivers and forgers, who have openly displayed their deceitful cards on occasions when they felt that doing so would pose no threat to their ill-gotten credibility. For example, in the fifth century, John Chrysostom in his *Treatise on the Priesthood, Book 1*, wrote:

And oft en it is necessary to deceive, and to do the greatest benefits by means of this device, whereas he who has gone by a straight course has done great mischief to the person whom he has not deceived.[193]

---

[193]Nicene and Post Nicene Fathers. 1-09. Philip Schaff . St. Chrysostom: On the Priesthood; Ascetic Treatises; Select Homilies and Letters; Homilies on the Statutes. Christian Classics Ethereal Library. (1886). p. 43.

Further, writing in the 16th century the famed father of the Protestant Church, Martin Luther said:

What harm would it do, if a man told a good strong lie for the sake of the good and for the Christian church ... a lie out of necessity, a useful lie, a helpful lie, such lies would not be against God, he would accept them.[194]

It would do us no harm to look beyond the words and testimonies of these self-confessed liars, so now let us examine the following evidences in a bid to establish the possibility that the Jews, in their *Talmud*, their *Tosefta* and their *Toledoth Yeshu*, may hold the keys to understanding the possible historical origins of the mythical/legendary Jesus Christ. As early as 150 ce Justin Martyr, in his dialogue with a Jewish Rabbi called Trypho, demonstrated that he was aware of at least portions of the Jewish traditions found in both the *Talmud* and the *Toledoth Yeshu*, saying:

...you have sent chosen and ordained men throughout all the world to proclaim that a godless and lawless heresy had sprung from one Jesus, a Galilean deceiver, whom we crucified, but his disciples stole him by night from the tomb, where he was laid when unfastened from the cross, and now deceive men by asserting that he has risen from the dead and ascended to heaven.[195]

Further, as can be witnessed in the writings of the third century Church Father Origen, who wrote against the famous second century Greek philosopher and Christian opponent Celsus, the traditions contained within the both the *Talmud* and the *Toledoth* can be shown to have been wide-spread during the second Century. Unfortunately the Church destroyed many of the works of non-Christian philosophers and anti-Christian scholars like Celsus and Porphyry, yet fragments of their critiques remain in rebuttals written by Christian apologists and Church fathers, like Origen's *Contra Celsum* or, *Against Celsus*. Celsus, having discoursed with certain Jews, is reported by Origen as contending the following:

---

[194]Martin Luther cited by his secretary, in a letter in Max Lenz, ed., Briefwechsel Landgraf Phillips des Grossmüthigen von Hessen mit Bucer, vol. I.
[195]The Apostolic Fathers with Justin Martyr and Irenaeus. Justin Martyr. (trans. Philip Schaff .) Justin Martyr Dialogue with Trypho. Christian Ethereal Library (1885). p. 411.

...[Celsus] accuses [Jesus] of having "invented his birth from a virgin," and upbraids Him with being "born in a certain Jewish village, of a poor woman of the country, who gained her subsistence by spinning, and who was turned out of doors by her husband, a carpenter by trade, because she was convicted of adultery; that after being driven away by her husband, and wandering about for a time, she disgracefully gave birth to Jesus, an illegitimate child, who having hired himself out as a servant in Egypt on account of his poverty, and having there acquired some miraculous powers, on which the Egyptians greatly pride themselves, returned to his own country, highly elated on account of them, and by means of these proclaimed himself a God.[196]

From the excerpt taken from this second century philosopher's attack on Christianity, many of the traditions contained within the *Toledoth Yeshu* can be seen to have been present in the second century. Accusations pertaining to Mary's adulterous nature, the bastardry of Jesus and his acquisition of miraculous powers in Egypt, details relayed much later in both the *Talmud* and the *Toledoth Yeshu*. Such traditions may further be shown to have been in circulation during the late second century, in the words of the famous Church Father Tertullian, who responded to the Jewish and Pagan criticisms of Christianity, said:

This, I shall say, this is that carpenter's or hireling's son, that Sabbath breaker, that Samaritan and devil-possessed! This is He whom you purchased from Judas! This is He whom you struck with reed and fist, whom you contemptuously spat upon, to whom you gave gall and vinegar to drink! This is He whom His disciples secretly stole away, that it might be said He had risen again... .[197]

Again here we see amongst a mixture of Gospel narrative components, one of which is particularly relevant to the matter at hand, the existence of stories describing Jesus as the son of a harlot, whose disciples had stolen his corpse to fraudulently claim that he had risen

---

[196]Philip Schaff . Ante-Nicene Fathers Vol. 4: Fathers of the Third Century: Tertullian, Part Fourth; Minucius Felix; Commodian; Origen, Parts First and Second. Grand Rapids, MI: Christian Classics Ethereal Library. p. 699.
[197]Philip Schaff . Ante-Nicene Fathers Vol. 3: Latin Christianity; Its founder, Tertullian. Grand Rapids, MI: Christian Classics Ethereal Library. p. 139.

from dead.[198] In commenting on this exhortation by Tertullian, Cambridge scholar and influential member of the Theosophical Society, G.R.S Mead said:

All these elements appear in order in the Toledoth and the carpenter's son and the harlot's son appear in the Talmud stories.[199]

Now all of this only takes the traditions of the *Toledoth* and *Talmud* back to the second century and as mentioned, does not constitute reliable historical evidence, either for the Gospel's Christ, nor our 100 bce Jesus. Even though we have hit a dead end, in terms of trying to establish whether or not Jesus was an historical person, let alone lived 100 years before the character depicted in the Gospels, we do have one last piece of historical evidence that presents us with a rather bizarre curiosity. In the fourth Century, a fanatical Church Father, by the name of Epiphanius, wrote, in his famous work, the *Panarion:*

...For the rulers in succession from Judah came to an end with Christ's arrival. Until he came the rulers were anointed priests, but after his (Christ's) birth in Bethlehem of Judaea the order ended and was altered in the time of Alexander (King Alexander Jannaeus), a ruler of priestly and kingly stock. This position died out with this Alexander from the time of Salina (possibly Queen Helena) also known as Alexandra... .[200]

For some reason, this fourth century Church Father believed that Jesus was born in the days of King Alexander Jannaeus 100 bce. Why would this ultra-fanatical heresy hunter take the word of his enemies, the Jews, when it came to testimony regarding his own personal saviour?

It does not seem to make sense, unless this tradition was floating around in Christian circles as well, but there seems to be no other evidence throughout the entire span of Christian history of anyone else asserting, in similitude to the *Toledoth Yeshu*, that Jesus was born in 100 bce.

---

[198]The Gospel of Matthew possibly written toward the end of the first century relates how the Jews "dishonestly" assert, that Jesus' followers snatched his body from the sepulchre and hid it to fraudulently claim that he had risen, which pushes back the date of this aspect of the *Toledoth* Yeshu story, to at least the end of the first century CE. (See Matthew 28:11-15).

[199]G.R.S Mead. Did Jesus Live 100 BC? Theosophical Publishing Society. (1903). p. 133.

[200]Einar Thomassen & Johannes van Oort. Translated By Frank Williams. The *Panarion* of Epiphanius of Salamis: Book 1 (Sections 1-46) Brill. (2009). p. 124.

Epiphanius even refers to his saviour's foster-father Joseph, as being known as, Joseph ben Pandera,[201] further showing that this Jewish tradition was not merely confined to the Jews, but also, at least to some degree, Christians believed that Jesus was called ben (son of) Pandera and that he was born during King Alexander Jannaeus' reign, somewhere around 100 bce. Heavy qualification must be made regarding Epiphanius' assertion that Jesus was born in King Alexander's reign, as the end of the above quoted passage from Epiphanius' *Panarion* continues:

… in the time of King Herod and the Roman emperor Augustus.[202]

Thus, Epiphanius placed these three historical events, *viz.* the reigns of King Alexander Jannaeus, King Herod the Great and the Roman Caesar Augustus, within the same year or so, when the rulerships of both Herod and Augustus were separated in time from King Alexander's reign by almost 100 years. Obviously, Epiphanius' testimony is unreliable and cannot be used to establish that Jesus lived in 100 bce, yet it demonstrates that this Jewish tradition was present among some Christians during the fourth century ce.

PSYCHOANALYZING CHRIST

Absent any reliable historical evidence for either the Jesus of the Gospels, or our much older Jesus ben Pandera, we are left no choice but to travel deeper into more abstract and speculative waters. We are given no choice but to suppose and hypothesize, yet, if such an approach was and still is, good enough for Christians to base an entire belief system upon, then surely it is good enough to form the bases of our admittedly circumstantial investigation into the Jesus who may have lived 100 years earlier than the legendary Christ and who could also possibly have been, the real human prototype upon which the mythical/legendary Jesus may have been built.

Here, I will attempt to show by use of the same grandiose speculation employed by Christians with regards to their interpretations

---

[201]G.R.S Mead. Did Jesus Live 100 BC? Theosophical Publishing Society. (1903). p. 404.
[202]Einar Thomassen & Johannes van Oort. Translated By Frank Williams. The *Panarion* of Epiphanius of Salamis: Book 1 (Sections 1-46) Brill. (2009). p. 124.

of their scriptures, that evidence of the accounts of Jesus' life as related in both the *Talmud* and the *Toledoth Yeshu*, can be shown to contain merit. Keep in mind that I will be using a Christian style of interpretation, which will require the reader's unconditional trust and faith in my (unsubstantiated) words and somewhat farfetched applications of both scripture and Christian tradition. Both the *Talmud* and the *Toledoth Yeshu* depict Jesus' mother Mary as being, let's say, less than virtuous with regards to her sexual proclivities; an adulteress, there I said it! The focus of this investigation will be to find out whether there is any evidence within the four official Gospels to support this less than flattering description of Jesus' mother. According to the Gospels, Mary was espoused to Joseph when she was allegedly impregnated by a "holy ghost." At this stage of the investigation we reach a three pronged fork in the road, so to speak.

Either Mary was impregnated by a holy ghost, in likeness to earlier sons of gods, like Hercules, Krishna, Horus, and many others, or she was an adulteress who came up with an excuse that would eventually form the basis of billions of people's faith. The third and most likely avenue is one which we will not investigate here, that being, the whole story is a fiction. Now, only two of the Gospels give details of Jesus' conception and birth, those two being Matthew and Luke, however Luke doesn't give us any detail as to Joseph's reaction to his wife's somewhat suspicious news. The Gospel of Matthew on the other hand, reports:

Now the birth of Jesus Christ was on this wise: When as his mother Mary was espoused to Joseph, before they came together, she was found with child of the Holy Ghost. Then Joseph her husband, being a just man, and not willing to make her a public example, was minded to put her away (divorce) privily. But while he thought on these things, behold, the angel of the Lord appeared unto him in a dream, saying, Joseph, thou son of David, fear not to take unto thee Mary thy wife: for that which is conceived in her is of the Holy Ghost.

~Matthew 1:18-20

The above extract from Matthew is the only source of evidence we have from the canonized Gospels with regards to Joseph's reaction to his wife's extra-marital pregnancy. Understandably, at first Joseph was ashamed, wanting to quietly divorce her until, it is alleged an angel came to him in a dream and told him that god had impregnated his wife. Not too many people spare a thought for poor old Joseph who, given no warning, had his wife taken by a god. This effectively robbed Joseph of any chance that he may have had to father a first born child with his beloved wife, not to mention, would have resulted in a severe inferiority complex when it came to pleasing his wife, conjugally speaking. Am I the only one who sees this act of Yahweh's as being a little rude. Perhaps on the seventh day he should have created some manners for himself before resting. Further, if human beings are all Yahweh's (God's) children, then this means two things. First, God committed incest by impregnating his own daughter Mary and secondly, that Jesus was inbred, as his father (God) was also his grandfather (Mary's father)!

Jokes aside, if the accounts of Jesus' life, contained within the Gospels were historical events embellished with mythology and Jesus was nothing more than a mere mortal prophet/heretic, as many early Christians believed, then Mary would have been lying to her husband when she told him that God had impregnated her, if the story be at all true. This means that both the accounts of Jesus' life told in the *Toledoth Yeshu* and the *Talmud* may have been closer to the truth than the Christian Gospels. If so, then Mary was in fact an adulteress and that she may have lied to cover up her indiscretion(s). As bizarre as an assumption as the following may be, let's assume for a moment that heavenly creatures and ghosts cannot impregnate mortal virgins and that Jesus' mother was merely a poor, sexually promiscuous woman who gave birth to a bastard that, due to his charisma, managed to gain followers and begin his own cult, loosely based on Jewish teachings. It is not completely incomprehensible. We know there have been many historical figures in the past that have risen to prominence, only to have the literal story of their lives decorated with mythology. Just look at Alexander the Great and the story of his birth which reads like Christ's or Pythagoras,' or even the records of Emperor Vespasian, who was said to have performed miracles similar to those performed by Jesus. All I'm saying is that it is possible that the Gospel accounts of Jesus' life are fictions based upon actual characters and events, as Ehrman and other historicists often assert.

Imagine a poor little illegitimate and socially outcast Jewish boy growing up with a promiscuous mother and a step-father who would have more than likely resented him, due to the fact that he was the seed of another man. What kind of animosity and resentment would this child eventually harbour toward his shameful mother? There is evidence of this animosity and resentment between Jesus and his mother within the official Gospels. The author of Luke tells us that when Jesus was twelve years old, he ran away from his parents who both failed to realize he was missing until around twenty-four hours later (see Luke 2:42-46). After losing him for approximately three days in total, they finally found him, at which time his mother said to him;

Son, why have you treated us so? Behold, your father and I have been looking for you anxiously, (see Luke 2:48) to which young Jesus snidely responded; How is it that you sought me? Did you not know that I must be in my Father's house? (see Luke 2:49). Jesus' contemptuous response does indicate that he lacked respect for both his mother and his "father." Further, he does seem to be taking an underhanded dig at Joseph. Notice that when Mary said to Jesus, your father (Joseph) and I have been looking everywhere for you, Jesus responded by saying; that they need not have looked for him because he was in HIS father's house. In other words; "Joseph is not my father, I am in MY father's house".

According to the narrative, what Jesus meant was that he was the son of Yahweh and the Synagogue was and is Yahweh's house, thus he was in his father's house. This should have been perfectly obvious to both Mary and Joseph who were both told Jesus was the son of Yahweh by angels and who both knew from their tradition that the Synagogue was God's house, however the narrative continues thusly:

And they did not understand the saying which he spoke to them. (see Luke 2:50).

This absurdity aside, it is clear that from an early age Jesus was contemptuous of his mother. This part of the narrative contains the last reference to Joseph being with either Jesus or Mary and, in all future events in which Jesus comes across his relatives, Joseph is absent. Could Joseph have left for Babylon as the *Toledoth Yeshu* reported? Make of this what you will, but if one is to subscribe to the view that the Gospels are legendary/mythical narratives written for the purposes of embellishing the account of a true historical character, then perhaps the *Tosefta* and *Toledoth Yeshu* hold the keys to answering the riddle of why Joseph seemed to want nothing further to do with Mary or Jesus, after the temple incident.

The next piece of evidence comes from John and relates to the events which took place during the famous marriage feast at Cana. When the wine gave out, the mother of Jesus said to him:

They have no wine.

And Jesus said to her:

O woman, what have you to do with me? My hour has not yet come.

His mother said to the servants:

Do whatever he tells you.

~John 2:3-5

The following piece of evidence can be found in all three of the synoptic Gospels and is as follows:

While he was still speaking to the people, behold, his mother and his brothers stood outside, asking to speak to him. But he replied to the man who told him, "Who is my mother, and who are my brothers?" And stretching out his hand toward his disciples, he said, "Here are my mother and my brothers!"

~Matthew 12:46-50, Luke 8:19-21, Mark 3:31-35

Clearly Jesus wanted nothing to do with his mother, nor anyone whom she had spawned. The following example of Jesus' indifference to his mother comes from a passage in John, which narrates the events that occurred whilst Jesus was allegedly on the cross. The passage in question does not seem to demonstrate contempt for his mother so much, but rather an apathy toward her, as he refers to her as "woman", rather than "mother", or "mummy":

When Jesus saw his mother, and the disciple whom he loved standing near, he said to his mother:

Woman, behold, your son!

~John 19:26

The final pieces of evidence which seem to indicate a strained relationship with his mother, comes from Jesus' anti-family teachings (see

Matthew 10:35-37, 19:29-30, Luke 12:51-53 & 14:26) and from the fact that upon his alleged resurrection, he does not appear to his mother, the "holy virgin," the very woman whom the holy ghost had chosen of all of the billions of women living on earth to impregnate, but rather to his favourite "prostitute," Mary Magdalene.

This brings us to the final aspect of this investigation in which we see that there is evidence, albeit tenuous in nature, to support the proposition that Jesus' mother was a promiscuous woman. For this part of the interpretation we will need to turn to the works of renowned psychologist Carl Gustav Jung for an analysis. According to Jung, the personality type we chose to partner with in adulthood is pre-determined by the personality of one or both of our parents. In his collected papers on "Analytical Psychology", Jung states:

The first attempts to assume friendship and love are constellated in the strongest manner possible by the relation to parents, and here one can usually observe how powerful are the influences of the familiar constellations. It is not rare, for instance, for a healthy man whose mother was hysterical to marry a hysteric, or for the daughter of an alcoholic to choose an alcoholic for her husband.[203]

It is quite well known that when we mature and form adult relationships, be they social or marital, we often tend to seek out those who reflect the qualities present in our early childhood role models. For most men, their mother is the personal archetype upon which they either subconsciously or even consciously use as a personality template when seeking future partners and for most women it is their father. So what female was Jesus said to have had the closest relationship with? According to a mix of both a creative application of scripture and Christian tradition stemming back to the sixth century Pope Gregory "the Great", it was none other than the famous prostitute, Mary Magdalene.

Whether or not Jesus and Mary were actual people, or even as Dan Brown and other fiction writers have suggested, were married, is irrelevant. What is important to the point at hand is that

---

[203]Carl. G. Jung. Collected Papers on Analytical Psychology. Bailliere, Tindall & Cox. (1920). p. 127.

the Gospels tell us that Jesus and Mary had a unique and special relationship. Mary Magdalene is mentioned approximately fourteen times in the Gospels and from the narrative we can see that she occupied a special and even exalted place amongst Jesus' disciples. They first met after she had been possessed by seven demons (see Luke 8:2). It is from this moment onwards that the narrative contained within the Gospels tells us that both she and Jesus developed a special relationship. She is the only person to have received the honour of anointing Jesus with holy oils, an event of symbolic significance, as the oils were those known as "Genuine-nard" the very oil used to anoint kings and priests (see John 12:3). Following this, Judas Iscariot gets angry at Mary for wasting such expensive oils on Jesus, at which time Jesus jumps to her defence (see John 12:7). She, unlike Jesus' famed twelve disciples, was present at his crucifixion and in both Matthew (27:55) and Mark (15:40), is mentioned first in the list of those present. She was also there watching as his corpse was wrapped in white linen and entombed by Joseph of Arimethea (see Matthew 27:59-61 and Mark 15:47). Mary Magdalene also headed to Jesus' tomb the first chance she got to anoint his dead body with spices and oils (see Matthew 28:1) and she was the first person Jesus appeared to after his resurrection (see Mark 16:9-10). It is curious that Jesus chose her to be the first witness of his resurrection and not his own mother or Peter, the very rock on which he was said to have built his church. Psychologists would argue, with strong evidence, that Jesus' choice to form a close bond with a "prostitute" was the result of early childhood influences, most likely stemming from his mother. Thus, Jesus' choice to form a close bond with the "prostitute" Mary Magdalene indicates that his mother, Mary, must have possessed similar qualities which appealed to Jesus in his adulthood. From this evidence, we can establish that Jesus' mother was possibly a promiscuous woman and that the *Talmud*, the *Toledoth Yeshu* and Celsus' account of his life were more accurate than the Gospels. Of course, this is all based upon speculation which is founded upon the testimony of witnesses who were far removed from the time of Jesus' alleged life and at the end of the day, serve no other purpose than to entertain our imaginations.

CONCLUSION

The issue of whether or not the Jewish rabbinical texts provide evidence for the historicity of Jesus is a matter which seems to have no positive answer. Either, they were based upon Christian sources and written centuries later in a bid to deride and make fun of the Christian's Messiah, in which case, they cannot be considered impartial and reliable historical testimonies, but rather, satirical works, based upon long established Christian traditions. Or, they are historically valid and are derived from Jewish oral traditions that described a real human Jesus of 100 bce. Given their timing and the fact they contain quite a number of historical discrepancies, like placing Jesus' birth during the reign of both King Jannaeus (100 bce) and at the same time, toward the end of King Herod's reign (4-6 bce), it does seem that the former proposition may be the most likely. It could however, be possible that having been written centuries after the fact, they contain a mix of truth and mythological fiction. Perhaps they do provide a historically accurate account of the Jesus of 100 bce and it may just be that, the Jesus of the Gospels was originally Jesus ben Pandira, a mortal that was born in the days of King Alexander Jannaeus. Christian apologists seem to be rather confused and divided over the issue of whether the Jewish rabbinical texts provide evidence for a historical Jesus. Some claim that they are reliable, in which case, we must take these Jewish texts at their word and call Jesus' mother an adulteress and admit that Jesus' dead body was hidden and later discovered. While other, perhaps more learned apologists, assert that the Jewish accounts of Jesus were written centuries later in a bid to counter Christian articles of faith. Yet, would we be unjustified amidst all of this apologetic speculation, to put forward our own, somewhat original hypothesis?

What if these Jewish texts were not written to counter the articles of faith set forth in the Christian Gospels, but that truth of the matter is in fact the opposite? What if the Gospels were written to counter the harsh and painful truths relayed by Jewish oral tradition regarding the true character upon whom the Christian's saviour was based? Picture a poor little Jewish rebel, whose mother was a promiscuous adulteress and he, Jesus ben Pandera, was neither the son of the Jews' god, nor did he rise from the dead like many more ancient sons of god, from Greece and Egypt. Is it really that absurd to propose such a scenario? If you think so, then weigh it against the claim that a holy ghost came down from the stars and impregnated a virgin without her consent, a kind of divine rapist if you like, whose off spring was a hybrid between man and raping-god, a hero who could bring the dead back to life and heal the sick with a magic touch. Add to this, the nightmarish and somewhat B-grade horror story of the bodily resurrection of his corpse and weigh the probabilities of both propositions against one another. I am not saying that one can prove, nor should believe, that Jesus was originally a character from 100 bce, but in the same tempered frame of mind, neither would I ask you to believe that he was a super god-man whose mother was a Jewish virgin and whose father was the Jewish God of the entire universe. Whatever the case may be, one must concede that the Jewish sources do not provide us with any real evidence for a historical Jesus and thus the Christian god-man Jesus, is, at least for the moment, more appropriately relegated to the realms of mythology.

JESUS AND THE NUMBER FOURTEEN

Many people are aware that there exists a contradiction between Luke's genealogy of Jesus and Matthew's. Whilst Matthew records "forty-two" generations from Jesus back to Abraham, (see Matthew 1:2-16 Vs Luke 3:23-38), Luke says there were fifty-seven and many of these ancestors were different people. (Luke 3:23-38). Before getting to the contradiction which forms the basis of this little piece, we should also be aware that Luke's genealogy of Jesus is also in contradiction with 1 Chronicles 3:16-19 and Matthew's is also in contradiction with 1 Chronicles 3:9-15 (which lists eighteen generations from David to Babylonian Exile, not fourteen as Matthew errantly claimed).

At Matthew 1:17, the pseudonymous author asserts:

> *Thus there were fourteen generations in all from Abraham to David, fourteen from David to the exile to Babylon, and fourteen from the exile to the Christ.*

Now, if we were to take him/her at their word, that every fourteen generations, some big event takes place which alters the course of the nation of Israel, we might be led to believe that there is some divine plan behind this nation's history, but why every fourteen generations? What is, or was, significant about the number fourteen?

It could be that the number numerologically represents the doubling of the "holy" seven, which frequently occurs throughout both the *Old Testament* and *New Testament*, not to mention more ancient Pagan religions and philosophies and forms the basis of the septenary (seven primary planets), from which we derive our days of the week.

In the words of Aristotle:

> *Since the number 7 neither generates nor is generated by any of the numbers in the decade, for this reason they also said that it was Athene. For the number 2 generates 4, 3 generates 9 and 6, 4 generates 8, and 5 generates 10, and 4, 6, 8, 9 and 10 are generated, but 7 neither generates any number nor is generated from any; and so too Athena was motherless and ever virgin.*[204]

Or, it could be something more relevant to Hebrew and the "history" of Israel. Looking to the Hebrew language, we may find a probable answer to this riddle. Hebrew is an alpha-numeric language, meaning that the letters double as numbers, each letter carrying a specific numeric equivalent or value.

1= 1 א ALEPH
2= 2 ב BETH
3= 3 ג GIMEL
4= 4 ד DALET
5= 5 ה HE
6= 6 ו VAV
7= 7 ז ZAYIN
8= 8 ח HET

---

[204]Jonathon Barnes & Gavin Lawrence. The Complete Works of Aristotle. Vol. 2. Fragments. Princeton University Press, (1984), p. 71.

9= 9 ט TET
10= 10 י YOD
11= 20 כ KAF
12= 30 ל LAMED
13= 40 מ MEM
14= 50 נ NUN
15= 60 ס SAMEKH
16= 70 ע AYIN
17= 80 פ PE
18= 90 צ TSADI
19= 100 ק QOF
20= 200 ר RESH
21= 300 ש SHIN
22= 400 ת TAV[205]

Further, if we take two other factors into consideration, we may get a clearer picture of the intentions of the pseudonymous author of Matthew.

(1) Hebrew did not use vowels in its manuscripts, so to give you an example, the name for one of their tribal gods, Yahweh, who henotheisticially became the sole god, into which the others were incorporated, appears in the Hebrew texts as, YHWH, with the vowels (AEIOU) omitted.

(2) The second being that the messiah was supposed to be descended from the House of David. (see; Isaiah 9:5-7, Psalms 89:3-4, 132:11 Jeremiah 23:5-6)

The name David, in the Hebrew texts appears without vowels as 'DVD' or Dalet, Vav, Dalet. If you consult the chart I have supplied above and add together the value of David's name, you will see that Dalet has a value of 4 and Vav, 6, giving a total of 14.

The pseudonymous author of Matthew, who seems to have been the most traditional out of the other two synoptic authors and the more Gnostic/Hellenistic John, in some regards, may have been

---

[205]http://www.smontagu.org/writings/HebrewNumbers.html

attempting to allude to the fact that Jesus was the thrice great (see Hermes Trismegistus for a comparison, re: thrice great and numerological significance of 3) David, the divinely appointed messiah (3) from the House of David (14), so he made Jesus' birth come after 3 lots of 14 generations.

With regards to this possibility, nay probability, Professor of *New Testament* Studies, Bart D Ehrman, said:

> *Also, in ancient Hebrew no vowels were used. So the name David was spelled D-V-D. In Hebrew, the letter D (daleth) is the number 4 and the V (waw) is 6. If you add up the letters of David's name, it equals 14. That may be why Matthew wanted there to be three groups of precisely fourteen generations in the genealogy of the son of David, the Messiah, Jesus. Unfortunately, to make the numbers work he had to leave out some names. I might also point out that if Matthew was right in his fourteen-fourteen-fourteen schema, there would be forty-two names between Abraham and Jesus.*[206]

Here is where we get to the error made by Matthew. Remember, in Matthew 1:17 he asserted three generations of fourteen, now I will leave you with his own version of the genealogy of Jesus and see if you can spot the mistake:

1. Abraham begat
2. Isaac;
3. Jacob;
4. Judas
5. Phares and Zara
6. Esrom;
7. Aram;
8. Aminadab
9. Naasson
10. Salmon;

---

[206]Bart D Ehrman. Jesus Interrupted. Harper Collins (2005) p. 38

11. Booz
12. Obed
13. Jesse;
14. David the king

1. Solomon
2. Roboam
3. Abia
4. Asa;
5. Josaphat
6. Joram
7. Ozias;
8. Joatham
9. Achaz
10. Ezekias;
11. Manasses;
12. Amon
13. Josias
14. Jechonias

1. Salathiel
2. Zorobabel
3. Abiud
4. Eliakim
5. Azor
6. Sadoc
7. Achim
8. Eliud
9. Eleazar
10. Matthan
11. Jacob
12. Joseph
13. Jesus

~Matthew 1:2-16

◆

THE GOSPEL OF MATTHEW CONTAINS ONE TOO MANY ASSES

Matthew was not only unfamiliar with the Hebrew language as demonstrated by his misuse of the term "almah" (young woman), to mean virgin ("Betulah"), when attempting to apply the "prophecy" of Isaiah (7:14) to Jesus' "virgin-birth," but he was also unfamiliar with Hebrew literary devices used in the *Old Testament*. This fact is highlighted at Matthew 21:2-7 where the author of Matthew has Jesus riding an ass (donkey) and a Colt (baby donkey) at the same time, so as to fulfil yet another "prophecy" from the Hebrew Scriptures. The author of Matthew was drawing from Zechariah 9:9, which is as follows:

> *Rejoice greatly, O daughter of Zion; shout, O daughter of Jerusalem: behold, thy King cometh unto thee: he is just, and having salvation; lowly, and riding upon an ass, and upon a colt the foal of an ass.*

The above passage is not describing a King riding two animals, but one. You may be wondering why it says he was "riding upon an ass and upon a colt the foal of an ass". Well, if one has an understanding of Hebrew literary techniques, one will understand that the last line, "and upon a colt the foal of an ass" is being used to emphasize the previous line "riding upon an ass". To put it simply, the author of this passage was actually saying that the King is not only riding a donkey, but a baby donkey, which in this context is being used to demonstrate the king's humility. This poetic technique is known to textual critics as "Synonymous Parallelism" and was a Hebrew literary device used to emphasize an important point within a given passage. There are many examples of this literary device throughout the *Old Testament*.

Here are just a few examples:

> *Yahweh hath rent the kingdom out of thy hand, And given it to thy neighbour (David), even to David.*
>
> ~1 Samuel 28:17

> *Your word is a lamp to my feet and a light to my path.*
>
> ~Psalm 119:105

And he declared unto you his covenant (the Ten Commandments), which he commanded you to perform, even the Ten Commandments.
~Deuteronomy 4:13

Thou also, son of man, take thee a tile, and lay it before thee, and portray upon it the city (Jerusalem), even Jerusalem.
~Ezekiel 4:1-2

The author of Matthew ended up creating a fictional story around this mistake, asserting:

And when they drew nigh unto Jerusalem, and were come to Bethphage, unto the mount of Olives, then sent Jesus two disciples, Saying unto them, Go into the village over against you, and straightway ye shall find an ass tied, and a colt with her: loose them, and bring them unto me. And if any man say ought unto you, ye shall say, The Lord hath need of them; and straightway he will send them. All this was done, that it might be fulfilled which was spoken by the prophet, saying, Tell ye the daughter of Sion, Behold, thy King cometh unto thee, meek, and sitting upon an ass, and a colt the foal of an ass. And the disciples went, and did as Jesus commanded them, And brought the ass, and the colt, and put on them their clothes, and they set him thereon.
~Matthew 21:1-7

Picture it, two animals of different heights, side by side and Jesus riding both at once. It does seem like Jesus was performing some kind of circus trick or dramatic stunt. The other three Gospel writers seemed to have understood this literary technique and in contradiction to Matthew, described Jesus entering Jerusalem on one ass, not two (see Mark 11:7, Luke 19:35, John 12:14).

ONE OF MATTHEW'S MANY MISAPPROPRIATED PROPHECIES - RACHEL IS CRYING FOR HER CHILDREN, NOT YOURS.

In Matthew 2:18, Herod's alleged decree to kill all the Children under two years of age in and around Bethlehem was seen as the fulfilment of a prophecy uttered by the prophet Jeremiah (see Jeremiah 31:15). As we will see, this erroneous application of prophecy is both illogical and slightly mischievous on the part of Matthew.

A voice was heard in Ramah, Lamentation, weeping, and great mourning, Rachel weeping for her children, refusing to be comforted, because they are no more.

~Matthew 2:18

This is where Matthew's use of Jeremiah's words comes to an abrupt ending. One could read this passage as quoted by Matthew and almost see how he was attempting to apply this *Old Testament* prophecy to the slaughter of the children of Bethlehem. Especially if one reads the deliberate mistranslation in the Revised Edition of the Good News *Bible*, which has Matthew saying at the end of Jeremiah's prophecy "because they are dead", instead of "they are gone", which is contrary to Jeremiah's version in the *Old Testament* of the same *Bible*. If one examines the matter further, more defects begin to emerge. We may also wish to note, that the slaughter of all of the children in Bethlehem by King Herod has not been recorded by any historian contemporary to Herod or later. Even in Josephus' vast literary work, *The Antiquity of the Jews*, in which he portrays Herod as a scoundrel and a monster, there is no mention of this event, which would have certainly ranked as one of his most despicable deeds. In fact, the only mention of this event is in the Gospel "According to Matthew" and nowhere else. So let's take a look at the source verse from the *Old Testament* in comparison with Matthew's application of it, and see if there are any gaping holes in logic and/or misuses of Jewish scripture to substantiate the divinity of Yahweh's supposed son.

A sound is heard in Ramah, the sound of bitter weeping. Rachel is crying for her children; they are gone, and she refuses to be comforted. Stop your crying and wipe away your tears. All that you have done for your children will not go unrewarded; they will return from the enemy's land. There is hope for your future; your children will come back home. I the lord have spoken.

~Jeremiah 31:15-17

When read in context we see that Jeremiah was referring to the exiled "children of Israel" who were being held captive in Babylon, "the enemy's land" and not the murdering of children, as it was applied by the author of Matthew. It should also be obvious to the reader that present tense is being used to convey a current event. "A sound IS heard in Ramah, Rachel IS weeping for her children", meaning that Rachel is weeping for children (possibly, children in the figurative sense as in "the children of Israel") and in her time, not hundreds of years after her death. The author of Matthew has once again, taken an *Old Testament* passage out of context to support the alleged divinity of Jesus. The application of Jeremiah 31:15 is a little mischievous as he ends the prophecy with, "for they are dead", when it is plain to any reader that Jeremiah 31:16 continues by saying, that her children will come back to her from the enemies land. Thus, the application of this verse to the alleged events that supposedly took place in Bethlehem is completely illogical on two grounds. One, the verse states that the children of Israel will return from their enemies land and thus cannot be dead and two, Herod resided in Bethlehem the children's land, and so the reference to the "enemy's land" in this context is nonsensical. By applying only part of Jeremiah 31 as prophecy, Matthew has taken the verse out of its original context in a very crude attempt to justify its application to the fore- telling of the fictitious slaughter of the innocents by Herod the Great.

PUTTING THE FREE WILL EXCLUSION CLAUSE TO BED.

(AKA: IT'S NOT GOD'S FAULT FALLACY)

When confronted with arguments from non-believers that demonstrate unequivocally, that their perfect creator has created an imperfect product, the human being, and that this illustrates the illogicality of the notion of a perfect creator, theists will jump to the free will argument. They argue that you cannot hold the manufacturer liable for "His" work, because he has installed "free will" into his product, a free will that, with all of his omnipotence and omniscience, he has no control over. This little piece is designed to put that argument to bed.

FREE WILL & THE BIBLE

There are almost as many verses in the *Bible* that contradict the doctrine of free will, as there are that support it. This is because the *Bible*, being a collection of books (biblia - Greek Plural – "little books" or "booklets") was not constructed and inspired by one single perfect mind, but many fallible and conflicting ones over a long span of time. We not only see theological and ideological conflicts between the Old and *New Testaments*, but between the Gospels themselves and between these Gospels and the Epistles of Paul. So, which verses from the "Word of God" conflict with the notion of free will?

According to a number of books contained within the *Bible*, God is all-knowing (see Job 28:24, 37:16, Psalm 139:4, 147:5, 1 Samuel 2:3, Isaiah 46:9, 55:9, 1 John 3:19-20, Hebrews 4:13, Matthew 10:30, for example), all-powerful (see Genesis 1:1, Exodus 35:1-35, Job 36:26, 37:23, 42:2, Psalms 139:1-13, 147:5, Isaiah 40:28, 44:24, Jeremiah 10:12, 32:27, Daniel 2:20-22, 4:35, Amos 4:13, Mark 10:27, Matthew 10:29, 19:26, Luke 1:37, Romans 1:20, 4:17, 8:28-29, 14:36, 1 Corinthians 1:25, Hebrews 1:3, Ephesians 1:19-22 & Revelation 19:6, for example), and, "He" has a plan and manipulates events in accordance with that plan (see Jeremiah 1:5, 29:11, Proverbs 3:5-6, Romans 8:28, 12:2, Isaiah 40:31, 58:11, Ecclesiastes 3:1-22, Ephesians 3:20) . So, how can free will exist in the presence of such an overbearing and perfect planner? The short answer is that it cannot, for everything we do, according to these passages and verses, is predestined and set in proverbial stone. This is why many Church fathers and scholars from Saint Augustine of Hippo (354-430 ce), to the founders and early proponents of the Protestant reformation, i.e., Luther and Calvin (sixteenth Century), argued against free will being an absolute doctrine. In fact, Luther in his *On The Bondage of the Will* argued strongly against free will in order to refute Erasmus' work, *On Free Will* and in so doing relied heavily on the following verse from Ephesians:

> For it is by grace you have been saved, through faith—and this is not
> from yourselves, it is the gift of God—not by works, so that no one

can boast. For we are God's handiwork, created in Christ Jesus to do good works, which God prepared in advance for us to do.

~Ephesians 2:8-10

This theological schism is not something which is confined to the past, as it still rages today amongst various denominations that draw their theology from the Calvinist school of thought and quite a number of other sects as well. So, free will is not a universally accepted doctrine within Christendom and is therefore a shaky approach for any theist wishing to argue from this stance.

Over and above the verses and passages cited, there are others in the *Bible*, particularly in the *New Testament*, which expressly conflict with the notion of free will. I will give you three examples:

2 Thessalonians 2:11-12:

For this reason God sends them a powerful delusion so that they will believe the lie and so that all will be condemned who have not believed the truth but have delighted in wickedness.

Romans 9:18

Therefore God has mercy on whom he wants to have mercy, and he hardens (manipulates) whom he wants to harden.

Romans 9:19-21

One of you will say to me: "Then why does God still blame us? For who is able to resist his will?" But who are you, a human being, to talk back to God? "Shall what is formed say to the one who formed it, 'Why did you make me like this?' Does not the potter have the right to make out of the same lump of clay some pottery for special purposes and some for common use?

If everything we do is the result of this twisted potter's design and plan, then we cannot be held accountable for the evil we do and therefore the theist in arguing that free will excuses their imaginary God's negligence and or wilful malice, has not even their own Scripture to Support them.

◆

PORPHYRY'S PROBLEMS WITH CHRISTIANITY

Porphyry was a third century Neo-Platonic philosopher, born in Phoenicia (modern day Lebanon).[207] He edited and published *Enneads*, written by the founder of the school of Neo-Platonic philosophy, his teacher, Plotinus, who was one of the most renowned philosophers since Aristotle.[208] Porphyry also wrote many works himself on a variety of topics. His *Isagog'* is an introduction to logic and philosophy and was the standard textbook on logic throughout the middle ages.[209] Needless to say, he was a profound philosopher and a brilliant logician.

PORPHYRY'S CRITICISMS OF CHRISTIANITY

Porphrey's Criticisms of Christianity were focused largely on the wide range of scriptural absurdities found within the Gospels and Epistles (letters) of Paul. Many modern textual critics and sceptics of Christianity are still asking the same questions he did, all those centuries ago. He had a sharp wit and on at least one occasion, dared those aspiring to become part of the clergy to prove their faith in the promises allegedly made by Jesus in the Gospel of Mark, by drinking deadly poison (Mark 16:18). On another occasion, he accused the apostles of lacking any real faith, asserting that their faith was unable to actually move mountains, as per the promise made in the Gospel of Matthew (see Matthew 17:20).

PORPHYRY'S CRITICISM OF CAMELS AND NEEDLES

As a philosopher and logician, Porphyry observed the sayings and stories in the Gospels through a lens refined by a clear and present mind. His irreverence was his strength and his powers of perception, for his time at least, were his greatest tools. He noted the danger of the

---

[207]Jorge Rupke. A Companion to Roman Religion. Blackwell Publishing. (2007). p. 364.
[208]John Boardman, Jasper Griffin & Oswyn Murray. The Oxford History of the Classical World. Oxford University Press. (1986). p.590.
[209]Ibid. p.675.

following saying of Jesus,' regarding the impossibility of a rich man gaining access to heaven, saying:

Let us examine another saying even more baffling than these, when He says, "It is easier for a camel to go through a needle, than for a rich man to enter into the kingdom of heaven." If it be indeed the case that anyone who is rich is not brought into the so-called kingdom of heaven though he have kept himself from the sins of life, such as murder, theft, adultery, cheating, impious oaths, body-snatching, and the wickedness of sacrilege, of what use is just dealing to righteous men, if they happen to be rich? And what harm is there for poor men in doing every unholy deed of baseness? For it is not virtue that takes a man up to heaven, but lack of possessions! For if his wealth shuts out the rich man from heaven, by way of contrast his poverty brings a poor man into it. And so it becomes lawful, when a man has learnt this lesson, to pay no regard to virtue, but without let or hindrance to cling to poverty alone, and the things that are most base. This follows from poverty being able to save the poor man, while riches shut out the rich man from the undefiled abode.

Wherefore it seems to me that these cannot be the words of Christ, if indeed He handed down the rule of truth, but of some poor men who wished, as a result of such vain talking, to deprive the rich of their substance. At any rate, no longer ago than yesterday, reading these words to women of noble birth, "Sell what thou hast, and give to the poor, and thou shalt have treasure in heaven," they persuaded them to distribute to poor men all the substance and possession which they had, and, themselves entering into a state of want, to gather by begging, turning from a position of freedom to unseemly asking, and from prosperity to a pitiable character, and in the end, being compelled to go to the houses of the rich (which is the first thing, or rather the last thing, in disgrace and misfortune), and thus to lose their own belongings under the pretext of godliness, and to covet those of others under the force of want.[210]

As brilliant an observation as this is, I feel that Porphyry missed something or at least failed to express one of the most likely reasons

---

[210]T.W. Crafer. D, D. The Apocriticus of Macarius Magnes. The MacMillan Company. (1919). pp. 69–70

for this alleged saying attributed to Christ. The idea behind this saying is that a wealthy person should give away their possessions to charity, a noble act to be sure. However, we must ask a question; to whom were these wealthy converts encouraged to hand their estates? Was it directly to the poor? Or, were they entreated to surrender their estates to the Church,[211] who promised to administer their bounty and who, eventually, through these kinds of manipulative tactics, became one of the wealthiest institutions on the face of the earth. They did give some to charity, but this charity, as will be demonstrated later on, was meant, in part, to exploit the norm of reciprocity and coerce conversions by playing on the obligation of the receiver, thereby turning seemingly benevolent charity into a clever investment.

PORPHYRY'S CRITICISM OF CHRIST'S SHY RESURRECTION

In an article I wrote entitled; *Christianity: A New Type of Myth*, I compared Professor Elizabeth Vandiver's academic definition of myth, to the narratives underscoring the Christian religion. One of the elements in her definition was "remoteness". With regards to this element she says:

Myths are stories set in the past. Myths do not deal with what is happening today, or this week, or even last year, we don't have myths about current time. Myths are set in the past, often in the very remote past.[212]

Although Professor Vandiver was describing classical myths, which are often set in the remote past, I took this idea and applied it in the following manner:

The word "remote", as it relates to the term, "remote past", is defined by the World English Dictionary, as being:

distant in time[213]

---

[211]Susan R. Holman. Wealth and Poverty in Early Church and Society. Holy Cross Greek Orthodox School of Theology. (2008). pp. 231–233.

[212]Professor Elizabeth Vandiver. Classical Mythology. Lecture 2: What is Myth? The Teaching Company. (2002).

[213]Collins English Dictionary - Complete & Unabridged 10th Edition 2009 © William Collins Sons & Co. Ltd. 1979, 1986 © HarperCollins Publishers 1998, 2000, 2003, 2005, 2006, 2007, 2009; cited at: http://dictionary.reference.com/browse/remote.

This is a rather vague definition and doesn't help us understand what Professor Vandiver meant when she said; "a myth is often set in the remote past." The etymological root of the word, "remote", may be of more assistance. The English word, "remote" stems from the Latin "remotes", being the past participle of the word, "remove".[214] So, the remote past is a time in the past, which is removed from the present. If one accepts this definition of the "remote past", then we could say, for the purpose of our investigation that; myths are often set in a time in the past, which is removed from the present.

This makes sense when we look at the creation myths of the Egyptians, Babylonians, Hebrews, and many other cultures, it fits the descriptions of myths such as Hercules/Herakles and his twelve labours, Demeter and Persephone, Osiris and Isis, and even Noah and his Ark, all being set hundreds and sometimes thousands of years, from the time they were alleged to have transpired. But the Christian myth was written down just over half a century after the purported events were claimed to have transpired. So is this shorter span of time long enough to qualify as, "remote"? Keep in mind, our definition; "a time removed from the present". To provide some context here, we should acknowledge the fact that, what qualified as the remote past 2,000 years ago is different from what we would describe as the remote past today. The reason for this difference is that, today and over the last few centuries, there has been a proliferation of chroniclers and chronicles. Since the advent of Gutenberg's printing-press in the fifteenth century, history has been more accurately documented, as a result of the increased media capacity of the modern era. Thus, fifty years ago, say during the 1960s, would not be considered the remote past, as we are not too far removed from it. We have video footage, newspaper archives, books, poems, and a plethora of various forms of media that serve to keep us in touch with that time. 2,000 years ago however, this was not the case.

One of the reasons we should distinguish between what constituted the remote past 2,000 years ago, from what we would consider the remote past, today, is that literacy rates 2,000 years ago were much lower than they are today. This means that there were less people to

---

[214]Ibid.

record history or keep people in touch with the past, during the first part of the first century, particularly in such a rustic and remote location as Palestine.[215]

The reason I drew attention to these two aspects of remoteness (remoteness of time and location), was to establish one of the possible reasons for the utilization of such remoteness, that being; it is impossible to disprove something very few people have witnessed, and so the lie becomes easier to protect, especially when belief joins the party.

We now come to Porphyry's criticism of Jesus' somewhat shy resurrection:

But He appeared to Mary Magdalene, a coarse woman who came from some wretched little village, and had once been possessed by seven demons, and with her another utterly obscure Mary, who was herself a peasant woman, and a few other people who were not at all well known. And that, although He said: "Henceforth shall ye see the Son of man sitting on the right hand of power, and coming with the clouds." For if He had shown Himself to men of note, all would believe through them, and no judge would punish them as fabricating monstrous stories. For surely it is neither pleasing to God nor to any sensible man that many should be subjected on His account to punishments of the gravest kind.[216]

In other words, Christ could have saved countless lives and thwarted innumerable controversies and violent schisms amongst his own followers, if only he had appeared to the primary chroniclers of his day. And what is stopping him from making himself visible to everyone today? He could appear on CNN or perhaps over the past 2,000 years he may even have learnt to read and write and could write a new, *New Testament*, relevant to today's world or at the very least, he could compose a letter to the various religious leaders and put an end to hostilities between the various sects and religions of the world. Better still, he could speak the same words to everyone simultaneously

---

[215]http://michaelsherlockauthor.blogspot.jp/2012/06/christianity-new-type-of-myth-part-1.html

[216]T.W. Crafer. D, D. The Apocriticus of Macarius Magnes. The MacMillan Company. (1919). pp. 43–44.

so that we could all confer with one another and establish beyond any reasonable doubt, that he is more than myth. How much suffering could have been averted, had he not been so remote?

PORPHYRY'S CRITICISM OF MATTHEW'S ERRANT GENEALOGY OF JESUS

Porphyry also highlighted the error in Matthew's genealogy of Jesus, which is missing a generation according to Matthew's own testimony. The author of Matthew claimed that there were fourteen generations from Abraham to David, fourteen generations from David to the Babylonian Exile and another fourteen generations from the Babylonian Exile to Jesus, however, the third lot of fourteen is missing a generation, which contradicts Matthew's own words:

So all the generations from Abraham to David are fourteen generations; and from David until the carrying away into Babylon are fourteen generations; and from the carrying away into Babylon unto Christ are fourteen generations.

~Matthew 1:17

Here is the list of Jesus' alleged ancestors taken from the King James *Bible*, a compilation of texts based on Father Jerome's very own Vulgate *Bible*:

Abraham begat	Solomon	Salathiel
Isaac;	Roboam	Zorobabel
Jacob;	Abia	Abiud
Judas	Asa;	Eliakim
Phares and Zara	Josaphat	Azor
Esrom;	Joram	Sadoc
Aram;	Ozias;	Achim
Aminadab	Joatham	Eliud
Naasson	Achaz	Eleazar
Salmon;	Ezekias;	Matthan
Booz	Manasses;	Jacob
Obed	Amon	Joseph
Jesse;	Josias	Jesus
David the king	Jechonias	

~Matthew 1:2-16

You can read any version of the *New Testament* and see for yourself that the third lot of fourteen generations begins with Salathiel and ends with Jesus, in which there are only thirteen generations, even though the author of Matthew claimed there were fourteen. This was a clear and definite error which Porphyry noticed and pointed out. Jerome's response to this charge, in which he tried to create an extra person by inserting the name of Jehoiakim to fill in the gap left by the author of Matthew, was as follows:

And it is for this reason that in the Gospel according to Matthew there seems to be a generation missing, because the second group of fourteen, extending to the time of Jehoiakim, ends with a son of Josiah, and the third group begins with Jehoiachin, son of Jehoiakim (Nowhere in the Bible does it say this!). Being ignorant of this factor, Porphyry formulated a slander against the Church which only revealed his own ignorance, as he tried to prove the evangelist Matthew guilty of error.[217]

Unfortunately the *Bible* doesn't agree with this church father, but I will let the reader examine Jerome's response to Porphyry's allegation and decide for themselves, on which side of the fence the truth falls with regards to this matter.

There is nothing so easy as by sheer volubility to deceive a common crowd or an uneducated congregation.[218]

~St. Jerome

PORPHYRY'S CRITICISM OF THE DEMON PIG STORY

Another tale found in the Gospels did not pass before the scrutinizing glance of this competent logician. This was the story of Jesus casting out the demons from the man, or two men (depending on which Gospel you read, see Mark 5:2 vs. Matthew 8:28) and into a herd of pigs. To Porphyry, this story lacked credibility upon the basis of both fact and logic. I think most rational people would agree from the outset, that such a tale is devoid of real and factual truth.

[217]Father Jerome. Commentary on Daniel. Chapter 1.1: cited at: http://www.tertullian.org/fathers/jerome_daniel_02_text.htm
[218]Father Jerome's Epistle to Nepotian. Cited in: Philip Schaff. Nicene and Post Nicene Fathers: Series 2, Volume 6. Christian Classics Ethereal Library. (2009). p. 250.

For one, demons probably don't exist, two, a son of a god, born of a human virgin and an ethereal ghost, more than likely didn't exist and finally, it would be unlikely to find such a large herd of pigs in a country in which they were regarded as the most taboo creature. On this note, Porphyry says:

And if we would speak of this record likewise, it will appear to be really a piece of knavish nonsense, since Matthew says that two demons from the tombs met with Christ, and then that in fear of Him they went into the swine, and many were killed. But Mark did not shrink from making up an enormous number of swine, for he puts it thus: "He said unto him, Go forth, thou unclean spirit, from the man. And he asked him, What is thy name? And he answered, Many. And he besought him that he would not cast him out of the country. And there was there a herd of swine feeding. And the demons besought him that he would suffer them to depart into the swine. And when they had departed into the swine, they rushed down the steep into the sea, about two thousand, and were choked; and they that fed them fled!" (Mark v. 8, etc.). What a myth! What humbug! What flat mockery! A herd of two thousand swine ran into the sea, and were choked and perished!

And when one hears how the demons besought Him that they might not be sent into the abyss, and how Christ was prevailed on and did not do so, but sent them into the swine, will not one say : "Alas, what ignorance ! Alas, what foolish knavery, that He should take account of murderous spirits, which were working much harm in the world, and that He should grant them what they wished." What the demons wished was to dance through life, and make the world a perpetual plaything. They wanted to stir up the sea, and fill the world's whole theatre with sorrow. They wanted to trouble the elements by their disturbance, and to crush the whole creation by their hurtfulness. So at all events it was not right that, instead of casting these originators of evil, who had treated mankind so ill, into that region of the abyss which they prayed to be delivered from, He should be softened by their entreaty and suffer them to work another calamity.[219]

---

[219]T.W. Crafer. D, D. The Apocriticus of Macarius Magnes. The MacMillan Company. (1919). p. 62–63.

No doubt a believer will respond to such attacks by saying something like; "well, you can't disprove this story's occurrence!" But is the burden of proof to be laid upon the inquirer? Is it the sceptic's obligation to disprove incredible assertions? I would argue that it is not an inquirer's obligation, but rather, that the burden of proof rests on the believer. If I make a statement regarding tomorrow's weather, the proof of my statement will be forthcoming. However, if I allege that a son of god was born 2,000 years ago in a remote backwoods village, in an equally remote country, inhabited by an intellectually remote people; who was said to have been miraculously born of a virgin and the God of the universe, who could turn water into wine, heal the sick, raise the dead and cast out demons from humans and place them into pigs, then such a statement is incapable of proof and thus hides and survives in the obscurity of the innumerable possibilities of the unknown. Therefore, it is not the inquirer's obligation to disprove the incredible, but the asserter's. Bertrand Russell once gave an analogy to describe the appropriate place for such a burden of proof, in his teapot analogy:

Many orthodox people speak as though it were the business of sceptics to disprove received dogmas rather than of dogmatists to prove them. This is, of course, a mistake. If I were to suggest that between the Earth and Mars there is a china teapot revolving about the sun in an elliptical orbit, nobody would be able to disprove my assertion provided I were careful to add that the teapot is too small to be revealed even by our most powerful telescopes. But if I were to go on to say that, since my assertion cannot be disproved, it is intolerable presumption on the part of human reason to doubt it, I should rightly be thought to be talking nonsense. If, however, the existence of such a teapot were affirmed in ancient books, taught as the sacred truth every Sunday, and instilled into the minds of children at school, hesitation to believe in its existence would become a mark of eccentricity and entitle the doubter to the attentions of the psychiatrist in an enlightened age or of the Inquisitor in an earlier time. It is customary to suppose that, if a belief is widespread, there must be something reasonable about it. I do not think this view can be held by anyone who has studied history.[220]

---

[220]http://www.cfpf.org.uk/articles/religion/br/br_god.html

PORPHYRY'S CRITICISM OF CHRISTIANS AND CIRCUMCISION

The following excerpt from Porphyry's work relates to an illogicality found within the doctrines of Christianity, in particular, the contradiction between Paul's version of Christianity and its primary parent religion, Judaism:

…how, although he (Paul) called circumcision "concision," he himself circumcised a certain Timothy, as we are taught in the Acts of the Apostles (Acts xvi. 3). Oh, the downright stupidity of it all! It is such a stage as this that the scenes in the theatre portray, as a means of raising laughter. Such indeed is the exhibition which jugglers give. For how could the man be free who is a slave of all? And how can the man gain all who apes all? For if he is without law to those who are without law, as he himself says, and he went with the Jews as a Jew and with others in like manner, truly he was the slave of manifold baseness, and a stranger to freedom and an alien from it; truly he is a servant and minister of other people's wrong doings, and a notable zealot for unseemly things, if he spends his time on each occasion in the baseness of those without law, and appropriates their doings to himself.

These things cannot be the teachings of a sound mind, nor the setting forth of reasoning that is free. But the words imply someone who is somewhat crippled in mind, and weak in his reasoning. For if he lives with those who are without law, and also in his writings accepts the Jews' religion gladly, having a share in each, he is confused with each, mingling with the falls of those who are base, and subscribing himself as their companion. For he who draws such a line through circumcision as to remove those who wish to fulfil it, and then performs circumcision himself, stands as the weightiest of all accusers of himself when he says: "If I build again those things which I loosed, I establish myself as a transgressor.[221]

Porphyry was highlighting the contradiction between Paul's words, his actions and the doctrines of this saviour's religion. On the one hand, Paul condemned circumcision (see Galatians 5:1-4, 6:12-13, Philippians 3:2) even though his own Lord and Saviour, Jesus Christ,

---

[221]Father Jerome's Epistle to Nepotian. Cited in: Philip Schaff. Nicene and Post Nicene Fathers: Series 2, Volume 6. Christian Classics Ethereal Library. (2009). p. 15.

had been circumcised in accordance with his own laws (see Luke 2:21). What's more, Paul, on another occasion, performed a circumcision on a fellow Christian by the name of Timothy (see Acts 16:3). Porphyry was also decrying the fact that Christianity adopted a rather confounded blend of both Judaism and paganism, which resulted in irreconcilable contradictions of fact and faith.

Having pointed out this illogicality and others like it, Porphyry became viewed as one of the most dangerous enemies of the Church.

Theologian and historian, Philip Schaff, described the opinions of the early Church toward Porphyry, saying:

Porphyry, the celebrated Neo-Platonic philosopher, regarded by the early Fathers as the bitterest and most dangerous enemy of the Church, wrote toward the end of the third century a work against Christianity in fifteen books, which was looked upon as the most powerful attack that had ever been made, and which called forth refutations from some of the greatest Fathers of the age: from Methodius of Tyre, Eusebius of Cæsarea, and Apollinaris of Laodicea; and even as late as the end of the fourth or beginning of the fifth century the historian Philostorgius thought it necessary to write another reply to it (see his H. E. X. 10).

Porphyry's work is no longer extant, but the fragments of it which remain show us that it was both learned and skilful. He made much of the alleged contradictions in the Gospel records, and suggested difficulties which are still favourite weapons in the hands of sceptics.[222]

For this reason, Porphyry became the target of degrading attacks from early fathers, one of whom, the aforementioned, Saint Jerome, derided him as a "rabid demon,"[223] who dishonestly, "misrepresented Christian Scripture" and who, "vomited out his madness" against the Christian religion. In truth, Porphyry's only crime was that, as a philosopher and logician, he saw errors and contradictions within the texts of the New Testament and pointed them out for all to see.

---

[222]Eusebius. Pamphilius. Eusebius Pamphilius: Church History, Life of Constantine, Oration in Praise of Constantine. Phillip Schaff. (1890). p. 39.

[223]Philip Schaff. Nicene & Post Nicene Fathers: Series 2; Vol. 6. Grand Rapids MI; Christian Classics Ethereal Library. (1819–1893) p. 916; Philip Schaff. Nicene and Post Nicene Fathers: Series 2; Vol. 3. Christian Literature Publishing Co. (1892). p.530

If truth is Christianity's most beloved principle, then no amount of criticism or inquiry can pose a danger to it. Falsities and fantasies are the only casualties of intellectual inquiry and it is usually such inquiry, which inspires defensive retaliations from the believer, whose ego becomes threatened by simple questions and criticisms. The real threat Porphyry posed, was not to the truth, but to the lie, the lie which permeates the entire foundation of the Christian religion and it is for this reason, that he received monstrous insults from apologists, whose sole purpose was to undermine his character and his integrity, for want of nothing more than the protection of belief-induced egocentrism.

◆

THE GOSPEL OF MARK & THE PIG'S MARATHON

They came to the other side of the sea, to the country of the Gerasenes. And when he stepped out of the boat, immediately a man out of the tombs with an unclean spirit met him. And the unclean spirits came out and entered the swine; and the herd, numbering about two thousand, rushed down the steep bank into the sea, and were drowned in the sea.

~Mark 5:1-2/13

The problem with this famous story is that the Sea of Galilee is about 60km northeast of Gerasa, the land of the Gerasenes. This means that Jesus could not have "immediately" (Ancient Greek: '"ufus") met the possessed man in the land of the Gerasenes, after stepping out of the boat. It also means that the pigs would have had to run an epic 60km from the land of the Gerasenes, before arriving at the bank of the Sea of Galilee, where they were reported to have drowned. One can imagine the eyewitness watching Jesus cast out the demons from the men in Gerasa, then quickly grabbing his papyrus and chasing the pigs 60 km with his writing scribe and papyrus in hand to document their demise in the Sea of Galilee. I wonder what he would have missed on his long walk back!? Perhaps Jesus said something of great importance for mankind like; "don't be cruel to animals, not even pigs, for they are my father's creation too."

Further, one could scarcely imagine Buddha's dismay at Jesus' inhumane and callus mistreatment of these beautiful and intelligent creatures.

Perhaps if Buddha had been present when Jesus sent these innocent pigs to their death, he may have offered Jesus some form of counsel regarding the importance of displaying compassion toward all living creatures. Getting back to the point at hand, to appreciate the significance of Mark's mistake, we need to ask an important question; what are the implications of this geographic error? The primary implication is that the author of this tale was ignorant of the geography of Palestine and thus, was more than likely foreign to that land. The person responsible for telling this story, whomever he might have been, had never been to Palestine and based, at least in part, the details of this fiction, on a crude map of Palestine or an errant manuscript, or even a distorted oral tradition.

At face value, this appears to be of little significance, but when trying to establish whether or not the author was an eyewitness to Jesus, or was relating the account of an eyewitness, it creates an insurmountable problem for believers. How could an eyewitness who was apparently a Jew and a native of Palestine, be ignorant of the distance between the Sea of Galilee and Gerasa? Wouldn't a native of this area have known that it would have been impossible for Jesus to immediately meet someone in Gerasa after stepping out of a boat on the shores of Galilee, when these two locations are separated by a 60 km walk?

The author of Luke tried to mitigate this error by saying that the event took place in Gerada (Luke 8:26), which is only about 15km from the shore, but this still doesn't support the claim that Jesus "immediately" met the man after stepping off the boat.

To illustrate this geographical error in a more modern context, let's put Jesus on trial. Imagine for the moment, that Jesus is not alleged to have exercised demons as the story says, but for the purposes of this parody, let's say that he is on trial for shooting a man in the land of Gerasa.

The State of Reason vs. Mr Christ

Facts: A pig farmer is found murdered in Gerasa and there is no evidence against the defendant (Mr Christ), but for the alleged eyewitness testimony of man who claims to have been present when Mr Christ allegedly shot the pig farmer in cold blood. The prosecution's case rests solely on the eyewitness testimony of this witness and nothing else. There is no physical evidence linking the defendant to the crime, no other witnesses, no prior relationship between the defendant and the deceased, no weapon and no apparent motive.

Judge: "Would the defence like to cross examine the eyewitness?"

Public Defender (PD): "Yes, Your Honour."

PD: "Mr… Ahh! It says here your name is just Mark! No last name?"

Mark: "No, I don't have a last name, just Mark, or John if you like!"

PD: "Mark and or John are your real names?"

Mark: "Yes!"

PD: "I'll stick with Mark. Mark, you claimed to have seen the defendant, Mr Christ, shoot the victim in the chest at point blank range with a 357 Magnum. Is that correct?"

Mark: "Yes, that's correct."

PD: "Could you please describe for the court, in your own words, what happened that day."

Mark: "Yes, I remember it clearly. It was a sunny day. I was sitting by the Sea of Galilee enjoying some wine and Psilocybin when I saw Mr Christ step off the boat where he was immediately met by the victim who approached Mr Christ in a threatening manner. Mr Christ took out a 357 Magnum and shot the victim in the chest."

PD: "What is the name of this place where you witnessed the shooting?"

Mark: "The place is called Gerasa, and we also call it the land of the Gerasenes."

PD: "Sorry, and once again you say you saw the defendant, Mr Christ, step out of the boat onto the shore of the Sea of Galilee where he was "immediately" approached by the victim? Is that right?"

Mark: "Yes, that's right."

PD: "I do apologize, but I'm a little confused. You are saying that you saw the defendant, my client, the man sitting over there, step off the boat and at that very moment, as soon as his foot touched dry land, in your words, 'immediately', he encountered the victim by the shore of the Sea of Galilee and shot him dead? Is that what you are saying?"

Mark: "Yes!! How many times do I have to tell you?!! Mr Christ exited the boat at which time he was immediately approached by the victim!"

PD: "Your Honour the defence would like to submit this map of the area in question as exhibit A.

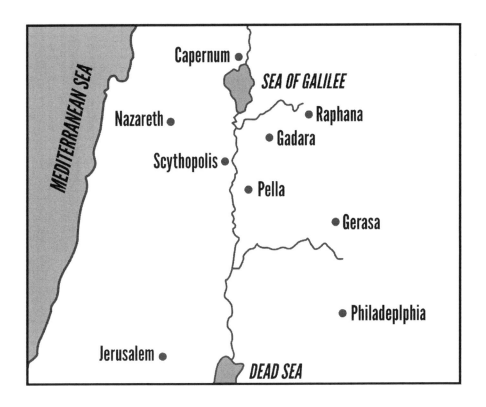

PD: Now Mark, this is a map of the area in question. Can you see the Sea of Galilee?"

Mark: "Yes, it's here!" (Mark points to the Sea of Galilee on the map)

PD: "And can you show me on this map, where Gerasa is?"

Mark: "Yes, it's here!" (Mark points to Gerasa on the map)

PD: "According to this map, Gerasa is about 60km away from the shore of the Sea of Galilee. It is in a completely different region! You are sure the victim immediately approached the defendant after he stepped out of the boat?"

Mark: "Yes! That's what I said!"

PD: "So how could the victim have immediately approached my client, on the shore by the Sea of Galilee, if Gerasa, the location in which the victim's body was found, is 60km away? Mr Christ would have had to have walked for nearly a day, before meeting the victim, but you are claiming he immediately met him after stepping out of the boat at the shore of Galilee. How can this be? Your Honour, the defence would like to call a witness to the stand."

Judge: "Who is the witness?"

PD: "The witness is a church father by the name of Papias, your Honour. I believe he will be able to shed some light on the witness and his testimony!"

Bailiff: "Do you swear to tell the truth, the whole truth, and nothing but the truth, so help you God?"

Papias: "I do!"

Bailiff: I thought you were forbidden from swearing oaths? (Matthew 5:33-37 & James 5:12)

Judge: Bailiff!

Bailiff: Sorry Your Honour, I couldn't resist.

PD: "Mr Papias, are you familiar with the alleged eyewitness, Mark?"

Papias: "Yes! I have heard from a source I trust, who had heard from a source they trusted, who had heard from a person they trusted, that Mark was a companion and scribe of the Apostle Peter, who was an eyewitness of Mr. Christ."

PD: "So, you are saying that you heard it from someone, who heard it from someone else, who had heard it from another person, that Mark heard from Peter, the so called eyewitness of Mr Christ, that he did in fact commit the act? Your Honour, this is nothing but hearsay upon hearsay. So upon your testimony, Mark was not an eyewitness at all, but merely an associate of an eyewitness, this Peter character?"

Papias: "Yes, although Peter was also called Simon."

PD: "That's very interesting because I also have here an affidavit signed by some of the leading biblical scholars that shows that the alleged eyewitness Mark, is not who he says he is either. Is any one of your Christian associates who they claim to be?"

Papias: "All I know is that Mark was not an eyewitness to the event!"

PD: "Your Honour the defence requests an acquittal, as the prosecution's case is based solely on the unreliable eyewitness testimony of a man who is not who he says he is and if he is in fact the Mark in question, then according to the defence's key witness, Papias, he was not an eyewitness at all." Also the event couldn't have transpired in the manner described by the witness as the location in which the victim was found was nearly a day's walk from the Sea of Galilee and so the witness' testimony is obviously false!

Judge: "There is clearly no evidence linking the defendant to this act and as such, the court has no choice but to grant the acquittal on the basis of a lack of evidence. Acquittal granted!"

◆

Now, if you think that the Judge in the above parody made the right decision due to the lack of evidence, then it is only logical that you also find the evidence of Mark's testimony insufficient, with regards to the story of Jesus and the demon pigs.

◆

THE GREAT VIRGIN ISIS – ANCIENT MYTHOLOGY IS NOT A CHEESEBURGER

The worship of the Egyptian goddess Isis spanned thousands of years, both in Egypt and abroad, travelling as far as Britain.[224] Throughout the vast expanse of both time and space, Isis collected and shed many qualities and attributes. Along the way, prior to the Common Era, Isis was given the title virgin on several occasions, and this article, which will present the works of both ancient and modern scholars, is an attempt to demonstrate this fact.

The main reason Isis' virginity has become a contended issue in relatively recent times, is largely due to the fact that, mythicists have used the virginity of Isis, to present arguments from similarity, against the historical Jesus Christ. They argue that, since Isis was depicted as the great virgin-mother of Horus, whose father was the Sun-god, Osiris, (the first recorded god to die and be resurrected), prior to the Christian era, then the similarity between these two myths, indicates that the later myth (Jesus Christ) was copied from the earlier (Isis, Horus and Osiris).

At this point, I should make a brief distinction between two separate, yet related issues. Those issues being; the arguments against an

---

[224]Rosalie A. David. *Handbook to Life in Ancient Egypt.* University of Manchester. Facts on File Inc. (2003). p. 178.

historical person named Jesus, known to mythicists as, the "Jesus Myth" and those concerned with undercutting the alleged truth of the "Christ myth," which pertains to the mythological components found in the Jesus Christ of the Gospels. As mentioned, these issues are related, but in my humble opinion, need to be addressed upon separate grounds. The Jesus myth, although containing some overlap with the Christ myth, for the primary historical sources we have for an historical Jesus, contain mythological components, needs to be addressed using historical methods. The Christ myth on the other hand, is exclusively a matter to be assessed and examined from the point of view of comparative mythology.

The virginity of Isis predominantly concerns the Christ myth, and is the focus of this article.

Now that we have a little context, we need only establish one thing. Was Isis considered a virgin prior to the Christian era? If so, then it makes no difference by whom, or in which country (so long as that country was proximate with the fomenters of Christianity), she was given this epithet, as we will have ascertained that this virgin-mother motif existed prior to its Christian reworking, thereby establishing the probability that the earlier version was the original. To put it simply, if this motif existed prior to the Christian era, and in a place that was connected to the initial regions in which Christianity was grown, then the probability of the Christians having adopted this mythology from the true originators, is high; as virgin mothers do not grow on trees, although in the ancient, especially Hellenistic world, they did seem to.

ANCIENT MYTHOLOGY IS NOT A CHEESEBURGER!

Ancient Mythology is not a Cheeseburger, may, at first glance seem like an odd statement to make. Please allow me to explain. Mythology involves the careful selection of living or fresh ingredients, which are carefully and thoughtfully woven together, folded over and over, so as to create a series of intricate and delicate layers. Finally, it is cooked slowly and tentatively over a long period of time. The result is a beautiful tapestry of symbols, ideas, philosophies and concepts that can be interpreted both subjectively and objectively, and on many different levels. Sadly, it is its complexity, which leaves many symbolically il-literate scholars and religionists alike, bewildered, yet belligerent in their resolve to endorse in exclusivity from the broader context, a mi-nor literal aspect of the myth. This problem was enunciated by Joseph Campbell's telling of the Buddhist parable of *The blind men and the el-ephant*. In this parable a group of men are molesting an elephant and the one who was touching the elephant's head declared that an ele-phant is like a water pot; the ones touching his ears said the elephant was like a winnowing basket; those feeling his tusks shouted, "No, indeed, he is like a ploughshare," and the men running their hands along the elephant's trunk were certain that he was like a plough pole. Further still, the men touching the elephant's stomach exhorted, "he is like a storage bin!" Other men touched his legs and argued that he was like pillars; the ones touching his tail said he was like a fan and so on and so on. Anyway, these men fought furiously over their incom-plete and competing descriptions of the elephant, but as the objective audience knows, they were all right, yet at the same time, wrong.[225]

We may contrast this complexity, to a degree at least, with theolo-gy. Theology is more like a Cheeseburger in that, it is uncreatively formed in haste, by hacking and slashing away at pieces of mythology that serve its purpose. Now, I am not saying that it doesn't develop and change over time, but that its foundations are established uncre-atively, by way of plagiarism, to use a modern term, and intellectual dishonesty. Once it has slaughtered its chosen myth, or collection of myths, it smashes the goodness out of the original ingredients, grounding them into a kind of psychological mince, rendering them unrecognisable. Following this, the theology adds artificial preserva-tives and poisons, like doctrine, dogma and faith, to ensure that it will maintain its structural integrity (emotional appeal), over an elongated period of time. Finally, it wraps this once beautiful creature, in a shiny paper packet, sets up neon lit franchises wherever it is able, and goes into the ultimate truth-selling business.

---

[225]Joseph Campbell. *The Masks of God – Primitive Mythology*. Secker & Warburg. (1960). p. 8.

Has this rant been merely the result of my missing breakfast this morning, or do I have a point to make!? Oh yes, that's right! When we analyse the mythology surrounding the goddess Isis, or Ast, as she was known to the Egyptians, we cannot gain an adequate understanding by hastily unwrapping the first version of the myth we encounter, and wolfing it down, only to spit it out all over the place in the guise of understanding, or McUnderstanding, as it should properly be called. We need to go into it, examine the symbolism, the various epithets and their meanings, the roots of their meanings, which are quite often astronomical/astrological in nature, as well as physiological and psychological, not forgetting that famous old Hermetic philosophy; "As above, so below". Moreover, we must not only examine the heart of the myth itself, but the entire corpus of surrounding myths, the myths which clothe the subject of the investigation. Only by doing so, may we gain an adequate understanding of the entire anatomy of not only the myth itself, but the various interplays between the myth in question and its surroundings. Only then can we begin to unlock some of the keys to understanding what and how this given myth was intended to be interpreted and conveyed.

Speaking on the deficiency of modern understanding as it relates to the myth, as it pertains to those myths found within the *Bible*, Professor Alvin Boyd Kuhn, once remarked:

That the sublime wisdom embodied in Greek myth and *Bible* allegory is still uninterpreted by the mind of the West to this day will prove to be the weightiest indictment of ignorance that history will present against the Christian civilization of this age. Barely less than laughable, will appear to later times, the spectacle of an age morally and spiritually dominated by the precepts of a Book the meaning of which was all the while uninterpreted and unknown.[226]

So let us continue an investigation into the question of Isis' virginity, with the above in mind.

THE MCISIS-$1.99: DEEP FRIED AND READY FOR APOLOGETICS!

The following represents one of the most popular versions of the Isis myth, one which apologists love to cough up on anyone who might

---

[226]Alvin Boyd Kuhn. *The Root of All Religion*. The Theosophical Press. (1936).

ask the question; was Isis a virgin? Now, I am in no way saying that this version of the myth is erroneous, cheap, or shallow. It is a beautiful myth, rich in symbolism and metaphor, and one which certainly fits the description of myth proper, furnished above. It is the manner in which it is quickly unwrapped, chewed, digested and regurgitated in exclusivity from the wealth of surrounding ingredients, which I aim to address.

In this version of the myth, Horus' evil uncle, Set, hosts a banquet for his good brother, the king of kings, Osiris. At this "Last Supper", Set, possessing an intention to betray his brother, produces a beautiful wooden box, in which he convinces Osiris to lay. Thereupon, Set nails the box shut, trapping Osiris inside. In a plan to ensure that his brother disappears forever, so that he might usurp his brother's throne, Set castes the coffin into the Nile and it floats away. Ignoring for now, the interplay of both the "sibling rivalry" and betrayal at the last supper motifs, which are present in many later myths, we now move onto the next part of the story.

Isis, the sister-wife of Osiris, is dismayed to discover what has happened and just as in the saga of the Babylonian Ishtar and Tammuz (Dhumzi), Isis goes in search for her loved one. She finds him, brings him back to life with her powerful magic. All appears to be right with the world until Set learns that his brother is alive and well. Set then begins a quest of his own, a quest to seek out Osiris and finish him once and for all. He succeeds in his fiendish endeavour, finds Osiris, cuts him into many pieces (14, 16, 42, etc.) and scatters the pieces of his dismembered corpse across Egypt. Surely, this is enough to deter Isis, Set thought. But blood is thicker than water, especially when it is mixed with incestuous passion, we may assume from the facts of this story. Isis then collects all the pieces of her dead husband-brother, bar her favourite piece, the phallus, and re-assembles him in a Frankensteinish experiment. Not being content to be married to a eunuch, Isis fashions a new phallus for her husband and then, whilst Osiris is still cold, makes passionate, incestuous and necromantic love with him, producing Horus.

There you go! She had sex with Osiris and was not a virgin! This was not an immaculate conception and she was no virgin, says the belief-induced apologist seeking to resolve their dissonance, in a bid to comfort both the fragile ego and the belief that resides therein. Unfortunately for the apologist however, this is not the end of our investigation into the matter.

A GODDESS WITH MANY NAMES- ISIS - A SOCIAL SECURITY NIGHTMARE!

In the centuries leading up to the alleged advent of Christ, the cult of Isis had already spread far and wide.

Egyptologist, Dr Rosalie David tells us that the Isis-Osiris mysteries were celebrated prior to the Christian era from Rome and as far west as Britain.[227]

As a result, Isis was incorporated into the mythologies of many different peoples. She meant many different things to many different people and was understood to represent varying qualities, depending on who was describing her. Subsequently, Isis became known by many names.

Discussing how Isis came to be adopted within the Greek Pantheon of gods, the ancient Greek historian, Herodotus (fifth century bce) tells us:

The relation between the Egyptian Isis and the Greek Io was probably this, that Phoenicians in early times had carried to Argos the worship of the moon, under the symbol of a heifer, or a woman with heifer's horns. The symbol itself and the name of Io, which is Coptic for the moon…the origin of it was forgotten, and the invention of the Greek mythologists supplied its place by the legend of an Argive princess, beloved by Jupiter, turned by him into a heifer, and driven through Phoenicia into Egypt, where she became the goddess Isis.[228]

So Herodotus is informing us that there was a connection between the Egyptian, Isis and the Greek, Io, and that both these forms, symbolically represent the moon. What we may also take away from Herodotus' statement is that, the source of the Io/Isis connection

---

[227]Rosalie A. David. *Handbook to Life in Ancient Egypt*. University of Manchester. Facts on File Inc. (2003). p. 178.
[228]John Kenrick. *The Egypt of Herodotus*. B. Fellowes (1841). p. 64.

predates Herodotus' own time by many years, as the origin of this amalgamation seems to have been lost in the wastes of time, leading this proud Greek historian to attribute Isis' origins to his homeland.

In their examination of the complex nature of the goddess Io, who we now know was Isis under another name, the two Oxford Emeritus Professors, Mark Morford and Robert Lenardon, say:

Io was originally a goddess; she may have been a form of Hera herself. Herodotus, who himself visited Egypt, said that Isis was identified there with Demeter, whose image Io had first brought there, and that Isis was always represented as a woman with cow's horns (in this being similar to the great Phoenician moon goddess, Astarte).[229]

Dr Jenny March, in her award winning, *Cassell's Dictionary of Classical Mythology* elaborates upon Morford and Lenardon's description of Io, reporting:

She was the virgin-priestess of HERA at Argos, and was so beautiful that ZEUS himself desired her.[230]

Further, reading from the ancient Greek tragedy, *Prometheus Bound*, written in the seventh century bce, by Aeschylus, we learn that Io was noted for her somewhat stubborn adherence to virginity:

Again and again in the night, visions would appear to me (Io) in my room and entice me with seductive words: "O blessed maiden, why do you remain a virgin for so long when it is possible for you to achieve the greatest of marriages?"[231]

So we see that not only was the older Egyptian Isis, transformed into the Greek Io, but that she was certainly worshipped as a virgin.

In the ancient novel, *The Golden Ass*, or *Metamorphoses*, as it was often called, Apuleius (second century ce), furnishes us with the following description of Isis:

...my divinity is adored throughout all the world in divers manners, in variable customs and in many names, for the Phrygians call me the mother of the Gods: the Athenians, Minerva: the Cyprians,

---

[229]Mark P.O. Morford & Robert J. Lenardon. *Classical Mythology*. Oxford University Press (2003). pp. 516–517.
[230]Jenny March. *Cassell's Dictionary of Classical Mythology*. Cassell & Co. (1998). p. 422.
[231]Mark P.O. Morford & Robert J. Lenardon. *Classical Mythology*. Oxford University Press (2003). p. 92.

Venus: the Candians, Diana: the Sicilians, Proserpina: the Eleusians, Ceres: some Juno, others Bellona, other Hecate: and principally the Ethiopians which dwell in the Orient, and the Egyptians which are excellent in all kind of ancient doctrine, and by their proper ceremonies accustom to worship me, do call me Queen Isis.[232]

Morford and Lenardon, commenting on Apuleius' work, say:

Cybele, Athena, Aphrodite, Artemis, Demeter, Persephone, Hera—the ancient Queens of Heaven and Earth—are here, through the process of syncretism, included in the great Egyptian goddess, Isis. Apuleius, whose evidence is almost certainly reliable, shows us how in the second century (he was born about A.D. 120) the figures of Greek and Roman mythology had given way to the idea of a single divine power.[233]

Isis became Demeter, the mother of the virgin, both Persephone and Io, the unfortunate virgins, Athena-Parthenos, Parthenos being a Greek epithet, to which we will come in just a moment, Artemis (a symbol of virginity), Hera, the goddess who renewed her virginity once a year by bathing,[234] along with many other goddesses. Now, even though Apuleius wrote this work around 120 ce, we may safely conclude from the earlier sources, like Herodotus and others, that these goddesses, whose origins span many centuries into the past, were already associated with the chief of all the goddesses, the Mother-Superior, Isis/Ast.

To show that Isis was associated with the virgin goddess Persephone, prior to Apuleius' time, we have the testimony of the first century Greek historian Plutarch, who tells us:

For Serapis they say is no other than Pluto, and Isis the same with Proserpine; as Archemaclius of Euboea informs us, as also Heraclides of Pontus, delivers it as his opinion that the oracle at Canopus appertains to Pluto.[235]

---

[232]Apuleius. (trans. William Adlington). *The Golden Ass of Apuleius*. David Nutt. Pub. (1893). p. 233.

[233]Mark P.O. Morford & Robert J. Lenardon. *Classical Mythology*. Oxford University Press (2003). p. 366.

[234]Price, Theodora Hadzisteliou. Kourotrophos: Cults and presentation of the Greek Nursing Deities. Leiden: E.J. Brill. (1978). p. 203.

[235]Dr William W. Goodwin. Plutarch's Morals. Little Brown and Company. (1878). p. 88.

In quoting Heraclides of Pontus, Plutarch, although living and writing in the first centuryce, was relaying an opinion of Isis dating back to the fourth century bce, at least.[236] But Proserpine or Persephone, as she was known to the Greeks, was not a virgin, she was raped by Hades.[237] Here is where we need to explore the more subtle undertones and broader characteristics of the landscape of classical mythology, so as not to forsake the overall context with regards to how the ancients viewed their gods and goddesses. Remember, we are not dealing with a cheeseburger. Notwithstanding Persephone's unfortunate encounter with Hades, she was still regarded and worshipped as a virgin goddess, and as a tragic symbol of innocence lost, of flowers cast to the ground.

Furthermore, many of these ancient Hellenistic gods and goddesses were considered "parthenos," meaning, "virgin."[238] This was not so much a literal epithet, although it was used as such, but a symbolic one, describing the purity of the gods, whether they were technically virgins or not, remembering Gerald Massey's wise words, *All that is non-natural and impossible as human history, is possible, natural and explicable as Mythos.*[239].

There were more Hellenistic manifestations of Isis that received the parthenos epithet, like Athena, whose name in full was usually, Athena-Parthenos. A second century Roman coin, currently held at the British museum, testifies to the amalgamation of Isis and Athena-Parthenos and is inscribed with the name, "Isis-Athena".[240]

The virgin-goddess, Artemis also became fused with Isis prior to the Christian era and it would benefit us here to conduct a brief examination into this Hellenistic goddess and her integration with Isis, in order to develop an understanding of how a goddess, could be both mother and virgin.

---

[236]http://plato.stanford.edu/entries/pythagoreanism/
[237]Mark P.O. Morford & Robert J. Lenardon. Classical Mythology. Oxford University Press (2003). p. 20.
[238]Ibid. p. 158.
[239]Gerald Massey. The Historical Jesus and Mythical Christ. A Lecture. (1880). p. 5.
[240]http://www.forumancientcoins.com/moonmoth/noncoins/athisistyche_bm_001.html.

Artemis was worshiped as both a virgin and a mother, in similitude to Isis. To fully appreciate just how this could be, we need to dive a little deeper into the rich waters of the psyche of the mythographers of the ancient world. If we examine and compare other Hellenistic myths which involve a similar interplay of the motifs of virgin and motherhood, we come upon the very core (Kore) of just how these gods and goddesses were understood. A good example to draw upon here would be Demeter and Persephone, who was also called, "Kore", meaning "young girl", and it is in this form that she was worshipped as the innocent virgin. Demeter is the mother and Kore/Persephone is the virgin. This seems simple enough, yet this is only a "cheeseburger analysis" of this mythical daughter and child duo.

Looking further into the matter, we discover that Demeter and Kore/Persephone were not seen as entirely separate goddesses, but rather, they described a single principle in two parts. This may be likened to Jesus being described as one aspect of the holy trinity. He is merely one aspect, or quality of a triune principle. We see the same with Horus and Osiris, both are one, and Horus would have been well within his mythological rights to declare, "I and my father are one."

In his attempt to reveal the secret of the complexity of the symbolism surrounding both Artemis and Isis, following a description of Artemis as a fertility goddess, associated with sex and motherhood, Dr Reginald E. Witt, explains that the key to decoding the holistic duality of such characters lies in the thinking of the Mediterranean world in the early Mycenaean age. Witt teaches us that the Great Goddess was worshipped as both a mother and a virgin, drawing upon the above cited example of Kore and Demeter. For Witt, as with many other classical scholars, the most obviously virginal character in classic myth is Artemis, despite the fact that her role was the promoter of male and female wedlock and she was seen as the midwife of the ancient mythical world.[241]

Morford and Lenardon support Witt's analysis of the duality associated with Artemis, seeing the root of this duality, as best explained by the lunar attributes of both Artemis and Isis, commenting:

---

[241]Reginald E. Witt. Isis in the Ancient World. Baltimore: Johns Hopkins Press. (1997). P. 141.

As in the case of other goddesses worshiped by women (e.g., Hera), this link with the moon may be associated with the lunar cycle and women's menstrual period. Thus the evident duality in Artemis' character and interests definitely links her with the archetypal concept of the virgin/mother.[242]

Finally, Dr Witt sums up the relationship between Isis and Artemis, saying:

How soon Artemis and Isis became amalgamated cannot be known with certainty. The 'Oxyrhynchus Litany' shows us that Isis was invoked as Artemis both in Crete at Dicte and in the Cyclades as the goddess 'of threefold nature'. We may think at first of an apparent stumbling-block, the declared resolve of Artemis to remain a virgin. But this virginal aspect, as we have seen, is but one of two, for at Ephesus she personifies female fruitfulness. Nor is Isis without another guise in her Egyptian setting. She and her sister Nephthys can be mimed in a piece of religious pageantry by two women, brought on to the scene 'with pure body' and each of them virgo intacta.[243]

But promoting virginity as a virtue was a Greek custom, not an Egyptian one, as the Egyptians did not see virginity and chastity as a divine mandate![244] Whilst this may have been the case at some points throughout Egyptian history, contrary to popular and unscholarly opinion, the Egyptians did have a word for virgin in their language,[245] and they did not hesitate to apply it to Isis, if only symbolically.

ISIS IN EGYPT: "THE GREAT VIRGIN"

Many apologists and unread commentators on Egypt are of the mistaken opinion that the ancient Egyptians did not, at any stage of their existence, have a word in their language for virginity, which is

---

[242]Mark P.O. Morford & Robert J. Lenardon. Classical Mythology. Oxford University Press (2003). p. 208.

[243]Reginald E. Witt. Isis in the Ancient World. Baltimore: Johns Hopkins Press. (1997). p. 143.

[244]Konrad H. Kinzl. A Companion to the Ancient Greek World. Blackwell Publishing (2006). p. 353.

[245]Sir E. A. Wallis Budge. An Egyptian Hieroglyphic Dictionary: Vol. 2. John Murray Pub. (1920) p. 1247.

transliterated as *hwt.n*, by the way. These ill-informed "experts" are of the opinion that there were no tales of virgins, for how could you have a story about a concept which did not exist in your language? Yet, according to both primary sources and scholarly appraisals of those sources, the concept of not only virginity, but the virgin-born god, was known and represented by the ancient Egyptians.

From Egyptian records, we know not only that the daughter of Ramesses VI(twelfth century bce), was one of the first known "virgin princesses" to hold that particular office,[246] but also, Herodotus tells us in the fifth century bce, that only virgins were allowed to act as priestesses at the temples of Isis.[247]

It would be remiss of me at this point, not to refer to a second centurybce papyrus, held in the British museum, which reads:

Let there be brought forth two young women pure of body, virgins, plucked of all hair, head ornamented with a wig, a tambourine in hand, with their name written on their shoulder: Isis, Nephthys; and let them sing the verses of this booklet before the god.' [Papyrus Brit. Mus., 10, 188.][248]

Further, the late Professor of Mythology, Joseph Campbell, in his brilliant series, *The Masks of God*, points to a late Egyptian papyrus of around 1600bce to demonstrate that the concept of the virgin birth (parthenogenesis) existed at a very early stage of Egyptian history.[249]

I could go on listing other primary sourced scholarship on this issue ad infinitum, but let us move along, as for some reason, I'm starting to develop a craving for a cheeseburger.

Summing up what we have discovered thus far, Isis was considered a virgin in her various cross-cultural manifestations, well before the Christian era. The virgin birth, as a mythological motif, was represented amongst ancient Egyptian sources as well. So, now all there is

---

[246]Morris L. Bierbrier. Historical Dictionary of Ancient Egypt. Scarecrow Press. (2008) p. 195.
[247]Edward I. Bleiberg. World Eras, Vol. 5: Ancient Egypt 2615-332 BCE. Gale Group. (2002) p. 202.
[248]Serge Sauneron. The Priests of Ancient Egypt. Evergreen Books Ltd. (1960). p. 69.
[249]Joseph Campbell. The Masks of God, Vol. 2: Oriental Mythology. Secker & Warburg. (1962) p. 98.

left to establish is that Isis was, in Egypt, expressly described as a virgin. If we can accomplish this, the issue of Isis as one of the oldest virgin mothers, whose tales inspired the birth of the Virgin Mary myth, will be put to bed once and for all (pun intended).

Before moving into the final part of this discussion, I must re-emphasize the complex nature of the mythos surrounding Isis. Yes, she was the wife of Osiris and the protective mother of Horus, but she was also considered to be the mother of Osiris and creation itself.

From a fourth century bce inscription in the temple of Isis, in Philae Egypt, we read that Isis was the:

Mighty one, foremost of the goddesses
Ruler in heaven, Queen on earth…
All the gods are under her command.[250]

In some regards, she may be likened to the goddess, Tiamat of the ancient Babylonians, in that she was described as the first cause of all creation, notwithstanding the fact that ancient records also refer to Isis as the daughter of Nut and Geb. In the words of Dr Reginald E. Witt:

The Egyptian goddess who was, equally, the Great Virgin (hwnt) and Mother of the God, was the object of the very same praise bestowed upon her successor [Mary, Virgin Mother of Jesus].[251]

Further, Witt tells us that Isis was directly associated with the resurrection of the dead and that in the Osiris Hymn, she was referred to as, ..."the Great Virgin," she was…the female embodiment of the Nile's annual reawakening.[252]

Keeping in mind the symbolic duality of opposites which Isis represented, we refer once again to the work of Dr Rosalie David, learning that Isis was considered the supreme mother-goddess.[253] Being that she was considered the supreme mother-goddess, coupled with the fact that both Horus and Osiris were interchangeable, Horus

---

[250]Richard H. Wilkinson. The Complete Gods and Goddesses of Ancient Egypt. Thames and Hudson. (2003). p. 146.

[251]Reginald E. Witt. Isis in the Ancient World. Baltimore: Johns Hopkins Press. (1997). p. 273.

[252]Ibid. p. 15.

[253]Rosalie A. David. Handbook to Life in Ancient Egypt. University of Manchester. Facts on File Inc. (2003).p. 152.

symbolically becoming Osiris in death, and Osiris becoming Horus in rebirth, Isis was both Osiris' wife and sister, as well as being his mother, the mother of Horus, and the Great Virgin. I told you! We are not dealing with a cheeseburger here, but a sophisticated ensemble of symbols, motifs and allegorical associations, all slowly cooked over thousands of years.

Commenting on an ancient Egyptian text, Dr Maulana Karenga observes:

She (Isis) is defined as mother of the divinities and of humanity, protector and resurrector of Osiris, mother and protector of the king and warrior "who is more effective than a million soldiers" (iabkar 1988, 61). But most striking and instructive is her definition as the Creator, herself. And although similar conceptions of the Creator as female exist in other African cultures (Mbiti 1970), this is clearly not the case in Judaism, Islam and Christianity. The text defines Isis in the following terms:

She is mistress of Heaven. earth and the otherworld.

Having brought them into being by what her heart/mind conceived And her hands created (Zabkar 1988, 51 .no.IV).[254]

Having established Isis' complex nature, let us now look at a thirteenth century bce text, from the temple dedicated to Isis, at Abydos in Egypt. The text, although not specifying Isis, as the enunciator, contains a statement we may rightfully conclude, was ascribed to Isis. The relevant portion of the text reads as follows:

I am the Great Virgin.[255]

The late Theologian, *Old Testament* scholar and Dean of the Theological Faculty at the University at Bonn, Dr G. Johannes Botterweck, in the second volume of his fifteen volume series, *Theological Dictionary of the Old Testament*, although not wishing to expressly reveal Isis as the subject of a text found in this thirteenth century bce temple, said:

---

[254]Maulana Karenga. Maat: The Moral Ideal in Ancient Egypt - A Study in Classical African Ethics. Routledge. (2004).

[255]G. Johannes Botterweck. Theological Dictionary of the *Old Testament*, Vol. 2. William B. Eerdmans Publishing Co. (1975). p. 339.

...The Pyramid Texts speak of "the great virgin" (hwn.t wr.t) three times (682c, 728a, 2002a...); she is anonymous, appears as the protectress of the king, and is explicitly called his mother once (809c). It is interesting that Isis is addressed as hwn.t in a sarcophagus oracle that deals with her mysterious pregnancy.[256]

We have the ancient testimony of the Pyramid Texts, which speak of the "great virgin," who is described as the "protector" and "mother of the king," both of which were almost exclusively applied to Isis, found in the temple dedicated to Isis, no less. This is almost certainly Isis, the virgin mother of Horus/Osiris.

CONCLUSION

Isis was considered a virgin, both in and outside of Egypt, prior to the Christian era. A wealth of evidence exists to demonstrate this, if one has the eyes and the mind to seek. Sadly, those whose beliefs impede their ability to seek the truth beyond the constrictive and restrictive boundaries of their ego inhabiting beliefs, go looking for and ultimately find, a Cheeseburger.

Unfortunately, due to constraints of both time and space, I have been unable to discuss the broad range of issues surrounding Isis' status, as the virgin mother of god. I have forgone discussions on her manifestation as Cybele, the virgin mother of the Phrygian Attis, her transformation into Minerva, Juno and many others, and I have had to subtract the bulk of archaeological artefacts and features that further support the well documented fact of her virginity. I have left off discussions which describe the more symbolic subtleties of her/his character and in so doing, have, to some degree, sought to fight Cheeseburger with Cheeseburger. Having said this, I thought it sufficient to run briefly over the more obvious scholarship on this Great Queen of Heaven, and leave the rest for the reader to investigate. As the great Galileo once remarked, it is easier to let people discover things for themselves, than to teach them, or words to that effect.

---

[256]Ibid. pp. 338–339.

I would like to conclude this little article with the wise words of the brilliant professor of Mythology, Joseph Campbell:

No good Catholic would kneel before an image of Isis if he knew that it was she. Yet every one of the mythic motifs now dogmatically attributed to Mary as a historic human being belongs also-and belonged in the period and place of the development of her cult-to that goddess mother of all things, of whom both Mary and Isis were local manifestations: the mother-bride of the dead and resurrected god, whose earliest known representations now must be assigned to a date as early, at least, as circa 5500 B.C.· It is often customary in devotional cults to limit the view of the devotee to a single local manifestation, which then is honoured either as unique or as the primary, "truest," form of the divinity represented.[257]

THE RECENT RISE IN ISLAMIC CONVERSIONS – MISPLACED SYMPATHIES

The point of this article is not to assume a direct connection between "terrorism," whatever that may be, and Islam. Let me assure both Muslim and non-Muslim readers, that my opinions on the "war on terror" would be in-line with most Muslims.

Islam, according to more than a few commentators (both Muslim and non-Muslim) is on the rise in western countries. Ignoring the anti-Muslim rhetoric inherent within the reporting on American Media Networks and in western Newspapers, an article in the Washington Post in September of 2007 stated:

The number of converts, it seems, is definitely on the rise," said Michael Taarnby, a terrorism researcher at the Danish Institute for International Studies. "We've reached a point where I think al-Qaeda and other groups recognize the value of converts, not just from an operational viewpoint but from a cultural one as well." Converts are a tiny subset of the Muslim population in Europe, but their numbers are growing in some countries. In Germany, government officials estimated that 4,000 people converted to Islam last year, compared with

---

[257]Joseph Campbell. Masks of God: Vol. 3 – Occidental Mythology. Penguin Books. (1976). p. 43.

an annual average of 300 in the late 1990s. Less than 1 percent of Germany's 3.3 million Muslims are converts.[258]

Again, leaving aside the fear-mongering and anti-Muslim sentiment, which is all too common in western reporting these days, we do see that officials are finding the number of converts to Islam rising in recent times.

Furthermore, one Muslim website provides the following information and statistics regarding the recent rise of Islam:

According to statistics from the U.N., Islam is now the world's second largest religion after Christianity. The U.N. statistics state that the Islam annual growth rate of Islam is around 6.40% compared to 1.46% during the same time period for Christianity. Also according to these statistics, one in five people on the planet are Muslim (by birth or geographical reference).

Other statistics from the U.N.:

Islam in North America since 1989 increased 25%

Islam in Africa since 1989 increased 2.15%

Islam in Asia since 1989 increased 12.57%

Islam in Europe since 1989 increased 142.35%

Islam in Latin America since 1989 decreased -4.73%

And Islam in Australia and Oceania / Pacific since 1989 increased 257.01%

Major Religions of the World

Christian – 2,038,905,,000 – 32% (dropping)

Roman Catholics – 1,076,951,000

Protestants – 349,792,000

Orthodox – 217,522,000

Anglicans – 81,663,000

Other – 537,135,000

Muslims – 1,226,403,,000 – 21% (growing)

Hindus – 828,130,,000 – 13% (stable)

Chinese folk religionists – 389,543,,000 – 6%

Buddhists – 364,014,,000 – 6% (stable)

---

[258]http://www.washingtonpost.com/wp-dyn/content/article/2007/09/14/AR2007091402265.html

Sikhs – 23,821,,000 – < 1%

Jews – 14,535,,000 – < 1%[259]

It seems rather obvious that Islam is on the rise. But what could account for the recent increase in converts? Is there anything history could teach us that might help explain this sudden rise in Islamic conversions?

Last year I was doing some research on early Christianity for the second volume in my three volume series *I Am Christ*, and I came across some very interesting information, regarding one of the major factors in Christianity's early success. According to some of the most esteemed historians of both past and present, one of the factors which contributed to the rapid increase in the numbers of Christian converts (prior to Constantine's conversion of the empire) was the public persecution of Christian martyrs.

The Regius professor of history at Oxford and Cambridge Universities, Henry Chadwick, described the impact of the persecutions of early Christians, saying:

From embodying a counter-culture to being seen as a mainly (not invariably) conservative social force was an extraordinary step. The number of martyrs did not need to be very large for their 'witness' to be public and 'newsworthy'. Remarkably soon the Church had recruits in high society, and as early as the middle of the second century was dreaming of a day when the emperor himself would be converted.[260]

This got me thinking about my own psychology, following the events which transpired as a result of the attacks on the World Trade Centre on 9/11 and the subsequent invasions of both Afghanistan and Iraq. I remember seeing old and frail Muslim clerics rounded up on the news in various western countries, images of burnt and brutalized Muslim children in those two invaded countries, and I can clearly remember being so incensed by this blatant persecution that I began to consider converting to Islam, just to show solidarity to these martyrs of the modern age. I hadn't even read the *Qur'an*, nor done any

---

[259]http://www.30-days.net/muslims/statistics/islam-growth/
[260]Henry Chadwick. The Church in Ancient Society: From Galilee to Gregory the Great. Oxford University Press. (2001). p. 1.

research on Islam whatsoever. I just wanted to express my utter contempt for these wrongful and unjust persecutions.

Following this increase in the unjust persecutions of Muslims, both the western and Islamic media were awash with stories of suicide bombers and clerics calling for violent Jihad (holy war) on the west. Osama Bin Ladin, the modern day Polycarp, was calling upon all Muslims to stand-up for Islam; using religious emotion and promises of heavenly virgins to convince peaceful Muslims to become violent martyrs for their faith.

Such was also the case close to 2,000 years ago, when the original Polycarp exhorted:

All the martyrdoms, then, were blessed and noble and took place according to the will of God. For it becomes us who profess greater piety than others, to ascribe the authority over all things to God. And truly, who can fail to admire their nobleness of mind, and their patience, with that love towards their Lord which they displayed? —who, when they were so torn with scourges, that the frame of their bodies, even to the very inward veins and arteries, was laid open, still patiently endured, while even those that stood by pitied and bewailed them. But they reached such a pitch of magnanimity that not one of them let a sigh or a groan escape them; thus proving to us all that those holy martyrs of Christ, at the very time when they suffered such torments, were absent from the body, or rather, that the Lord then stood by them, and communed with them. And, looking to the grace of Christ, they despised all the torments of this world, redeeming themselves from eternal punishment by [the suffering of] a single hour. For this reason the fire of their savage executioners appeared cool to them. For they kept before their view escape from that fire which is eternal and never shall be quenched, and looked forward with the eyes of their heart to those good things which are laid up for such as endure; things "which ear hath not heard, nor eye seen, neither have entered into the heart of man," but were revealed by the Lord to them, inasmuch as they were no longer men, but had already become angels.[261]

---

[261]Philip Schaff. Ante-Nicene Fathers. Vol. 1: The Apostolic Fathers with Justin Martyr and Irenaeus. The Martyrdom of Polycarp. Christian Ethereal Library. (1885).p. 66

This horrible conversion device was seized upon by early church leaders, who, like the corrupt clerics of Islam today, promoted and encouraged voluntary martyrdom with promises of salvation and reward as a means of gaining converts... to the point that it became a widespread problem in the first few centuries of the Christian era. Again, Henry Chadwick informs us that voluntary and aggressive martyrdom was primarily the result of the manipulation engendered by promises of celestial joy.[262]

Isn't this exactly what we are seeing in recent times with regards to Islam? And couldn't the persecution of Muslims, following 9/11 and the sight of this injustice, be one of the major factors in Islam's recent rise in western countries? I think it may be.

◆

TWO VICTIMS OF PROTESTANT INSANITY – THE STORIES OF MATTHEW HAMONT AND MICHAEL SERVETUS.

MATTHEW HAMONT: MURDERED FOR CHRIST AND COUNTRY

Matthew Hamont, a loving husband and father, was burned alive by the Church of England for the crime of holding an opinion of God that was outside the narrow purview of both the Anglican Church and Christianity, in general.[263]

Matthew Hamont was brutally tortured and snuffed out by the intolerant flames of a powerful church, for the crime of Deism.

Deists believe in a creator, yet they see no need for organized religion, a position which in Matthew Hamont's time, would have been very threatening to malign faith wielders and monarchists, who stood to forfeit immeasurable wealth and power, should Deism win the minds of the masses. The Deist's God is one who designed the universe and set the wheels in motion, so to speak, then stepped back to let the universe govern itself. Deists view miracles and prophecies as being the invention of human imagination and religious scriptures,

---

[262]Ibid. p. 67.
[263]Jeremy Collier, M.A. An Ecclesiastical History of Great Britain. Vol. 6. William Straker. (1811). pp. 608–609.

like the *New Testament* and the *Qur'an*, for example, as being little more than manmade fables.

In April of 1579, Matthew Hamont was taken from his wife and his only son, Erasmus, and dragged before the Ecclesiastical Court of the Church of England, by the bishop of Norwich, Edmund Freke.[264] The charges laid against Matthew were:

Denying Christ as the Saviour of mankind,

Accusing Jesus of being nothing more than a Jewish sinner,

Disbelieving in the existence of the Holy Ghost and

Asserting that the Gospels are fictitious fables.[265]

For these "crimes," Hamont was handed over to the Sheriff, at which time further charges of blasphemy were laid against him for uttering un-pleasantries about the Queen of England, who is believed by many to sit on the divinely appointed throne until Christ's return. For this additional crime, he had his ears cut off, before being burnt alive, the sentence of his initial crimes.[266]

One cannot begin to imagine the horrendous pain, the torment and the excruciating agony Matthew must have suffered in his final hours. Having his ears violently hacked off, feeling and hearing, if indeed he could still hear, his skin sizzle, as his nerves went into overdrive, sending a tsunami of excruciating messages to his pain receptors, until he could feel no more. Nor could one begin to fathom the emotional heartache and anguish of his beloved wife and only son, who not only suffered the unspeakable loss of a husband and father, but must have also felt the social effects and stigma of being associated with a convicted heretic. And for what!? Because those whose minds are so fixated, so certain, so overwhelmed by their own ideas, that they feel and believe they have the right to snuff out human lives with such callous disregard for the victim and their family? What kind of insanity is this that turns people into monsters? To answer in a word, belief.

---

[264]Alexander Gordon. Dictionary of National Biography. Vol. 24. (1895–1900).

[265]Robert Wallace. Antitrinitarian Biography. Vol. 2. E.T. Whitfield. (1850). Pp. 364–365.

[266]Ibid.

MICHAEL SERVETUS: CALVIN'S FURY!

If we were to use a single word to describe Michael Servetus, it would have to be, polymath. He was a mathematician, philosopher, astronomer, astrologer, theologian and a physician, among other things.[267] Despite his intelligence, he was a devout Christian, one who despised the pomp of the papacy and so was drawn to the Reformation. On at least two occasions he narrowly escaped the flames of the Catholic Inquisition and became despised by Lutherans, Calvinists and Catholics alike. Members of these various sects were constantly at war with each other over ridiculous theological/superstitious differences, however, as much as they each relished the idea of burning members of their rival sects, they harboured nothing less than a frenzied desire to see Michael Servetus tortured and finally scrubbed from this planet. Michael's three chief heresies were: that he believed the trinity to be false, which, in Servetus' day, was a belief that could have you murdered by any of the Christian churches; he did not believe in infant baptism, again a fatal belief to hold in such a dark and depraved age; and finally, he saw it as absurd that a person be saved by faith alone, or that faith naturally produces good works.[268] Officially, these were the reasons Calvin put Servetus to death for, however, if one examines the correspondences between Servetus and Calvin, another, even more insidious reason for this crime comes to light.

In the beginning, Servetus and Calvin's letters to one another were moderate and cordial however, as time went on more and more differences began to emerge between the Christianity of Calvin and his intellectual superior, Servetus. In the end, Calvin tried to put a stop to their correspondence by sending Michael his seminal and authoritative work entitled,'*The Institutes of the Christian Religion,* which he thought would make this heretic bow down before the "supreme intellect" of Calvin. It did not. In fact, Michael sent it back heavily annotated, drawing attention to errors of fact, logic and theology, by employing Christian Scripture and the works of the ante-Nicene

---

[267]Carl Theophilus Odhner. Michael Servetus: His Life and Teachings. J.B. Lippincott Company. (1910). p. 19.
[268]Ibid. p. 58–59.

fathers, to demonstrate where and how Calvin's central tenets were flawed.[269] Naturally, Calvin was infuriated wanting Servetus dead. In a letter to one of his friends, Calvin wrote:

There is hardly a page that is not defiled with his vomit.[270]

Following this event, Servetus sent other correspondences to Calvin and in one asked to come and sit with him to discuss their differences. Upon receiving this request, Calvin wrote to his chief Lieutenant, Farel:

Servetus lately wrote to me and sent me with his letters a great volume of his ravings, saying that I would see there things stupendous and unheard of until now. He offers to come here if I approve, but I will not pledge my faith to him. For should he come, if my authority avails, I should never suffer him to go away alive.[271]

Calvin's authority availed and he didn't suffer Michael to leave Geneva alive, for after a speech given by Calvin in Geneva, at which Michael was in attendance, Calvin had him arrested and put to death by the jealous and prideful flames of an intellectually dominated zealot.

The twentieth century church historian, Carl Theophilus Odhner, paints a rather vivid picture for us of the events accompanying Michael Servetus' murder, from contemporary accounts:

When he came in sight of the fatal pile, the wretched Servetus prostrated himself on the ground, and for a while was absorbed in prayer. Rising and advancing a few steps, he found himself in the hand of the executioner, by whom he was made to sit on a block, his feet just reaching the ground. His body was then bound to the stake behind him by several turns of an iron chain, whilst his neck was secured in like manner by the coils of a hempen rope. His two books,—the one in manuscript sent to Calvin in confidence six or eight years before for his strictures, and a copy of the one lately printed in Vienne,—were then fastened to his waist, and his head was encircled in

---

[269]Ibid. p. 21.

[270]R. Willis, M.D. Servetus and Calvin: A Study of an Important Epoch in the History of the Reformation. Henry S. King and Co. (1877). p. 168.

[271]Carl Theophilus Odhner. Michael Servetus: His Life and Teachings. J.B. Lippincott Company. (1910). p. 22.

mockery with a chaplet of straw and green twigs bestrewed with brimstone. The deadly torch was then applied to the faggots and flashed in his face; and the brimstone catching, and the flames rising, wrung from the victim such a cry of anguish as struck terror into the surrounding crowd. After this he was bravely silent; but the wood being purposely green, although the people aided the executioner in heaping the faggots upon him, a long half-hour elapsed before he ceased to show signs of life and suffering. Immediately before giving up the ghost, with a last expiring effort he cried aloud: "Jesus, Thou Son of the Eternal God, have compassion upon me!" All was then hushed save the hissing and crackling of the green wood; and by-and-by there remained no more of what had been Michael Servetus but a charred and blackened trunk and a handful of ashes.[272]

Had Servetus and Hamont's murders been the only ones we could lay at the feet of the Protestants, there would still be ample reason to condemn their belief-infatuated insanity, however, they were not and for proof of this, we need only read the records of the Protestant London Missionary Society, who lusted for Christ so desperately that their depravity in countries like Tahiti, New Zealand and Australia, saw no bounds. We may even cite examples such as, the widespread burning and drowning of young women accused of being witches, by the protestant puritans in

both Europe and America, or the brutal and inhumane African slave trade, overseen and encouraged by various non-Catholic churches. The list of crimes goes on and on, *ad infinitum*.

Anglican Rev. William Dean Inge adds:

The earlier Protestantism, in its chief forms, was certainly intolerant. Some of the minor sects pleaded for liberty of conscience, but minor sects always plead for liberty of conscience until they become major sects. On what principle were the Anabaptists, a body of Christian Socialists, persecuted by Lutherans and Calvinists? Why were the absolutely harmless Quakers maltreated both in Europe and in America, where four of them actually suffered death? Why did Calvin cause the Spaniard Servetus to be burnt

---

[272]Ibid. pp. 32–33.

alive? Why, above all, were many thousands of "witches" executed in Protestant countries?[273]

Surely, even if one innocent person has died as a result of Jesus' teachings, or those whom Jesus allegedly chose to represent him here on earth, then Jesus should be held to be vicariously liable for such crimes. The tragic truth of the matter is that it has not only been one innocent person who has suffered and died as a result of both the Catholic and Protestant churches, but millions upon millions of innocent people. Thus, once again it is argued, that if Jesus did in fact exist and reaching further into credulity, if he was the son of God, then he is either all-loving and impotent or all-knowing and apathetic. In either case, neither this Jewish god-man, nor his representatives on earth are worthy of our trust and devotion. As the ancient Jewish historian Philo noted regarding Epicurus' problem relating to the quandary of an allegedly all-powerful and all loving God, who is either unable or unwilling to prevent evil and suffering, said:

Epicurus' old questions are yet unanswered. Is he (God) willing to prevent evil, but not able? Then is he impotent. Is he able, but not willing? Then is he malevolent. Is he both able and willing? Whence then is evil?[274]

THE NUTS AND BOLTS OF THE CHRISTIAN SCAM

When analyzing Christianity, scholars and commentators view the religion in some of the following ways:

The result of a divine advent of the Son of God;

The corrupt manifestation of a divinely inspired mortal prophet's advent;

A sincere but misguided belief in a miraculous and magical son of God;

A misinterpretation of its parent religion, Judaism, or;

---

[273]W.R. Inge. (Dean of St. Paul's Cathedral) Christian Ethics and Modern Problems. G.P. Putnam's Sons. (1930). p. 189.
[274]Jordan Howard Sobel. Logic and Theism: Arguments For and Against Belief in God. Cambridge University Press. (2004). p. 436.

As a natural progression and derivation of earlier pagan and Jewish mythologies.

Not too many people view Christianity as being the result of a deliberate scam, undertaken for the purpose of gaining power and control over a mass of people. I do not believe that it was merely a scam and I do concede that this essay is somewhat facetious, however, I do think that the rise of Christianity and the circumstances that led to its success, share many aspects to which one could, albeit loosely, apply the term, scam. If Jesus was not the Son of God and the events surrounding his life recorded in the Gospels are fictitious, then someone, or a group of people, must have created these stories. If they did in fact create these stories from fictitious fruits, then the next question to ask is: "Why?" Some scholars are of the opinion that many if not most of the narratives of Jesus' life were never intended to be taken literally, but were intended as insightful allegories, scholars like Bruno Bauer, Arthur Drews, Paul-Louis Couchoud, G.A. Wells and Earl Doherty, for example.

Notwithstanding this credible hypothesis, the Christian mythographers either created these narratives and the religion of Christianity to deceive, or else, a group of men hijacked an allegorical system of thought, turning it into a literalized mythology, thereby transforming helpful and liberating teachings into a tool for imprisoning the mind of the meek. Either way, the prime suspects, whom scholars commonly refer to as the Proto-Orthodox Church, set themselves up as the intermediaries of a fictitious god and in so doing, set in motion a machine that would see millions slaughtered, imprisoned and otherwise harmed as a result.

Why?

Whoever controls people's perception of "god" becomes his intercessor and by proxy, gains "his" authority over all of those who surrender their minds, by way of their belief. When analyzing Christianity through such a lens, the similarities to a scam are remarkable. In this essay I will run through the nine primary elements that comprise the Christian scam, in order to illustrate this possibility for the reader. These elements are also components of successful businesses and so to avoid any confusion with regards to the business like terminology used, let me make it clear that I see no difference between a business which has been built upon dishonest terms and a textbook scam. Both are undertaken for the profit of the proprietor(s), to the detriment of the target(s) and both usually involve practices which are rooted in greed, deception and deliberate manipulation.

I will not attempt to prove beyond a reasonable doubt that the religion of Christianity is based exclusively upon a deliberate scam, however, I would like to illustrate the possibility of this notion for the consideration of the open minded reader.

LEGITIMACY - COCA-COLA SINCE 1886

One of the primary means by which products and companies gain legitimacy, is by the protracted length of time that has elapsed since their establishment. The longer a product or company has been in business, the more legitimacy they will have established in the marketplace. A religion is not too different. Take Christianity for example, it has been in business for almost 2,000 years and so today, it is seen as a religion with antiquity behind it. It is perceived as being a legitimate religion. Furthermore, it has around 30% of the earth's population as members,[275] affording it further legitimacy by way of its successful propagation over the millennia.

An error does not become truth by reason of multiplied propagation, nor does truth become error because nobody sees it.

~Gandhi

How did Christianity catch on and survive to the present age, if at one point in its history, it was a new and otherwise illegitimate fringe religion, one which had no antiquity behind it? The theoretical answer to this question will serve to illustrate the possible genius of the fomenters of this once fledgling theology.

CHRISTIANITY AND JUDAISM: HIJACKING LEGITIMACY

Christianity is theologically rooted in the more ancient religion of Judaism. When Christianity was beginning to flourish in the first few centuries of the Christian era, Judaism had been around for over 1,000

---

[275]https://www.cia.gov/library/publications/the-world-factbook/geos/xx.html

years and was relatively well-known to the non-Jews in the Near East, Asia Minor, the Mediterranean, Egypt, Persia and Greece.[276] Even though Judaism was viewed as a peculiar religion and was subjected to persecution from mobs in the Roman Empire on occasion, it was recognized as a legitimate religion by many of the pagans of the above mentioned regions.

The pagan philosopher Celsus, in his attack on Christianity said:

As the Jews, then, became a peculiar people, and enacted laws in keeping with the customs of their country, and maintain them up to the present time, and observe a mode of worship which, whatever be its nature, is yet derived from their fathers, they act in these respects like other men, because each nation retains its ancestral customs, whatever they are, if they happen to be established among them. And such an arrangement appears to be advantageous, not only because it has occurred to the mind of other nations to decide some things differently, but also because it is a duty to protect what has been established for the public advantage...[277]

Celsus acknowledged the legitimacy of Judaism for the reason that it was rooted in the antiquity of its people. This statement by Celsus serves to demonstrate the mindset of early non-Christians when it came to ascribing legitimacy to ideas and beliefs. If they had antiquity behind them and were derived from the participant's fathers, then, according to many of the pagans of the day, the religion or belief was considered to be legitimate. Not much has changed in the way in which people attribute legitimacy to beliefs and practices. Thus, if a group of people are attempting to start a new religion, as the Christians were, it is a good idea to use the legitimacy of a previously established theology, rooted in antiquity, to sell the new one to a hesitant and semi-sceptical society.

---

[276]Corpus Papyrorum Judaicarum (C.Pap.Jud.). Three vols. by V. A. Tcherikover published in 1957, 1960 (with A. Fuks) and 1964 (with A. Fuks and M. Stern), containing papyri that witness the presence of Jews in Graeco-Roman Egypt; cited in: David S. Potter. A Companion to the Roman Empire. Blackwell Publishing. (2006). p. 53; W.D. Davies & L. Finkelstein. The Cambridge History of Judaism, Vol. 1; Introduction; The Persian Period. Cambridge University Press. (1984). p. 326.

[277]Phillip Schaff. Fathers of the Third Century: Tertullian, Part Fourth; Minucius Felix; Commodian; Origen, Parts First and Second. Grand Rapids MI; Christian Classics Ethereal Library. (1885). p. 974.

Again, if we look at the slow growth of Scientology, in comparison to the faster spreading Baha'i faith, which is rooted in the three Abrahamic religions, the results speak for themselves. Even though the Baha'i faith has had over a hundred year head start on Scientology, the Baha'i, unlike the Scientologists, did not try to create a new religion from scratch, in which they would need to start from the ground and work their way up, they, like the Christians, simply targeted an existing marketed religion and gave it a unique twist.

In Stephen Key's book, *One Simple Idea*, this highly successful entrepreneur and licensing expert, shares one of his biggest secrets regarding the successful propagation of an idea, saying:

In my experience and the experience of countless others, the fastest, easiest, and most profitable road to…success is with an evolutionary idea, not a revolutionary one. It's with giving a new twist, a small tweak, or a unique value to a proven product. It's with a simple idea.[278]

Porphyry identified this "simple idea" approach, as it was utilized by the early Church father Origen, commenting:

But Origen, having been educated as a Greek in Greek literature, went over to the barbarian recklessness (Christianity). And carrying over the learning which he had obtained, he hawked it about, in his life conducting himself as a Christian and contrary to the laws, but in his opinions of material things and of the Deity being like a Greek, and mingling Grecian teachings with foreign fables. For he was continually studying Plato, and he busied himself with the writings of Numenius and Cronius, Apollophanes, Longinus, Moderatus, and Nicomachus, and those famous among the Pythagoreans. And he used the books of Chaeremon the Stoic, and of Cornutus. Becoming acquainted through them with the figurative interpretation of the Grecian mysteries, he applied it to the Jewish Scriptures.[279]

Upon an examination of the various errors made by Christians when applying the Hebrew Scriptures to their new religion, some of

---

[278]Stephen Key. One Simple Idea: Turn Your Dreams into a Licensing Goldmine. While Letting Others Do the Work. McGraw Hill. (2011). p. 37.
[279]Porphyry Book 3. Eusebius: Church History , in Nicene and Post-Nicene Fathers, 2nd Series, ed. Philip Schaff and H. Wace, (Grand Rapids MI: Wm. B. Eerdmans, 1955), Vol. 1, pp. 265–266.

which I highlight in my book, *I Am Christ: The Crucifixion – Painful Truths,* it may be that Christianity did not directly arise out of Judaism, but was adapted to it or may have even been a collaborative product of both Jews of the diaspora and Gentiles. This may have been done to hijack Judaism's legitimacy and develop a religion which was evolutionary, rather than revolutionary in nature.

If the people attempting to graft ancient religious scriptures onto their own, misinterpret, mistranslate and misunderstand simple literary devises, used by the already established religion, isn't it possible that the grafters have done so with no direct knowledge of those ancient scriptures? This serves to possibly demonstrate that the creator of such fanciful works was not proximate to the religion in which he was basing his new religion's legitimacy. He may have been attempting to establish his revelation as a pre-established and legitimate manifestation of a continuous and "legitimate truth." This continuous and legitimate truth in Christianity's case was that their founder was the Jewish son, of the Jewish creator of the more ancient Jewish religion. Despite their attempts however, if one looks closely enough at the Christian religion, one can see that it has been sloppily tacked onto the Jewish religion, possibly for the purpose of rooting itself in the antiquity of a more ancient and legitimate religion. It may be that once Christianity had established itself in its own right, it then turned on its source (Judaism), by way of scriptural, financial and physical persecutions, to protect its own ill-gotten legitimacy.

Think about it this way. Who could more thoroughly expose the Christian's errors with regards to the mistranslations and misapplications of Jewish Scripture? The Jews! Those "sons of Satan," "deceivers," those "liars!" Don't listen to them, they have forked tongues and eat their young! If they tell you that we have mistranslated their Holy Books and hijacked their prophecies for our own profit, remember, they are the brood of vipers that killed the saviour of mankind!

'UNIQUE SELLING POINT'

The next element in this scam is the "unique selling point". The new religion needs to have a distinctive character that separates it from earlier ones so as to offer something new and appealing. The unique aspect of the religion gives it the ability to claim that only its teachings are the "God-given truth." Christianity has quite a few unique characteristics. From its father religion it directly inherited the concept of a messiah (Greek: *Kristos;* Eng. "Christ"), but it reformed this concept by making the Christian messiah more fantastic and more appealing than the Jewish one. The Christian's messiah was no boring mortal sent to save Israel alone, but a super-human, endowed with magical powers, sent to save the entire planet. He could heal the sick, see the future, caste out demons, walk on water, turn that water into wine and he could have probably leapt tall buildings in a single bound as well. The Christians created a virtual super-messiah.

In order to create this superior messiah, the Christian mythographers had to become the Dr. Frankensteins of mythography and formulate a hybrid of both Jewish and non-Jewish heroes. Thus, he is said to be physically descended from King David, of whom the Jewish messiah must be a descendant and yet, he shares characteristics with more ancient gods such as; Zeus, Hercules, Dionysus, Bacchus, Mithras, Krishna, Buddha, Horus, Osiris and many other earlier pagan gods. These gods had been melded together to create a semi-original saviour of mankind that could be easily understood by the pagan masses to allow for the easy sale and re-sale of this theology, without appearing too similar to its mythological antecedents.

The only problem with this Frankenstein is that, in order to make Jesus superhuman, the Christians had to compromise his messianic lineage by forfeiting his actual descent from David. He cannot be the seed (Anc. Greek: *Sperma*) of David, because we are told that his foster father Joseph was the descendant of David and Jesus is not Joseph's son, but Yahweh's, thus, the Christians erred in this respect.

Another unique aspect of Christianity lay in the distinction made with regards to the so-called, "Laws of Moses," versus those allegedly given by Jesus. In the Gospels, as previously discussed, Jesus reversed some of the old Jewish laws prescribed by his omniscient father. This added an additional element of uniqueness to the Christian religion. In reversing these old laws they were able to give the people a hero rooted in the ancient and legitimate Jewish religion, without all of the tedious and restrictive conditions that were attached to Judaism, restrictions that were off-putting to many of the Gentile targets.

There were however, problems with overturning the Laws of Moses. The first problem is that in trying to establish legitimacy by attaching itself to Judaism, there had to be a continuation from the *Old Testament* to the *New Testament*, and we see this continuation not only in the theme which underscores the entire corpus of the narratives, but also within the various references to *Old Testament* laws, narratives, prophets and characters, particularly in the Gospel of Matthew, who attempts to apply *Old Testament* prophecy to the new religion's messiah at almost every turn.

Notwithstanding the various parallels and throw-backs to the Hebrew *Bible*, the overturning of God's laws by his own son/himself, creates an insurmountable contradiction for Christians. A contradiction that led the early Jewish opponent of Christianity, Trypho, to exhort:

Why do you select and quote whatever you wish from the prophetic writings, but do not refer to those which expressly command the Sabbath to be observed?[280]

They were not only claiming that Jesus was with God from the beginning (see John 1:1), but that he was in fact God/Yahweh as well (John 1:1-13 & 10:30, for example). If this is true, why would an all-knowing God, of whom it is alleged, knows the beginning from the end, (Isaiah 46:9-10) create laws that he claimed were of the utmost importance only to later reverse these fundamental laws? I guess we should all be grateful that he hasn't reversed the law of gravity. Given that "God" has never reversed any of the laws of nature, laws which according to the *Bible* are almost secondary to those regulating the superficialities of his chosen people; it doesn't seem to make sense that he would change his eternally wise mind.[281]

---

[280]Phillip Schaff. Ante-Nicene Fathers. Vol. 1. Justin Martyr. Dialogue with Trypho, Chapter (XLVIII). Christian Classics Ethereal Library. (1867). p. 328.
[281]Verses that indicate Yahweh doesn't change his mind:
For I am the Lord, I change not; therefore ye sons of Jacob are not consumed. Malachi 3:6; *God is not a man, that he should lie; neither the son of man, that he should repent: hath he said, and shall he not do it? or hath he spoken, and shall he not make it good?* Numbers 23:19, for example.

This paradox between the *Old Testament* laws and the *NewTestament*, is a little like the super messiah problem; just as they could not create a super messiah with a physical link to David, they were also unable to create a messiah who was the God from the *Old Testament*, without contradicting his previously established and omnisciently constructed laws.

For many Christian's these inconsistencies still go unnoticed today and if they are noticed, the "Complaints Department" or Christian apologetics, provide creative solutions to these inconsistencies.

The changes made to "God's laws" were essential in repackaging the old Jewish religion into one that could be sold to the whole world, no matter what the race or ethnicity of the target might be. One might be forgiven for assuming that the repackaging of Judaism was done for the purpose of mass-global marketing.

And he said unto them, Go ye into all the world, and preach the gospel to every creature.

~Mark 16:15

FAMILIARITY

We have to consider not only what was different about Christianity, but also what was similar to the other religions in the Greco-Roman world; and so that is the task before us; to see what it was about Christianity that made it attractive to the people, so that people would give up their pagan traditions...[282]

~Bart Ehrman

Familiarity is another vital element of this scam. Neither the new deity or demiurge nor the religion's doctrines can be too different from those already established and understood by the prospective targets. Generally speaking, people will only adopt new beliefs that are not too different from those they have previously known and believed and these new concepts need to be understandable. If the targeted convert is faced with something that is drastically different from anything he/

---

[282]Bart D. Ehrman. From Jesus to Constantine: A History of Early Christianity. The Teaching Company. (2004). Lecture 9: The Early Christian Mission.

she has encountered in the past and he/she cannot understand it, the scam will probably fail. Thus, Jesus and the Christian religion were based upon archetypes, motifs and teachings that were already well established amongst both the pagan and Jewish communities.

With regards to this element of the Christian scam, the renowned Egyptologist, E.A Wallis Budge, in relating the ease in which the conversion of the Egyptians to the Christian faith took place, said:

…the Egyptians who embraced Christianity found that the moral system of the old cult and that of the new religion were so similar, and the promises of resurrection and immortality in each so much alike, that they transferred their allegiance from Osiris to Jesus of Nazareth without difficulty. Moreover, Isis and the child Horus were straightway identified with Mary the Virgin and her Son…[283]

Budge went on to say:

Interesting, however, as such an investigation would be, no attempt has been made in this work to trace out the influence of ancient Egyptian religious beliefs and mythology on Christianity, for such an undertaking would fill a comparatively large volume.[284]

Suffice to say, there were similarities between the old pagan religions and the more modern religion of Christianity. Such similarities can be found in the symbols, practices, motifs, archetypes and teachings which gave the early Christians a head start when it came to converting new members to their cult. People could relate to "Jesus'" teachings and his life's story, because they had already heard similar teachings and stories from their ancestors about previous gods and sons of gods.

In his renowned work, *The Age of Reason,* Thomas Paine observed:

It is, however, not difficult to account for the credit that was given to the story of Jesus Christ being the Son of God. He was born when the heathen mythology had still some fashion and repute in the world, and that mythology had prepared the people for the belief of such a story. Almost all the extraordinary men that lived under the heathen mythology were reputed to be the sons of some of their gods. It was

---

[283]E.A Wallis Budge. The Gods of the Egyptians or Studies in Egyptian Mythology. Vol. 1. Methuen & Co. (1904). Preface, p. xv.
[284]Ibid. p. xvi.

not a new thing at that time to believe a man to have been celestially begotten; the intercourse of gods with women was then a matter of familiar opinion. Their Jupiter, according to their accounts, had co-habited with hundreds; the story therefore had nothing in it either new, wonderful, or obscene; it was conformable to the opinions that then prevailed among the people called Gentiles, or mythologists, and it was those people only that believed it.[285]

This component of the Christian scam also links in with the first element, legitimacy, for it is with this familiarity that an idea is granted the appearance of legitimacy, by way of its age.

This aspect of the Christian scam may also be observed in Justin Martyr's *First Apology,* in which he said:

And if we even affirm that He was born of a virgin, accept this in common with what you accept of Perseus. And in that we say that He made whole the lame, the paralytic, and those born blind, we seem to say what is very similar to the deeds said to have been done by Aesculapius.[286]

The early Christian mythographers did not only seek to pander to the beliefs of their targets, but they also provided for them the same places of worship, places which the Pagans had been worshipping for generations. The strategy of the adoption of pagan places of worship may have been undertaken not only to send the message that the old religions were now out of business, but also to provide a familiar environment for the targets to feel comfortable in, whilst they were being "converted" and practicing their new faith. Some may not be aware that the very site, upon which Saint Peter's Basilica (in Vatican City) stands, was for centuries prior to the Christian era, a temple of the pagan god Mithras.[287]

Another interesting, yet possibly fortuitous fact about Mithras was that the ancient myths surrounding his birth say that he was born

---

[285]Thomas Paine. The Theological Works of Thomas Paine. Age of Reason. Belford Clark and Co. (1882). Part 1, p. 8

[286]The Apostolic Fathers with Justin Martyr and Irenaeus. Justin Martyr. (trans. Philip Schaff.) First Apology. Chapter 21: Analogies of Christ. p. 171.

[287]Payam Nabarz. The Mysteries of Mithras: The Pagan Beliefs that Shaped the Christian World. Inner Traditions (2005). p. 52; see also the Basilica of St. Clement in Rome, which was formerly a temple for the cult of Mithras; John Henry Parker. The Archaeology of Rome. Oxford: James Parker and Co. (1877). p. 1426.

from a rock.[288] This fact, coupled with the location of the Mithraeum beneath the central headquarters of the Christian Religion, may give us cause to pause and ponder the following exhortation:

...upon this rock I will build my church...

~Matthew 16:18

With regards to the strategy of taking over pagan places of worship, Pope Gregory I, writing in the early seventh century, informs us that:

...the temples of the idols in that nation ought not to be destroyed; but let the idols that are in them be destroyed; let water be consecrated and sprinkled in the said temples, let altars be erected, and relics placed there. For if those temples are well built, it is requisite that they be converted from the worship of devils to the service of the true God; that the nation, seeing that their temples are not destroyed, may remove error from their hearts, and knowing and adoring the true God, may the more freely resort to the places to which they have been accustomed...[289]

Not only did early Christians view the ancient pagan temples as being well built, but the mythologies that inspired their initial construction were also deemed to be good building blocks for a new and ambitious religion.

MARKET ENTRY STRATEGY

The next obstacle faced by the early Christians was how to engage an overwhelmed religious marketplace. There was already a vast array of gods, faiths and philosophies floating around the Greco-Roman world, in the first few centuries of the Christian era, which made it difficult for a new religion, such as Christianity, to find a niche. This is where the seeming sociological genius of the Christian proselytizers came into play. Christians converted the poor and ignorant or forgotten classes of the society, which created a domino effect that propelled its mission up into the higher, more strategically important ranks of society.

---

[288]Roger Beck. The Religion of the Mithras Cult in the Roman Empire. Oxford University Press. (2006). p. 192.
[289]Saint Bede. Bede's Ecclesiastical History of England. Christian Classics Ethereal Library (673-735CE). p. 64.

In French philosopher, Nicolas Antoine Boulanger's book, *Christianity Unveiled*, he discussed Christianity's focus on converting the poor, saying:

The conquests of the Christian religion were, in its infancy, generally limited to the vulgar and ignorant. It was embraced only by the most abject amongst the Jews and Pagans. It is over men of this description that the marvellous has the greatest influence. An unfortunate god, the innocent victim of wickedness and cruelty, and an enemy to riches and the great, must have been an object of consolation to the wretched. The austerity, contempt gospel, whose ambition was limited to the government of souls; the equality of rank and property enjoined by their religion, and the mutual succours (assistances) interchanged by its followers; these were objects well calculated to excite the desires of the poor, and multiply Christians.[290]

Once this niche in the market had been acquired, the next step was to expand their share and begin to takeover other areas of the market. Such may have been the forward thinking and long term planning of these scam artists, that they marketed their god-man as both a poor man, born in a humble stable, so as to appeal to their initial targets, who were peasants and lower-class invisibles and also, as a divine ruler, the king of kings, born from the royal bloodline of the House of David, to entice rulers and emperors to adopt this religion once it had percolated up the social-strata. In this way, Christianity appealed to the whole spectrum of the society, from the meek to the majestic, leaving no spirit un-subjugated and no mind unmolested.

SALES PITCH/GIMMICK

Having established that the niche in this overwhelmed religious market were the poor, deprived and untapped masses, the Christian fathers needed to come up with a gimmick or sales pitch, aside from the communistic proprietary benefits, to kick-start their scam. They would need to put something on the table and bait their hooks with

---

[290]Paul Henri Thiry Holbach, Nicolas Antoine Boulanger. Christianity Unveiled. (Trans. W. M. Johnson) (1895). p. 31.

an offer that the poor would see as irresistible. As well as the miraculous healing powers and supernatural abilities promised by the early Christians, which included, but were not limited to; the ability to miraculously heal the sick and be healed, the ability to drink poisons and handle deadly snakes without coming to harm, there was one thing that Christians promised their potential converts that would have appealed to the disenfranchised multitudes of the first few Christian centuries more than anything else, wealth and comfort. Not in this life of course, but in the next. Yes, if you convert today, you may enter the kingdom of heaven and secure for yourself and your children, the life you were never able to have whilst you were here on earth! You will no longer worry about feeding and clothing your children, nor will you want for anything, for in heaven the jewels and thrones of kings will be available to you, the poor.

Imagine from the point of view of the poor, how seductive the verses found within the *New Testament* would have been, that describe heaven as a rich and magical place, a kingdom where the trees yield fruit on a monthly basis, where the walls are lined with precious stones and gold and where you will never go hungry or thirst again.

> *The wall was made of jasper, and the city of pure gold, as pure as glass. The foundations of the city walls were decorated with every kind of precious stone. The first foundation was jasper, the second sapphire, the third agate, the fourth emerald, the fifth onyx, the sixth ruby, the seventh chrysolite, the eighth beryl, the ninth topaz, the tenth turquoise, the eleventh jacinth, and the twelfth amethyst. The twelve gates were twelve pearls, each gate made of a single pearl. The great street of the city was of gold, as pure as transparent glass.*
>
> ~Revelation 21:18-21

> *To the thirsty I will give water without cost from the spring of the water of life.*
>
> ~Revelation 21:6

> *Then the angel showed me the river of the water of life, as clear as crystal, flowing from the throne of God and of the Lamb down the*

middle of the great street of the city. On each side of the river stood the tree of life, bearing twelve crops of fruit, yielding its fruit every month.
~Revelation 22:1-2

How enticing these passages must have been to the meek and gullible masses who were the initial targets of this hope and dream scam. What person, who toiled daily to find scraps to feed themselves and their children, would have been able to resist such an offer? All they had to do was to forgo their mental sovereignty and submit to the perpetuators of this scam and all the gold, fruit, waters of life and precious stones would be theirs for an eternity. No more would they have to suffer and sweat to survive, but they could sit up high in the clouds filling their bellies with the finest foods, whilst watching those who had exploited them here on earth, suffer in the burning fires of hell, for that is where their earthly masters were bound.

M.M Mangasarian, commenting on this aspect of the scam, said:

It is only for this world, however, that Jesus believes in poverty. In the next, his followers will receive a hundred-fold for every sacrifice made. They will be given thrones, crowns, jewelled streets to walk in and mansions of pure gold in which they will drink of the fruit of the vine. Heaven, in the opinion of Jesus, is like a bank which pays ten thousand per cent for every privation suffered in this world. The most pronounced commercialism even is not so extravagant as that. The heaven of Jesus is more materialistic than this world. It is often claimed that this doctrine of Jesus was a great comfort to the unfortunate, who were given something to look forward to. If they were poor, here, they could hope to be rich there. It is true to a great extent that Christianity won its way into the hearts of the masses by flattering them. "Unto the poor the Gospel is preached," said Jesus. And what was its message to them? You have lost this world, but the next will be yours. In my opinion this promise, while it sounds big, is a very empty one. It taught the poor to submit to oppression, instead of inspiring them to rebellion against injustice.[291]

---

[291]M.M Mangasarian. Is the Morality of Jesus Sound? A Lecture Delivered Before the Independent Religious Society. Orchestra Hall. pp. 18–19.

Blessed are the meek: for they shall inherit the earth.

~Matthew 5:5

SALES STRATEGY: SELLING THE SCAM

Once the niche in the market had been identified and the bait set, the Christians would have to formulate a successful sales strategy, to sell their beliefs to the masses. Any successful scam or business requires a well thought out sales strategy. The beauty of selling this religion was that it only required a short initial period of "cold sales" (selling to someone for the first time with no prior rapport) and then it went into an almost automatic "warm sell" (selling to someone you know and trust) mode.

Much like a sales person employed by a corporation, the Christian's job is and has always been, to sell the previously purchased doctrines of faith to new targets. As with any pyramid sales scheme, the faithful customer becomes the dedicated proprietor and sales person. They have been convinced of the products quality through clever rhetoric and hope profiteering and are encouraged to go forth and sell it to others. This advances the aim of the organization and bestows a feeling of importance upon the newly promoted sales person. Christians, like pyramid sellers, feel that it is their obligation and duty to sell this product to the best of their ability to as many people as possible. This means they must present the product in the best possible light to the prospective customer/convert. It is their job to convince and convert the target. This is why preachers and pastors are trained in sophistry, rhetoric or homiletics at seminary schools all over the world. Any faults or blemishes with the product must be hidden from the customer/convert's view and their attention drawn to its selling points. Very few preachers will point out discrepancies and contradictions which exist within the texts from which they preach, or refer to the brutal history of their religion. Instead, they do their utmost to sell the belief system to others.

Do you want to know the truth!? Do you have an empty feeling in your heart? Do you want eternal life? How about a place where all your dreams can come true after you die? Do you want to be rich in the afterlife and never hunger again? Do you want to be special? How about being amongst the chosen of the Almighty God? If all the above sounds appealing, just sign up today for our quick and easy "get saved plan", all for the low price of your mind, soul, complete obedience and of course, your future service.

As mentioned, selling something to someone you don't know is known as "cold selling". Cold selling requires more persuasion and skill on the part of the sales person, than selling to someone where there is an existing relationship. If you are fortunate enough to have avoided working in a job in which you were required to cold sell, which I confess, I have not, then, you will be unable to relate to the experience of smashing one's head against a wall daily, in order to convince a stranger to buy something that they don't need. You may have however, have experienced this tragedy from the converse point of view, if you have ever received a telephone call from a telemarketer or head-hunter.

I remember as a child, my father had two short and reliable scripts he employed to get rid of telemarketers and they worked every time. Whenever a telemarketer would call, he would pass the phone to me and I would repeat one of his two favourite scripts. "We can't talk right now, because we are in the middle of burying my grandma in the backyard" or, "My dad can't talk right now because he is trying to clean the blood off his shovel." Whether it was my convincing delivery or the fact that a sincere sounding child was saying such shocking things, the outcome was always the same. My father would never use these scripts when one of his friends called the house and herein lies the difference between cold and warm sales.

Now, compare the situation of a telemarketer trying to sell you something versus a situation in which a friend or family member recommends you buy something which they have bought. This form of sales is a lot more successful. This is where Christianity's true sales power can be found. Children are sold the doctrines of Christianity by their parents before their rational minds have a chance to defend against such nonsense; the very people in whom these children have the most faith, utilize that trust to sell them their theology's mental product.

Most Christian parents are unwitting participants in this "absolute truth pyramid selling scheme", as they were sold this product when they were also young and view this brainwashing as a positive kind of "teaching." The Christians of the first few centuries appeared to have taken advantage of this knowledge when they set up their initial sales strategy. Of course, it may simply be that they were selling a religion which, as with almost all other belief-systems and as an inherent consequence of such socially transmitted diseases, naturally weaved its way through society without too much deliberate thought being put into this aspect of the scam; but let us stick with the more facetious interpretation for now, as it is more entertaining.

The beauty of this technique is that it not only works within family networks, but also between close friends, weaving its way through the fabric of our social grids, which interlock at points and allow mental viruses like Christianity to spread throughout whole societies and beyond.

CUSTOMER RETENTION STRATEGY

Once a person is sold this product and accepts it as truth, they adopt it as an integral part of their identity. They have been "converted", "changed," "reborn" and have now become a Christian. Therefore, the majority of the work to keep this person faithful and loyal to the religion is done by the mechanisms of their own mind, mechanisms inherent within belief itself. Generally speaking, not too many people will question established beliefs, due to the emotional inhibiters found within the mechanics of belief itself. In this way, the person polices their own mind in order to conform to that, which they have already agreed. However, there are those who possess the higher qualities of mind and question even themselves. These people need a little more encouragement to stay onboard. Once this cult has the person's mind locked within the prison of belief, it tells them that if they do find the keys to go outside, they will suffer. It is too dangerous out there! You will go to hell! You will be lost without us! You need us! Christ died for you, you pitiful little sinful worm, don't you feel guilty!? It is the employment of such fear and guilt which acts as a kind of electric fence dissuading the person's mind from freeing itself.

Take for example the fear inducing speech of Tertullian, who, in the third century, addressed a group of prospective pagan converts and exhorted:

...expect the greatest of all spectacles, the last and eternal judgment of the universe. How shall I admire, how laugh, how rejoice, how exult, when I behold so many proud monarchs, and fancied gods, groaning in the lowest abyss of darkness; so many magistrates, who persecuted the name of the Lord, liquefying in fiercer fires than they ever kindled against Christians; so many sage philosophers blushing in red-hot flames with their deluded scholars; so many celebrated poets trembling before the tribunal, not of Minos, but of Christ; so many tragedians, more tuneful in the expression of their own sufferings; so many dangers ...[292] Or the second century Church father, Justin Martyr's threat:

[Jesus] shall come from the heavens in glory with his angelic host, when he shall raise the bodies of all the men who ever lived. Then he will clothe the worthy in immortality; but the wicked, clothed in eternal sensibility, he will commit to the eternal fire, along with the evil demons...[293]

Also writing in the second century, Theophilus of Antioch, warned:

For the unbelievers and for the contemptuous and for those who do not submit to the truth but assent to iniquity, when they have been involved in adulteries, and fornications, and homosexualities, and avarice, and in lawless idolatries, there will be wrath and indignation, tribulation and anguish; and in the end, such men as these will be detained in everlasting fire.[294]

Finally, we may draw upon the threats made by Saint Fulgentius in the late fifth century, aimed at terrifying mothers, whose children were yet to be baptized in Christ:

---

[292]Joseph Wheless. Forgery in Christianity. Psychiana (1930). p. 278.
[293]Philip Schaff. Ante-Nicene Fathers. Vol. 1: The Apostolic Fathers with Justin Martyr and Irenaeus. The Martyrdom of Polycarp. Christian Ethereal Library. (1885). p. 280.
[294]Philip Schaff. Ante-Nicene Fathers Vol. 2: Fathers of the Second Century: Hermas, Tatian, Athenagoras, Theophilus, and Clement of Alexandria (Entire). Christian Classics Ethereal Library. (1885). p. 143.

Be assured, and doubt not, that not only men who have attained the use of their reason, but also little children who have begun to live in their mothers womb and have there died, or who, having been just born, have passed away from the world without the sacrament of holy baptism, administered in the name of the Father, Son and Holy Ghost, must be punished by the eternal torture of undying fire; for although they have committed no sin by their own will, they have nevertheless drawn with them the condemnation of original sin, by their carnal conception and nativity...[295]

These are just a few of the many examples of how Christians have relied upon the useful device of fear to convert and maintain its flocks.

In addition to the fear and guilt barriers which keep the believer's mind fenced in, one cannot underestimate the powerful and coercive pressures inherent within social bonds as well. As Christians tend to socialize with other Christians, they stand to jeopardize social bonds, connections and their reputation, if they take the courageous step of growing beyond their own egocentric beliefs. For a person to shed their Christian label is often more frightening than the realization of the error of their belief and thus, even if they recognize inconsistencies and begin to internally question their religion's doctrines and its historical truth (have a "crisis of faith"), they will usually keep it to themselves, generally speaking, or else confess it to a trusted peer, who will more often than not, recommend higher doses of faith to fight off reason and rational inquiry. But what Christians call a crisis of faith, I call an epiphany.

So the customer retention strategy works through the person's own emotional inhibiters, such as fear, guilt and peer pressure, in order to stop them from questioning or at least publicly announcing their questions to their fellow believers. If they do leave the faith they have two choices;

To have a millstone tied around their neck and be hurled to the bottom of the sea, metaphorically speaking, or;

Return to the faith and be more adored than before.

As a catch-all, last resort policy for those few not moved by fear or guilt, there is the Christian "return and be more adored than before"

---

[295]Joseph Wheless. Forgery in Christianity. Psychiana (1930). p. 278.

THE BOOK OF HERESY

policy. That's right, if you leave and come back you will be shown so much more love and given so much more attention that you will not want to leave again.

How think ye? if a man have an hundred sheep, and one of them be gone astray, doth he not leave the ninety and nine, and goeth into the mountains, and seeketh that which is gone astray?

And if so be that he find it, verily I say unto you, he rejoiceth more of that sheep, than of the ninety and nine which went not astray.

~Matthew 18:12

THE CUSTOMER RELATIONS DEPARTMENT

The eighth element of the Christian scam was the establishment of their customer relations department or, apologetics. If there is a defect with a product or service, it is the customer relations department's job to console the customer and defend the integrity of the organization. This is where Christian apologetics comes in. If a believer or a non-believer finds a defect within the Christian Scriptures, or with a particular doctrine of Christian faith, it is referred to apologists, who do their best to come up with creative solutions to solve the problem for the customers/believers, thereby maintaining the perceived integrity of their organization/scam. The role of the apologist is to defend the faith and maintain the tenuous illusion of both scriptural and doctrinal reason. If outsiders challenge the Christian scam, the apologist is tasked with refuting the charges, by employing persuasive rhetoric and illogical arguments cloaked in a thin veneer of pseudo-logic. The purpose of this defence is not so much to convert new comers, although this may on occasion be the result, but it is more about protecting and shielding the already converted believers from the open minded critical analysis of their belief. The apologists are the bouncers at the door, forbidding entry to anyone who might bring logic and reason to their suggestible patrons.

I remember having a debate with a member of my wife's church and on almost every point of contention he referred me to various apologists. He begged me to read this apologist/s book and that apologist's book and when I read some of these books, I found that they all had one thing in common. They were all based upon tenuous supposition and extravagant creativity, which were employed to uphold the claim to the exclusive possession of absolute truth. In other words, they were all attempting to prove that their belief was in fact a truth and thus, they were seeking to change its very form. If it is a science or truth system, then it will be called as such, but it is not, it is called a belief system and for good reason. Until such time as it proves its claim in the more trustworthy realm of science, it remains a belief system. Therefore, no matter how hard someone fights to turn their unsubstantiated beliefs into truths, they will inevitably fail, for such is the futile nature of the unsubstantiated belief. When I was fortunate enough to engage in discussions with Christian apologists and ask them questions, for which they had no answer, I was accused of having a "hardened heart" and that there would be no point debating with me, for I was "blinded by the devil."

This brings us to the emergency procedure put in place by Christian apologists when they are faced with logic and criticism they are unable to circumvent with rhetoric and creative speculation. The Devil, aka, the Boogey Man!

Above, I proposed that to retain the membership of the believer, fear was and still is, employed by the Church, because fear, being an instinct which is vital for our survival, is one of the most powerful motivators and inhibitors within the psyche of the human being. Now, if fear is so powerful and we see that it is used to maintain the flocks within Christendom, then such a fact makes Satan the apologists' primary henchman. He has been invaluable when it has come to maintaining a believer's loyalty, who, being manipulated by a fear of the devil and hell, has handed over their psychological sovereignty to the creeds of Christendom. Without Satan, who would play the role of the bad cop, in order that one might confess and remain devoted to a belief, which is founded upon little more than error and fable. The maintenance of membership via direct threat is not Satan's only task however, for he is also charged with blackening the name of anyone who would dare question or undermine the beliefs held by Christians.

Those who seek truth beyond the deceptive realms of egocentric beliefs come into direct conflict with believers who often have little to offer in the way of rational retaliations to reasonable questions. As Thomas Paine once quipped: *To argue with a person who has renounced the use of logic and reason is like administering medicine to the dead.* So, if an apologist cannot adequately shield the fragile ears of his sheep, he will often engage his emergency protocols and make one simple statement, a statement so powerful and convincing to the mind of a believer that they will fall back in line with the rest of the sheep and ignore the intelligent challenge of an "accuser." "Satan confounds the minds of those not saved by our Lord Jesus Christ, for he is a deceiver and an extremely clever one, at that!" Exhortations along this line often have the desired effect, resulting in the believer turning his cheek to the enlightening fruit of free thought.

In Thomas Paine's brilliant and heretical work, *The Age of Reason*, a piece of literature which caused him to be harassed and hunted across entire continents, from England to Europe and eventually to the U.S.A, by various Christian Churches, who all sought to submit his body to the flames of their pious pyres, Paine enunciated the following:

The Christian Mythologists, after having confined Satan in a pit, were obliged to let him out again to bring on the sequel of the fable. He is then introduced into the Garden of Eden, in the shape of a snake or a serpent, and in that shape he enters into familiar conversation with Eve, who is no way surprised to hear a snake talk; and the issue of this tete-a-tete is that he persuades her to eat an apple, and the eating of that apple damns all mankind. After giving Satan this triumph over the whole creation, one would have supposed that the Church Mythologists would have been kind enough to send him back again to the pit; or, if they had not done this, that they would have put a mountain upon him (for they say that their faith can remove a mountain), or have put him under a mountain, as the former mythologists had done, to prevent his getting again among the women and doing more mischief. But instead of this they leave him at large, without even obliging him to give his parole- the secret of which is, that they could not do without him...[296]

---

[296]Philip S. Foner, PhD. The Complete Writings of Thomas Paine. The Citadel Press. (1945). p. 470.

Upon the word of the apologist, the Christian believer takes rest and does not need to worry about reasonable challenges to their faith, as these questions have already been answered, at least to their satisfaction, by the Christian Customer Relations Department.

TIMING

The final element of the Christian scam is timing. Any good scam requires precise timing if it is to take off and succeed. The timing can either be manufactured or opportunistic in nature. For example, if a pharmaceutical company deliberately spread an epidemic for which they alone possessed the cure and upon the outbreak of this epidemic, jumped to sell their cure, this would be a case of manufactured timing, as the company manipulated events to create the timing necessary for their scam to succeed.

However, if for example, a group of people set up a website for the purported purpose of taking donations for victims of a massive earthquake, but were really syphoning the funds into their own accounts, then this would be a case of opportunistic timing, as they did not create the earthquake, but merely took advantage of the situation to further their own economic interests. It is the latter example of timing which appears to reflect the early Christian scam, for it was not only the initial persecutions that helped propel their religion, but the widespread wars, plagues and other natural disasters present in the first few centuries of the Christian era.

Plagues and Promises

In the first few centuries of the Christian era there were many plagues and diseases which spread across the entire Roman Empire. The first big one was known as the "Antonine Plague", which was a smallpox pandemic that killed over ten million people and lasted from around 165 ce to 180 ce.[297] This pandemic was spread by Roman soldiers who fought in Mesopotamia and who, were later transferred to Syria and Italy, which spread the disease throughout the entire Empire.[298] Although there had

---

[297]Daniel T. Reff. Plagues, Priests and Demons. Cambridge University Press. (2005) p.13.
[298]Ibid. pp. 46–47.

been earlier plagues, this plague marked the beginning of many other plagues and diseases, which eventually engulfed Europe and created a tense and fearful environment conducive for the propagation of Christianity.

Seventy years after the devastating Antonine Plague, Europe was hit with a massive measles epidemic (251 ce). This plague was called the "Plague of Cyprian" and decimated huge parts of the Roman Empire leaving large populations impoverished and in fear.[299] Such fear was a primary ingredient, of which the Christian proselytizers took advantage when converting a multitude of newcomers to their ranks.

In between these two plagues there were many other diseases, like malaria, for example, which plagued Europe and resulted in extreme suffering and an atmosphere of desperation, amongst a war torn and broken people.

The plagues and wars which ravaged much of Europe during the first few Christian centuries seemed to work as an innocent, yet crucial co-conspirator, in the devolution of the Roman Empire and at the same time, created fertile soil in which to plant the delusionary seeds of hope embodied within the Christian faith. Like lawyers chasing ambulances, early Christians saw great opportunities in the horrible tragedies that befell the people of Europe, namely, the prospect of taking control of the social power packets of the Eastern Wing of the Roman Empire.

To give you a later example of this opportunism, we turn to Daniel T Reff, an anthropologist and associate Professor in the Department of Comparative Studies at Ohio State University, who, in his book, *Plagues, Priests and Demons,* reported that:

In 591 ce, Pope Gregory sent missionaries to vigorously convert the Lombards, who were dying from the plague. Five years later, the plague prompted Gregory to "at once" organize another mission, this time to Kent, where a small group of monks reportedly baptized ten thousand. According to Bede, "Almost at the same time that this kingdom had accepted the name of Christ, many of the kingdoms of Britain were attacked by a virulent plague.[300]

---

[299]Ibid. p. 49.
[300]Daniel T. Reff. Plagues, Priests and Demons. Cambridge University Press. (2005) pp. 94–95.

The Church seized upon the opportunities occasioned by such calamities and on the back of horrendous suffering, at a time when the victim's prayers to their healing god's like Aesclepius, were failing, they came rushing in to sell their mentally incarcerating belief and swell the ranks of their flocks with promises of healing and salvation.

And these signs shall follow them that believe...they shall lay hands on the sick, and they shall recover.

~Mark 16:16/18

Was it the wide spread illnesses and plagues which caused later Christian scribes to add verses such as these into the Gospels? We do not have the answer to this question, however, what we have been afforded by hindsight, is the knowledge that such promises contained within the Gospels and the writings of the early Church fathers, aided conversions all across Europe.

If your child was dying of a disease, which no doctor could cure, and a man came to your town promising a cure, if only you and your family would promise to convert to his religion, what would you do? Most people would and in the first few Christian centuries did, convert to Christianity as a result of such promises.

Stories of priests and Church fathers with miraculous healing powers, men who could anoint the sick and the dying with some oil and at once bring them back to health, had the desired outcome for the early Church.

Bart Ehrman, in his lecture series entitled, *From Jesus to Constantine: The History of Early Christianity*, reiterates this point, saying:

Why was Christianity succeeding in converting people to its faith? ...The success of Christianity had to involve the way in which it relayed its message to the pagans that it converted....Christianity was able to build upon the one thing that pagans expected out of religion, probably the main thing that pagans expected out of religion, was help for life in the present. Christians, by claiming that their god was the one true god, who had power over nature, who could do the miracles that were needed for life to be sustained; by claiming these things convincingly, they were able to convert people who of course wanted rain for their crops and personal health and healing from sickness and power over evil and victory over enemies, that is what people wanted...[301]

In addition, Daniel T. Reff gives an account of some of these miraculous stories found in early Christian literature. The following is an account of the life of Saint Germanus of Auxere, of whom it was reported had miraculous healing powers:

First the children, then their elders, began to succumb to a swelling in their throats that brought death after an illness of less than three days.

His congregation was being wiped out as if they were being slaughtered by the sword. No human measures brought any relief. . . . Immediately he blessed some oil and, at its touch, the internal swelling went down and a passage was thereby opened for breathing and swallowing. The heavenly remedy effected a cure as rapidly as the onslaught of the disease had brought death. (Constantius of Lyon's Life of Saint Germanus of Auxere, 478ce)[302]

The next account of miraculous healing comes from Jesuit annals written in the New World (the Americas):

Another Indian from the same pueblo was suffering from a constriction of the throat that was causing him a lot of pain. I had some holy water brought and, making two Crosses over the place where it hurt, I told him to trust in the Lord who had died on the Cross. Through this divine remedy (for there are few human remedies in this land) he and other sick people were healed. (Jesuit anua of 1601)[303]

Daniel T. Reff goes on to explain the reason for such stories and the correspondence of Christian conversion with the diseases which helped spread their faith:

The miraculous cure also had theological significance; it was an assertion of the most fundamental of all Christian beliefs, namely that through Christ's sacrifice and his gift of the sacraments, Christians could mobilize God to intercede on their behalf. However, as detailed

---

[301]Bart D. Ehrman. From Jesus to Constantine: A History of Early Christianity. The Teaching Company. (2004). Lecture 10: The Christianization of the Roman Empire.
[302]Daniel T. Reff. Plagues, Priests and Demons. Cambridge University Press. (2005). p. 233.
[303]Ibid.

in Chapters 2 and 3, the popularity of the miraculous cure also reflects the prevalence of epidemic disease, which was coincident with the spread of Christianity in Europe and the New World.[304]

These promises, propagated by the deliberate deception of Christian authors, were not fulfilled and their misleading stories of miracles may have even exacerbated the plagues and diseases of Europe. Such a sad scenario is made sadder by the fact that once the Christians had converted enough people and gained a majority in the affected countries, they rose to great heights of power, which they used to oppress, imprison and murder those who had once trusted these curators of Christ. There is a sizable amount of evidence to suggest that the plagues, wars and various other miseries suffered by those living in Europe in the first few centuries of the Christian era, afforded the timing and provided the opportunity to spread this belief more efficiently than would have otherwise been the case, absent these dramatic circumstances.

CONCLUSION

Having hijacked the Jewish religion's legitimacy and created a slightly unique character and story, we might consider the possibility that they began studying society to find an entry point or niche in the market; once they found this gap, they seized upon the opportunity provided by wide spread tragedy which afforded them with the perfect timing required to kick-start their campaign of cognitive coercion. Having established their entry point through the lower-classes, by promises of health and wealth, they employed a sales strategy that allowed the religion to sell itself automatically amongst these social networks. To keep their flock penned in, they developed a customer retention strategy which was rooted in fear, guilt and existing social pressures. The creation of the customer relations department was founded, we may assume, to serve the religion in times where it lacked the overt power to kill anyone who would dare to speak against it. This aspect of the scam was aimed at pandering to the illogical and

---

[304]Ibid. pp. 234–235.

stubborn nature of people's beliefs through the creative and imaginative use of pseudo-logical defences, which apologized for the illogicalities associated with their faith.

With all these components in place, Christianity eventually took control of the Roman Empire and they became one of the darkest and most destructive forces this earth had possibly ever witnessed. From the torture and slaughter of men, women and children, to the suppression of knowledge both ancient and contemporary, the Christians earned a reputation as being the main characters and proponents of the European Dark Ages.

NO REASON FOR JESUS – A NEW APPROACH TO THE CHRIST MYTH

Most people attempting to disprove the literal existence of Jesus Christ (mythicists) do so by demonstrating the plethora of parallels that exist between the Christ myth and the various earlier myths which were in circulation in and around the regions in which the Gospels were first produced. They point to the twice-born giver of wine and life, Dionysius, the resurrected Osiris, or the Son of God, Horus, who was one with his father, among many other examples. Mythicists also demonstrate, with solid evidence, the philosophical origins of Jesus' alleged revelations, which have been now established to have been first penned by more ancient Egyptians, Greeks and Persians, for example.

The purpose of this small essay is to attack the Christ myth from another angle, one which has been, by and large, overlooked.

THE REASON FOR JESUS CHRIST

Christ came, they say, to redeem mankind from their fallen and sinful state, which, according to Christian and Jewish theology, is the result of the "original sin" described in the "Fall of Man" narrative. The Fall of Man refers to the original disobedience of the first two humans allegedly created by the "one true God" and can be found in Genesis 3. It is an etiological (explanatory) myth, tacked onto the end of the creation myths found in Genesis 1 & 2, which serves to explain the evils of this world. The first three chapters of Genesis are linked to one another, albeit in a rather conflicting manner, so to begin, let us start at the beginning.

Genesis 1:1:

In the beginning, God created heaven and earth. No, wait, that's not right! The original Hebrew reads;

בְּרֵאשִׁית, בָּרָא אֱלֹהִים, חֵמַשָׁה תֵא, חֵמִימָשָׁה תֵא, סֵיהֵלֵא אֶרֶב, תֵישָׁאֵרֶב. (Read Right to Left)

Transliterated it reads;

Bur'ashyth Bur'a 'Elohim 'Ath HShamayim V'ath H'aurtsh

And correctly translated it reads;

In the beginning the gods created the heavens and the earth.

~Genesis 1:1

The gods (plural) *Elohim*, is an epithet applied by the so-called "E" writers of the *Old Testament* and it is a term used to describe multiple gods. Of course, there are defences for this polytheistic term, most of which have been thoroughly debunked by textual, historical and archaeological scholars.

Here are three such scholars:

Bart Ehrman (Biblical Scholar)

There is good evidence that at different periods of history, Jews in fact, believed that there were multiple gods. You can find this even within the Jewish Bible, the Hebrew Bible. Within the Ten Commandments, "you shall have no other gods before me," says the Ten Commandments, well, you need to think about that for a second…no other gods before me? Well, that presupposes that there are other gods, it's just that they're not to be worshipped before the god of Israel.[305]

Rev. Archibald Henry Sayce (Professor of Assyriology at Oxford)

Elohim is a plural noun, and its employment in the Old Testament as a singular has given rise to a large amount of learned discussion, and, it must also be added, of a learned want of common sense. Grammarians have been in the habit of evading the difficulty by describing it as a "pluralis majestatis," "a plural of majesty," or something similar, as if a term in common use which was grammatically a plural could ever have come to be treated as a singular, unless this singular

---

[305]Bart D. Ehrman. From Jesus to Constantine: A History of Early Christianity. The Teaching Company. (2004). Lecture 2: Religious World of Early Christianity.

had once been a plural....We may take it for granted, therefore, that if the Hebrew word Elohim had not once signified the plural "gods," it would never have been given a plural form, and the best proof of this is the fact that in several passages of the Old Testament the word is still used in a plural sense. Indeed there are one or two passages, as for example Gen. 1:26, where the word, although referring to the God of Israel, is yet employed with a plural verb, much to the bewilderment of the Jewish rabbis and the Christian commentators who followed them. It is strange how preconceived theories will cause the best scholars to close their eyes to obvious facts.[306]

Ze'ev Herzog (Professor of Archaeology at Tel Aviv University, Israel)

And it will come as an unpleasant shock to many that the God of Israel, Jehovah, had a female consort and that the early Israelite religion adopted monotheism only in the waning period of the monarchy and not at Mount Sinai.[307]

So, Jesus cannot be the one true son of the one true God, because the Jewish theology, upon which the Christian religion has been theologically established, was originally polytheistic, as has now been thoroughly established by archaeological, biblical, textual and historical scholars.

For sake of brevity, let us move past all of the other flaws and problems with the first pages of Genesis and go straight to the Garden of Eden and the so-called, Fall of Man.

THE FALL OF MAN, IN A NUTSHELL

Once upon a time God created a beautiful Garden, graced with every type of plant, fruit and animal (Genesis 2:8). There was every single kind of tree and plant pleasant to the sight, from tropical plants to temperate flowers, all side by side (Genesis 2:9). The tropical plants were maintained by a complex system of hydroponic lighting and heating,

---

[306]Rev. A. H. Sayce. The "Higher Criticism" and the Verdict of the Monuments. E. & J.E Young and Co. (1894). p. 84.
[307]http://archaeologynews.multiply.com/notes/item/15

whilst the temperate flora and fauna were cooled with outside air conditioners. There were dinosaurs and birds living in harmony and most importantly, there was man, and by man, I mean a male human being, created from dirt, a dirt-man, if you like (Genesis 2:7). Let us ignore the chapter before this one, in which we were previously told that men and women were created and blessed simultaneously (Genesis 1:27), for such nit-picking is only going to sully the narrative.

At first, the all-knowing and wise God thought the animals might make good companions for the man (Genesis 2:18), but soon discovered that this arrangement wasn't working too well, what with all the serious injuries Adam was sustaining due to his numerous advances toward some of the tigresses and lionesses, so the God decided to dose the man with divine drugs and put him in a deep sleep (Genesis 2:21). Whilst the man was sleeping, the God came down and removed one of his ribs (Genesis 2:21), filled a bathtub with ice and placed the unconscious man therein. When the man awoke to find himself in a bathtub full of ice, he was shocked and a little chilly, to say the least. Unaware of his missing rib, he gazed upon one of the most curious creatures he had ever seen and he called her "woman-where's my dinner!?" (Genesis 2:23). This "woman-where's my dinner" was created by the God to act as his slave (Genesis 2:20) and to help him populate the garden with human beings, for whom she would have to cook, clean, have sex and then, after all that, be told to shut up while they all watched TV, or whatever the equivalent was back then. We are unsure of the entirety of their exploits in the garden, but what we do know from the first chapter, is that the gods created them in their own image (Genesis 1:26), stupid, and without knowledge of good and evil (Genesis 2 – 3).

Notwithstanding their incompetent nature, these newborn children were left virtually unsupervised, which we might well forgive the God for, as he was a first time parent with a lot on his plate. Growing bored with the banality of watching these two fools frolic around day in and day out, the God decided to plant a tree in the middle of Garden, a tree that was endowed with magical fruit which bestowed upon the taster, the knowledge of good and evil (Genesis 3:6-7). Possessing an unwavering zeal for ignorance, the God warned these two newborns not to eat this fruit (Genesis 2:17). Naturally this warning was completely lost on these two ignoramuses, as they weren't the products of intelligent design, or at least, were not designed to be intelligent and so, with the help of a walking and talking snake, the most cunning beast of the field (Genesis 3:1), a creature that the God thought it wise to bestow such intelligence upon, they fell prey to temptation and ate the fruit (Genesis 3:6). These two infantile humans had no idea that disobedience was a bad thing, because they hadn't eaten the forbidden fruit yet, and given the negligence of the moronic God who placed these two idiots in a garden inhabited by the most cunning beast of the field, we might excuse their misdeed, but he did not and subsequently cursed every human descendent, even you and me. So there you have it, the Fall of Man, in a nutshell.

But what if this Fall of Man never took place? What if, as crazy as it may sound to some, this whole account is myth? What impact would this have upon Christianity, a religion that today, is intrinsically linked with human history? I shall reveal the consequences of this in just a moment, but first, let's look at a small fragment of the mountain of evidence that exists, which demonstrates beyond any reasonable doubt that both the Garden of Eden and Fall of Man are fictitious myths, myths adopted in large part from the more ancient religion(s) of the Babylonians and Sumerians.

Exhibit A – Contradictions

If the story of creation found in the first few chapters of Genesis is a real and reliable account of the divine creation of the universe, the earth, plants, animals and humans, then we would expect it to be without contradiction. If contradictions did exist, then this would indicate that the account is not the product of an infallible God, but that of fallible human authors.

If we compare the account of creation in chapter one of Genesis to the account of creation in chapter two, we notice irreconcilable differences. For example, in the first chapter of Genesis, the earth emerges from the water and is therefore saturated with moisture (Genesis 1:2, 6-7), whilst in the second chapter, the ground is dry and requires moistening (Genesis 2:5-6). In the first chapter, the order of creation is different to the second, with birds and animals being created before man

(Genesis 1:24-26). Fowls that fly are made from the waters in the first chapter and from the dry ground in the second (Genesis 1:20 vs. Genesis 2:19). In the first chapter man is created in the image of the gods (Genesis 1:26 vs. Genesis 3:22), whilst in the second he is made from dirt (Genesis 2:7) and only becomes like the gods after eating the forbidden fruit (Genesis 3:22). In the first, man is made to be the Lord of the whole earth (Genesis 1:26) and in the second, made only to dress and keep the garden in Eden (Genesis 2:15). Finally, man and woman are created as a set in chapter one (Genesis 1:27) and separately in chapter two, with woman being a kind of afterthought (Genesis 2:21-22).

Notwithstanding the different epithets applied to the gods in chapter one (Elohim – the gods) versus chapter two (Yahweh-Elohim – Lord of the gods), these are the primary conflicts that exist between the two separate etiological myths found in the first chapters of Genesis. This has a devastating impact upon the credibility of the second and third chapters of the book of Genesis, within which we find our Fall of Man narrative, for chapter two is impeached by chapter one and chapter three cannot stand without chapter two, as these two chapters are intrinsically linked.

Exhibit B – The Garden in Eden

If the Garden of Eden was not a real place, then the setting for the Fall of Man is erased from reality and subsequently, the event itself is left as nothing more than a fictitious myth. The present consensus amongst archaeologists, Assyriologists and scholars of comparative mythology, is that the Garden of Eden narrative was adopted by the Hebrews from their Babylonian captors sometime during the exilic or even post-exilic period (from the 6th century~).

The location of the Garden of Eden is described in the book of Genesis as being close to the Tigris and Euphrates rivers, which just happens to be the exact location of ancient Babylonia, or Sumer, the land of the Chaldeans. George Smith's mentor at the British Museum, Assyriologist, Sir Henry Rawlings, noted that there is not only a striking similarity between the Babylonian region of Karduniyas or Ganduniyas with the Garden of Eden mentioned in the *Bible*, but also an agreement with regards to the ancient Chaldean account of the sword guarding the garden which turned in all directions.

So he drove out the man; and he placed at the east of the Garden of Eden Cherubims, and a flaming sword which turned every way, to keep the way of the tree of life.

~Genesis 3:24

Referring to this sword and the Garden of Eden, George Smith stated that:

Eden is a fruitful place, watered by the four rivers, Euphrates, Tigris, Gihon, and Pison, and Ganduniyas is similar in description, watered by the four rivers, Euphrates, Tigris, Surappi, and Ukni. The loss of this portion of the Creation legend is unfortunate, as, however probable it may be that the Hebrew and Babylonian traditions agree about the Garden and Tree of Knowledge, we cannot now prove it. There is a second tree, the Tree of Life, in the Genesis account (3:22), which certainly appears to correspond to the sacred grove of Anu, which a later fragment states was guarded by a sword turning to all the four points of the compass.[308]

The description of this sword guarding the tree of life that turns in all directions represents a peculiar and obscure detail, one which indicates that it was directly copied by the Hebrews.

With regards to the Chaldean origin of the Garden of Eden, George Smith concluded:

There are coincidences in respect to the geography of the region and its name which render the identification very probable; the four rivers in each case, two, the Euphrates and Tigris, certainly identical, the known fertility of the region, its name, sometimes Gan-dunu, so similar to Gan-eden (the Garden of Eden), and other considerations, all tend towards the view that it is the Paradise of Genesis. There are evidences of the belief in the tree of life, which is one of the most common emblems on the seals and larger sculptures, and is even used as an ornament on dresses; a sacred tree is also several times mentioned in these legends, but at present there is no direct connection known between the tree and the Fall, although the gem engravings render it very probable that there was a legend of this kind like the

---

[308]George Smith. The Chaldean Account of Genesis. Scribner, Armstrong and Co. (1876). p. 88.

one in Genesis.[309] As a final note on the parallels between these two mythological gardens, let us look at the name ascribed to the famous garden in the book of Genesis; The Garden of Eden. If we examine the title of this famous garden, we will notice that it is not a garden called Eden, but rather, a Garden in a place called Eden (see Gen. 2:8). But where is this Eden? The Bible gives us references to its location, being somewhere proximate to the Tigress and Euphrates Rivers, as well as two other rivers, the Pishon and the Gihon:

Now a river flowed out of Eden to water the garden; and from there it divided and became four rivers. The name of the first is Pishon; it flows around the whole land of Havilah, where there is gold. The gold of that land is good; the bdellium and the onyx stone are there. The name of the second river is Gihon; it flows around the whole land of Cush. The name of the third river is Tigris; it flows east of Assyria. And the fourth river is the Euphrates.

~Genesis 2:10-14

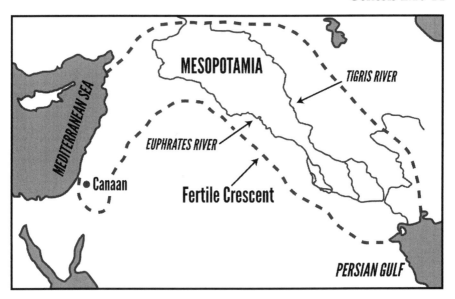

Looking at the map above we see that both the Tigris and Euphrates Rivers are located in Mesopotamia. As for the other two rivers, their locations are not so easy to pin-point, for no extra-biblical

---

[309]Ibid. pp. 305–306.

records exist that describe their true locations, which has led to much speculation over the centuries. No one knows the location of the River Pishon, or the land it supposedly flowed around, Havilah, as both the River Pishon and the land of Havilah are only found within Jewish Biblical and Apocryphal writings. Thus, the location of these two land marks are either fictitious or have been lost to us in the wastes of time. But what of the River Gihon and the land called Cush, the second set of coordinates mentioned in Genesis?

Cush or Kush is mentioned in the *Bible* and has been said by some biblical scholars to describe the land we now call Ethiopia.[310] However, there are no water ways which connect the Tigress and Euphrates rivers in Mesopotamia to any river on the separate continent of Africa, where the land of Ethiopia sits. Thus, it is impossible that the River Gihon, said to surround the entire land of Cush, could be a reference to a river which is both proximate to the Tigress and Euphrates Rivers and at the same time, encircle the country of Ethiopia.

There is another explanation as to the possible location of Kush, one which keeps the mythological Garden of Eden in Mesopotamia, close to the Tigress and Euphrates rivers and at the same time hints at the true origins of the Eden myth.

Kush may have originally been pronounced "Kish". If so, then Kush or Kish, would more than likely find its etymological root in the name of a very famous ancient Sumerian city, Kish, which would make a lot more sense with regards to the description of a place close to both the Tigress and Euphrates Rivers. It is probable that the authors of Genesis chapter two were describing a land somewhere in Mesopotamia, for the reason that we have two definite landmarks which still exist today, those being the aforementioned, Tigress and Euphrates Rivers.

Hebrew and Semitic vowels can be interchangeable, as they do not appear in written texts. For example, the name David, appears in the Hebrew Texts, transliterated as DVD, and Yahweh as YHWH, etc. Thus, the 'U' in Kush, may have originally been an 'I,' or 'Y' making it Kish/Kysh, the name of our well known Mesopotamian city in

---

[310]Zenaide A. Ragozin. The Story of Chaldea: From the Earliest Times to the Rise of Assyria. The Knickerbocker Press. (1886). p. 189.

Sumer. Further, in support of this proposition we may observe that the word Kush, as it is popularly transliterated into English, is rendered, "KVSH", however the "V" or Hebrew character, "Vav", when substituting a vowel as is the case here, acts as the "U" sound, and is interchangeable with the "Yod", or "Y",'which, if substituted, would render the transliteration, KYSH, pronounced Kish. For evidence of these interchangeable characters, we may cite the work done by two nineteenth century professors of theology and Assyriology, F. Delitzsch and C.F. Keil, who in discussing the interchangeable nature of these two Hebrew characters, demonstrated that the Hebrew word "Havah", meaning "Eve", was interchangeable with Hebrew term 'Hayah', which also means Eve, demonstrating that the Vav and Yod characters were interchangeable.[311]

This makes more sense, especially when we discover that the person called Kush or Kish, in chapter ten in the book of Genesis, who was the grandson of Noah, was also the father of both Havilah (Gen. 10:7), the very name of the land described as being encircled by the Pishon River in Genesis chapter two, and Nimrod, "the mighty one" (Gen. 10:8-10), of whom it was said:

The first centres of his (Nimrod's) kingdom were Babylon, Uruk, Akkad and Kalneh, in Shinar (Sumer). From that land he went to Assyria, where he built Nineveh, Rehoboth-Ir, Calah and Resen, which is between Nineveh and Calah—which is the great city.

~Genesis 10:10-12

Kush/Kish, is the father of Nimrod, who, according to the biblical legend, was the first King of Mesopotamia, which means that his father, Kish, was the Patriarch of Mesopotamia, possibly referring to an ancient Sumerian character, from whom the name of the real city of Kish was derived. It may have been that the author(s) of Genesis was attempting to assert that the original patriarch of Mesopotamia, which is often called, the "cradle of civilization" was Ham, the father of Kish and grandfather of Nimrod, the first Mesopotamian King. This may also be supported by the fact that Ham is also described as the father

---

[311]C.F. Keil & F. Delitzsch. Biblical Commentary on the *Old Testament*: Vol. 1. T&T Clark. (1885). p. 106.

or original patriarch of the land of Canaan (see Gen. 9:18), a land whose people were the political, social, philosophical, theological and possibly even the biological descendants of not only the Egyptians, but of the Mesopotamians as well, the two largest, most influential and ancient empires in that region.

Based on the evidence above and the fact that the Tigress and Euphrates Rivers are located in Mesopotamia, we may assert with some confidence, that the author(s) of the second chapter of Genesis, or at least the relevant parts thereof, alleged that the Garden in Eden was located somewhere in ancient Sumer, or Babylonia.

This brings us back to the question at hand; where was Eden? If, as we have seen, the authors of the book of Genesis were trying to establish that Eden was in Mesopotamia, then we must investigate the issue upon Mesopotamian terms, so to speak. We can do so by asking one simple and logical question. From a mythological point of view, what would have existed in that area called Eden, before God planted a garden there? Prior to the planting of the garden in Eden, the area would have been nothing more than a desolate land, an open country, an uncultivated steppe or plain, which is exactly what the word "Eden", or "Edin" means in the ancient Sumerian language.[312]

The *Harper Collins Bible Dictionary* concurs with both the scholars at Oxford and the compilers of the Jewish Encyclopaedia, saying:

Although traditionally identified with the Hebrew word meaning "luxury, pleasure, delight" {eden), Eden is more probably to be related to a Sumerian word meaning "plain, steppe" or the like [edin).[313]

Reading through the ancient Sumerian tales contained on the tablets discovered in Mesopotamia and deciphered by various Assyriologists at Oxford University, it becomes apparent that the origins of the Eden myth are to be found within the ancient Sumerian

---

[312]The Electronic Text Corpus of Sumerian Literature. Faculty of Oriental Studies. Oxford University. (2006); Glossary (E); http://etcsl.orinst.ox.ac.uk/edition2/etcsl-lemma.php?sortbylemma=lemma&letter=e; Fred Skolnik & Michael Berenbaum. *Encyclopaedia Judaica* 2nd Ed. Vol. 7. Thompson Gale. (2007). p. 388.

[313]Paul. J. Achtemeier. Harper-Collins *Bible* Dictionary Revised Edition. Harper Collins, (1989). p. 267.

mythology, which date back to somewhere around the middle of the fourth millennium bce.[314]

He (The god Enki) raised a holy crown over Eden. He fastened a lapis-lazuli beard to the high Eden, and made it wear a lapis-lazuli headdress. He made this good place perfect with greenery in abundance. He multiplied the animals of the high Eden to an appropriate degree, he multiplied the ibex and wild goats of the pastures, and made them copulate. Enki placed in charge of them the hero who is the crown of the high Eden, who is the king of Eden, the great lion of the high Eden, the muscular, the hefty, the burly strength of Enlil – Šakkan, the king of the hills.[315]

♦

Its vineyard "Black garden in Eden", planted near the house, is a mountain oozing wine and grows in a place with fearsomeness and radiance.[316]

♦

Ninegala, the holy….With her, Eden is filled with a glorious garden.[317]

So we see that not only were primary narrative components copied from the earlier polytheistic religions of the Babylonians and Sumerians, but that the very word itself, Eden, was also adopted as the title of this mythical land.

NO REASON FOR JESUS

Let us now travel full circle and re-examine the alleged reason for Jesus' earthly advent, based on the information we have canvassed and in light of his inherent ties to these now debunked myths.

From its earliest writer, Paul, Christian theology has linked the reason for Jesus' earthly incarnation with the Fall of Man. From Paul's Epistle to the Romans we read:

---

[314]Leonard W. King. A History of Sumer and Akkad. Chatto and Windus. (1923). p. 65.
[315]The Electronic Text Corpus of Sumerian Literature. Faculty of Oriental Studies. Oxford University. (2006) http://etcsl.orinst.ox.ac.uk/edition2/etcslgloss.php?lookup=c113.349&charenc=gcirc
[316]Ibid. http://etcsl.orinst.ox.ac.uk/edition2/etcslgloss.php?lookup=c217.779&charenc=gcirc
[317]Ibid. http://etcsl.orinst.ox.ac.uk/edition2/etcslgloss.php?lookup=c40816.C.11&charenc=gcirc

But the gift is not like the trespass. For if the many died by the trespass of the one man (Adam), how much more did God's grace and the gift that came by the grace of the one man, Jesus Christ, overflow to the many! Again, the gift of God is not like the result of the one man's sin: The judgment followed one sin and brought condemnation, but the gift followed many trespasses and brought justification.

~Romans 5:15-16

Following this, Christian commentators, theologians and preachers throughout the centuries have propagated this theological position. It is the central axis upon which rests, the Christ myth.

In the late second century, Ireneaus linked not only Christ with Adam, but Eve with Mary, saying:

As Eve was seduced by the word of an angel and so fled from God after disobeying his word, Mary in her turn was given the good news by the word of an angel, and bore God in obedience to his word. As Eve was seduced into disobedience to God, so Mary was persuaded into obedience to God; thus the Virgin Mary became the advocate of the virgin Eve. Christ gathered all things into one, by gathering them into himself. He declared war against our enemy, crushed him who at the beginning had taken us captive in Adam, and trampled on his head, in accordance with God's words to the serpent in Genesis: I will put enmity between you and the woman, and between your seed and her seed; he shall lie in wait for your head, and you shall lie in wait for his heel.[318]

Irenaus was describing the fallascious "proto-evanglium", which attempts to esoterically link Genesis 3:15 with Jesus' advent, making prophecy out of nothing and misinterpreting Hebrew Scripture to turn a mythical snake into Satan, for which there is absolutely no theological justification.[319] Regardless, it does demonstrate how Christian theology is and has always been, rooted in the first few chapters of Genesis, without which, Jesus' purpose is rendered redundant and obselete. For if there was no fall, then there was never a need for redemption and subsequently, no need for a redeemer.

---

[318]Irenaeus. Against the Heresies. Book 2.
[319]Paul. J. Achtemeier. Harper-Collins *Bible* Dictionary Revised Edition. Harper Collins, (1989). p. 975.

CONCLUSION

Christianity, at least as it has come down to us today, is hinged upon its alleged historicity, both with regards to the Christ myth itself and its theological basis; the Fall of Man. Subtract its historical foundations and you obliterate its legitimacy. To this end, many mythicists have focussed their attention on demonstrating the lack of genuine historical testimony for both the human Jesus and the Jesus Christ of the Gospels; they have roundly established the adopted nature of the mythos that forms the very substance of the Christ myth and in so doing, have aided efforts to erradicate the collective coma of Christianity from contemperory society. But if the very reason for Jesus Christ's advent comes from the first few chapters of Genesis, which most would agree it does, then attacking the reason for Jesus is in my opinoin, the next frontier in mythicism.

If, as we have seen, the first chapter of creation impeaches the second, then key narrative features central to both the second and the third chapters (the creation of the tree of knowledge, the creation of Eve after Adam and the Fall itself) are rendered unreliable accounts of the past. This being the case, the credibility of the Fall of Man narrative is left as an unhistorical event, thereby cutting away at the very root of the allegedely historical Christ. Finally, in discovering that the Garden of Eden, the very setting of the Fall narative, was an adopted myth, we have successful undermined the existence of original sin, the fall and most importantly from the mythicist's point of view, the reason and subsequent existence of Christ himself.

FORGING THE HISTORICAL JESUS - THE JOSEPHUS FORGERIES

The primary secular authority whom Christians use as testimony with regards to the historicity of Jesus is, Flavius Josephus. Josephus was an elite Jew, born in Jerusalem a few years after Jesus' alleged crucifixion. He served as a Jewish military leader in Galilee, the very place alleged to have been home to Jesus. Josephus' father Matthais was of Jewish royalty and lived during the alleged life of Jesus in

Jerusalem, the very town in which many of Jesus' main events were supposed to have transpired. It is curious that Josephus' father never mentioned a miracle worker by the name of Jesus of Nazareth. Josephus was a Jewish historian who penned volumous works on Jewish history. Two of his most renowned works were; *Antiquities of the Jews* and *The Jewish Wars*. From these works it is plain to see that, despite his desire for self-preservation, he was a very proud and devout Jew. Before we begin to examine the two alleged references to Jesus which appear in his work entitled *Antiquity of the Jews* (90 ce – 94 ce), it is both relevant and necessary to note that he made mention within that work, of approximately twenty different people, all with the name of Jesus, and that some of these characters included; Jesus the son of Sapphias, Jesus the son of Gamala, Jesus the son of Phabet, Jesus the son of Sie, Jesus the son of Fabus, Jesus the son of Thias, Jesus the son of Gamaliel, Jesus the son of Damneus, Jesus the brother of Onias, Jesus the brother of John, Jesus the Galilean (who was a great military commander) and many others.

JOSEPHUS - THE JEW

Given that we know Josephus remained a devout Jew for the entire span of his life, we should take a quick look at the Jewish position regarding the coming messiah. Judaism, whether pharisaic or orthodox, rejects the notion that Jesus was a messiah/Christ. A prominent Jewish Website enunciates the Jewish belief regarding the future arrival of the messiah, saying:

Belief in the eventual coming of the 'moshiach' (messiah)... is part of the minimum requirements of Jewish belief. In the 'Shemoneh Esrei' prayer, recited three times daily, we pray for all of the elements of the coming of the moshiach: gathering of the exiles; restoration of the religious courts of justice; an end of wickedness, sin, and heresy; reward to the righteous; rebuilding of Jerusalem; restoration of the line of King David; and restoration of Temple service.[320]

---

[320]"Moshiach: The Messiah." The Messianic Idea in Judaism. Judaism 101. Sept. 10, 2009. <http://www.jewfaq.org/moshiach.htm

Furthermore, Judaism has certain scriptural requirements for the coming messiah which have yet to be fulfilled. What is the Messiah supposed to accomplish? The *Bible* says that he will:

A. Build the Third Temple (Ezekiel 37:26-28).

B. Gather all Jews back to the Land of Israel (Isaiah 43:5-6).

C. Usher in an era of world peace, and end all hatred, oppression, suffering and disease. As it says; *"Nation shall not lift up sword against nation, neither shall man learn war anymore."* (Isaiah 2:4)

D. Spread universal knowledge of the God of Israel, which will unite humanity as one*: "God will be King over all the world on that day, God will be One and His Name will be One"* (Zechariah 14:9).

If an individual fails to fulfil even one of these conditions, then he cannot be regarded as the Messiah. Because no one has ever fulfilled the *Bible*'s description of this fictitious future King, Jews still await the coming of the Messiah, even though I do concede that on one occasion, Josephus referred to the Roman Emperor Vespasian as the messiah.[321]

Now that we have established the Jewish position, with regards to Jesus as the Messiah, let's have a look at the two alleged references to Jesus in *Antiquity of the Jews,* beginning with the most famous, found within what is known as, the *Testamonium Flavium.*

The Testamonium Flavium

Now there was about this time Jesus, a wise man, if it be lawful to call him a man; for he was a doer of wonderful works, a teacher of such men as receive the truth with pleasure. He drew over to him both many of the Jews and many of the Gentiles. He was [the] Christ (Messiah). And when Pilate, at the suggestion of the principal men amongst us, had condemned him to the cross, those that loved him at the first did not forsake him; for he appeared to them alive again the third day; as the divine prophets had foretold these and ten thousand other wonderful things concerning him. And the tribe of Christians, so named from him, are not extinct at this day.[322]

Problems with the Above Reference to Christ.

Arguments from Silence.

---

[321]Flavius Josephus, Jewish Wars. 6.312-313
[322]Josephus Antiquities of the Jews, VIII, iii, 3

The second century Church father and apologist, Justin Martyr (*circa* 100 – 165 ce), who had pored over Josephus's works, made no mention of the *Testamonium Flavium*. In an address to the Greeks, Justin referred to Josephus' *Antiquities of the Jews* to support his argument with regards to the antiquity of Moses, yet we are expected to believe that he somehow missed the passage which provides non-Christian evidence for his Saviour. Further, he wrote a Treatise against Trypho, a Jew who was critical of this new religion called Christianity and yet he failed to mention Josephus' confession regarding the messiah-ship of Jesus. If the passage in Josephus' work had of existed at this time, Justin would have no doubt, used it against his Jewish opponent Trypho. Here is one of your own, a fellow Jew who has admitted that Jesus was the Messiah! Other early church fathers who failed to mention the reference to Christ in the *Testamonium Flavium* included: Theophilus Bishop of Antioch (180 ce), Irenaeus (120/140 – 200/203 ce), Clement of Alexandria (150–211/215 ce), Origen (185 – 254 ce), who stated that Josephus did not believe Jesus was "the Christ." (*Contra Celsum, Book 1. Chapter XLVII*)[323], Hippolytus (170 – 235 ce), Minucius Felix (250 ce), Anatolius (230~270/280 C.E), Saint John Chrysostom (347 – 407 C.E) and Photius (820 – 891 ce).

So how is it that early church fathers, familiar with the very work in which Josephus allegedly referred to Jesus as the Christ, made no mention of it? This is a serious problem for Christian apologists.

Arguments from Compromised Transmission.

In fact, the very first mention of it comes from Eusebius in the fourth century, who was a motivated church father and known forger. In Joseph Wheless' work, *Forgery in Christianity*, he relays the following regarding letters to and from Jesus that were forged by Eusebius himself and spread amongst the gullible believers of the day:

...the Catholic Encyclopaedia, which again describes them, and proves that they 'Were forged by their great Bishop of Caesaria (Eusebius): "The historian Eusebius records [HE. I, xii], a legend which he himself

---

[323]"For in the 18th book of his Antiquities of the Jews, Josephus bears witness to John as having been a Baptist, and as promising purification to those who underwent the rite. Now this writer, although not believing in Jesus as the Christ…"

THE GOSPEL OF ATHEISM AND FREETHOUGHT

firmly believes concerning a correspondence that took place between Our Lord and the local potentate (Abgar) at Edessa. Three documents relate to this correspondence: (1) the Letter of Abgar to Our Lord; (2) Our Lord's answer; (3) a picture of Our Lord, painted from life.[324]

He goes on to say:

But it is not true, as we have seen already confessed, that Eusebius innocently believed that these forgeries were genuine- for they were all shamelessly forged by Eusebius himself: "who vouches that he himself translated it from the Syriac documents in the archives of Edessa. [325]

The *Bible* scholar, Professor Bart Ehrman, reports on Eusebius' dishonest character in the following words:

Eusebius stands at the end of this process. It was his rewriting of history that made all later historians think that his group (Orthodox Christianity) had always been the majority opinion. But it did not really happen that way.[326]

Eusebius appears to have been a zealous fraud who, given the chance to advance his own religious beliefs, would seize upon such an opportunity with the tenacity of a starving gutter rat.

Literary Problems

Christ Interrupts the Narrative

In the passage before Josephus seems to be drooling over Christ, with all the adoration of an adoring Christian, he is reporting on the tragic events which befell the Jews when Pontius Pilate violently suppressed a Jewish rebellion. This dramatic event was narrated by Josephus in a very dark and tragic tone. This paragraph is then followed by the cheerful reference to the wonderful works of Christ, following which, the next paragraph begins; *About the same time also another sad calamity put the Jews into disorder*. The manipulated order of this text makes it seem like Josephus was saying that the wonderful advent of the Jewish Messiah was a sad calamity, when his use of words in describing Jesus were anything but sad. Minus the Christ paragraph, the "sad calamity" becomes the

---

[324]Joseph Wheless. Forgery in Christianity. Psychiana. (1930). p. 109.
[325]Ibid.
[326]Bart D. Ehrman. Jesus Interrupted. HarperCollins. (2009). p. 214.

violent suppression of the Jews by Pontius Pilate which makes a lot more sense. So to sum up the order of his narrative:

1. The Jews are violently suppressed by Pilate.
2. Jesus' amazing character and messiah-ship and his loyal and wise followers.
3. Another Sad calamity put the Jews in disorder.

If we subtract the second "Christ passage", the narrative not only flows continuously but also makes a lot more sense. Remsburg summed up the opinion of the Christian community, saying:

Bishop Warburton declares it to be a forgery: "If a Jew owned the truth of Christianity, he must needs embrace it. We, therefore, certainly conclude that the paragraph where Josephus, who was as much a Jew as the religion of Moses could make him, is made to acknowledge Jesus as the Christ, in terms as strong as words could do it, is a rank forgery, and a very stupid one, too" (Quoted by Lardner, Works, Vol. I, chap. iv). [327]

The Rev. Dr. Giles, of the Established Church of England, says:

Those who are best acquainted with the character of Josephus, and the style of his writings, have no hesitation in condemning this passage as a forgery (Christian Records, p. 30). [328]

The Rev. S. Baring-Gould, in his Lost and Hostile Gospels, says:

This passage is first quoted by Eusebius (fl . A.D. 315) in two places (Hist. Eccl., lib. i, c. xi; Demonst. Evang., lib. iii); but it was unknown to Justin Martyr (fl . A.D. 140), Clement of Alexandria (fl . A.D. 192), Tertullian (fl . A.D. 193), and Origen (fl . A.D. 230). Such a testimony would certainly have been produced by Justin in his apology or in his controversy with Trypho the Jew, had it existed in the copies of Josephus at his time. The silence of Origen is still more significant. Celsus, in his book against Christianity, introduces a Jew. Origen attacks the argument of Celsus and his Jew. He could not have failed to quote the

---

[327] John E Remsburg. The Christ: A Critical Review and Analysis of the Evidences of His Existence. The Truth Seeker Company. (1909) pp. 32–35.
[328] Ibid.

words of Josephus, whose writings he knew, had the passage existed in the genuine text. He, indeed, distinctly affirms that Josephus did not believe in Christ (Contr. Cels. i).[329]

Dr. Chalmers ignores it, and admits that Josephus is silent regarding Christ. He says:

The entire silence of Josephus upon the subject of Christianity, though he wrote after the destruction of Jerusalem, and gives us the history of that period, in which Christ and his Apostles lived, is certainly a very striking circumstance. (Kneeland's Review, p. 169)[330]

The following, from Dr. Farrar's pen, is to be found in the Encyclopaedia Britannica:

That Josephus wrote the whole passage as it now stands no sane critic can believe.[331]

Eusebian Style and Language

It has been noted by a number of textual critics, that the above passage does not fit the style or grammar used in any of Josephus' other works. The *Testamonium Flavium* uses the Greek term *"poietes"* with the meaning "doer" (as part of the phrase *doer of wonderful works*), but elsewhere, Josephus only uses the term *"poietes"* to mean "poet", while it is Eusebius who uses *"poietes"* to mean "doer", as in *doer of wonderful works*, when referring to Jesus in some of his other works.[332]

Further, in the *Testamonium Flavium,* Josephus refers to the Christians as a tribe. Elsewhere however, he only uses the word tribe to describe an ethnic, rather than a religious group. Again we find that Eusebius, the one responsible for first producing this Testamonium, was the one who used the word tribe to describe Christians as a group.[333] Are we to regard the following three facts as mere coincidence?

---

[329]Ibid.

[330]Ibid.

[331]Ibid.

[332]Eusebius, Demonstration of the Gospels, 3:5; Eusebius, History of the Church, 1:2:23; Ken Olson, Eusebian Fabrication of the Testimonium (2001).

[333]Flavius Josephus. Complete Works of Josephus. Vol. 3: Antiquities of the Jews. Bigelow Brown and Co. Inc. Ant. Book Pg. 12/Ant, Book 18, Pg.94/Ant. Book 20, p. 274/Jewish Wars; Book 1, p. 510/Book 2, p. 610; Phillip Schaff . Eusebius Pamphilius: The Life of Constantine with Orations by Constantine and Eusebius. Grand Rapids: Christian Ethereal Library. (1890). p. 651.

1. Eusebius is the first recorded person to publish the *Testamonium Flavium*
2. He uses the words, *"poietes"* and "tribe" in a manner which matches the misapplication of Josephus' common usage of those very terms, and;
3. Eusebius has been charged with forging letters to and from Jesus to a King of Syria and accused by other biblical scholars and historians, for rewriting and altering historical record to support his beliefs.

A Further Stylistic Implication - Brevity

Finally, Josephus was in the habit of writing volumous works, in which he would go into lengthy discourses about everyone from High priests to commoners. If Josephus did believe Jesus to be the Jewish Messiah, as the interpolation suggests, he would have given more ink to him than to some of the robbers and commoners he devoted pages to. Take for example, his commentary on Judas, the son of Ezekias, who was a robber. This comparatively insignificant character was given fifteen lines in Book Seventeen of his *Antiquities of the Jews*.[334] A further example is Simon the slave of Herod who in the same book had thirty-six lines written about him.[335] Josephus' Messiah only receives twelve short sentences. Coupled with the other tell-tale signs of forgery, the brevity of this reference to Josephus' "beloved" and "miraculous" messiah, also indicates interpolation of the crudest nature. To further illustrate the unsophisticated nature of this Christian interpolation, I will provide the reader with a similar example of my own creation. The following interpolation will be inserted into a speech made by Malcolm X.

Malcolm X: Black Man's History Speech (December, 1962)

Now all of a sudden our people of all complexions are not apologizing for being black but bragging about being black. So there's a new thinking all over America among the so-called Negroes. And the one who is actually the author of this new thinking is The Honourable

---

[334]Flavius Josephus. Complete Works of Josephus. Vol. 3: Antiquities of the Jews. Bigelow Brown and Co. Inc. pp. 60–61.
[335]Ibid. pp. 62–63.

Elijah Muhammad. It is what he is teaching that is making our people, for the first time, proud to be black, and what's most important of all, **for the first time the French people, who are becoming more and more obsessed by negroid ideas, represent a threatening menace to the existence of the white race in Europe because they are bound up with the Jewish campaign for world-domination by infecting the white race with the blood of an inferior stock.** It makes our people want to know more about black, want to know why black is good, or what there is about black that is good.[336]

After reading this example, one may have observed a number of peculiarities. All of a sudden Malcolm changes the topic from what is happening in America to what is happening in France. He appears to be using a different style of language ("Negroes" vs. "Negroid"), his beliefs are severely compromised by the interpolation from Hitler's *Mein Kampf* and if the interpolated passage is subtracted, the speech makes more sense and flows continuously.

THE SECOND REFERENCE TO JESUS IN JOSEPHUS' ANTIQUITIES

The second reference Josephus allegedly made to Jesus Christ also appears in *Antiquities of the Jews*, book 20, chapter 9:

Festus was now dead, and Albinus (the Roman procurator of Judea) was but upon the road; so he (The high priest Ananus) assembled the Sanhedrin of judges, and brought before them the brother of Jesus, (who was called Christ), whose name was James, and some others; and when he had formed an accusation against them as breakers of the law, he delivered them to be stoned. [337]

As previously mentioned, Josephus referred to around twenty different people named Jesus and upon a further examination of the context of this passage, we see that the Jesus in question, may have in fact been, Jesus the son of Damneus. The passage quoted above describes the illegal execution of a number of people by the high priest Ananus, one of whom

---

[336]http://www.malcolm-x.org/speeches/spc_12__62.htm;   Adolf   Hitler.   Mein Kampf. Chapter 2.
[337]Flavius Josephus. Antiquities of the Jews. Book 20 Chapter 9.

was a person named James, who had a brother called Jesus. The problem with this execution was that it angered many of the locals, who appealed to the Roman procurator, pointing to the fact that Ananus had not sought the approval of his Roman overseer Albinius, thus rendering the execution illegal. To this, Albinius agreed and sent Ananus an angry letter, placing pressure on the ruling Enthrach of Judea, Agrippa, to oust Ananus from the post of high priest. Agrippa did this and in his stead made Jesus the son of Damneus, the new high priest.[338]

If we understand that the person who ended up ascending to the throne of high priest following the illegal execution of "James the brother of Jesus," was Jesus the son of Damneus, then it makes sense that James' death would have been mitigated by the Enthrarch, in a bid to quell the subsequent unrest in Judea, who, by placing his brother Jesus, the son of Damneus, in the position of high priest, not only brought peace back to his land, but at the same time, won a political point with his Roman overlord, Albinius. Upon this logic, we may argue that the Jesus "who was called Christ" phrase may have originally read, Jesus "the son of Damneus," and that this was changed by someone, possibly even by the first ever Christian to quote this passage, the third century Church father, Origen, although such an allegation against Origen is merely speculative and circumstantial at this stage. Origen quoted this passage from Josephus' *Antiquities of the Jews* twice in his works, once in his commentary on the Gospel of Matthew in which he said:

And the wonderful thing is, that, though he (Josephus) did not accept Jesus as the Christ, he yet gave testimony that the righteousness of James was so great; and he says that the people thought that they had suffered these things (fall of Jerusalem approx. 70 CE) because of James. [339]

And secondly, in his apologetic treatise against the Pagan Celsus, in which he said:

Now this writer (Josephus), although not believing in Jesus as the Christ, in seeking after the cause of the fall of Jerusalem and the destruction of the temple, whereas he ought to have said that the conspiracy against Jesus was the cause of these calamities befalling the

---

[338]Ibid.
[339]Philip Schaff . Ante-Nicene Fathers Vol. 9: Origen-Commentary on the Gospel of Matthew. Grand Rapids,MI: Christian Classics Ethereal Library. (1885). pp. 820–821.

people, since they put to death Christ, who was a prophet, says nevertheless—being, although against his will, not far from the truth—that these disasters happened to the Jews as a punishment for the death of James the Just, who was a brother of Jesus (called Christ),—the Jews having put him to death, though he was a man most distinguished for his justice. [340]

In both of the above cited quotes from Origen, we see that whatever copy of Josephus' Antiquities he was reading from, he was given the distinct impression that Josephus neither accepted, nor believed that Jesus was the Christ/Messiah, contrary to the alleged account found within the Testamonium Flavium, in which the forger made Josephus say; "he was the Christ!" Further, Origen equates the James of this passage in Josephus' Antiquities, with the James from the Christian Scriptures, which seems to me to be a little problematic, logically speaking. If the James spoken of by Josephus was the Christian James identified throughout the Christian Scriptures, then the Jewish rabble would not have been likely to protest his execution, nor even care that he was executed. Such a person would have been branded a heretic by the masses for worshiping, or even being associated with Jesus, an act, the *New Testament* and early Christian writings tell us, was something the majority of Jews saw as offensive. Yet according to Josephus' account, so many Jews protested James' execution, that both the Roman procurator and the Enthrarch of Judea were forced to intervene, resulting in the deposing of the high priest Ananus and the insertion of Jesus the son of Damneus in his place.

It seems to me that the initial reading of Jesus "who was called Christ" would have been likely to have been, Jesus "the son of Damneus" as it makes a lot more sense in the context of the story. All a Christian forger would have had to do was substitute "the son of Damneus" for the phrase; "who was called Christ", and they would succeed in convincing future apologists and the Christian laity alike, that this was in

---

[340]Philip Schaff. Ante-Nicene Fathers. Vol. 4: Fathers of the Third Century: Tertullian, Part Fourth; Minucius Felix; Commodian; Origen, Parts First and Second; Origen-Contra Celsum. Christian Classics Ethereal Library. (1885). p. 714.

fact, an historical reference to their god-man. If we look at the situation from an investigative point of view, the Christians had the means to manipulate this passage, in that they controlled and manipulated the texts of various ancient authors on several other occasions, including the *Testamonium Flavium,* in this very same document mentioned above. They had motive, for there is no greater witness to their historical messiah than this renowned first century Jewish historian and they had opportunity, in that they possessed and controlled this ancient historian's works for centuries, with the first mention of the *Testamonium Flavium* coming from the pen of the fourth century church father Eusebius and the first mention of the second reference to Jesus "called Christ" coming from the third century Church father, Origen. Means, motive, opportunity and a proven penchant for altering and even destroying the works of ancient authors whose versions of history did not conform to their belief system, is enough evidence to at least consider that the references to Jesus within the works of Josephus, were forgeries.

TIMING

The final problem in using either of these possibly spurious references to Jesus Christ as historical evidence is their timing. Josephus' Antiquities of the Jews' was written at the end of the first century some sixty years after the alleged crucifixion of Jesus Christ and as such, even if there had been no forgery, this account would fail the historical test of contemporanity.

CONCLUSION

If these two fleeting references to Jesus are subtracted from the historical record, which, we may rightly contend they should be, then Christians are left with no valid historical source for the earthly existence of their god-man. Before you jump up and say, what about the Gospels, I would urge you to provide a satisfactory defence in the face of the fact that such "historical" testimony is written beyond the scope of contemporanity, is affected by bias, plagued with inconsistencies and riddled with forgeries; then, and only then, may you produce these religious manuscripts as historical evidence for a mundane human Jesus, and nothing more.

REASON'S WAR ON CHRISTMAS - IS JESUS THE REASON FOR THE SEASON?

During the Christmas period the media is awash with fundamentalists screaming about the so-called "War on Christmas." Slogans like, "Keep Christ in Christmas" and "Jesus is the reason for the season," are chanted by the faithful, *ad nauseam*. On top of all the protestations from Church leaders and run of the mill preachers, FOX news presenters and media pundits are doing their best to keep reason out of the season. But what is the reason for the season? Let's take one of the above mentioned slogans and really look at the evidence in a bid to establish the real reason for the season.

JESUS IS THE REASON FOR THE SEASON!

Is Jesus the reason for the season? To answer this question we must dissect it using all of the available evidence, for no reason exists beyond reasonable evidence. Who was Jesus Christ? What is the season? Once we have answered these two questions, we may be able to ascertain with sufficient certainty, whether or not Jesus is the reason for the season.

Who was Jesus Christ?

Who was Jesus Christ? The question seems simple enough, but the devil or truth, one might say, is in the details. To the devout Christian, he was the Jewish son of the creator of the entire universe and everything in it; the Messiah, the saviour of humanity, and the light of the world; the redeemer, the sacrificial Lamb of God, born to be slaughtered for the world's sins and the founder, next to Paul, of Christian religion. His words and deeds, Christians believe, are recorded in the four official Gospels of the *New Testament*; Matthew, Mark, Luke and John, four faithful and accurate testimonies that have been inscribed with the names of the actual eyewitnesses to this miraculous earthborn god incarnate. According to these Gospels, he was the son of a Jewish virgin named Mary and foster son of Joseph, a descendent of King David (see Matthew 1 & Luke 3), born in Bethlehem toward the end of Herod the Great's reign, which the first century Jewish historian,

Josephus, helps us date to around four bce, although some scholars are of the opinion that Herod died in 1 bce,[341] which would cause problems for the present consensus with regards to the year of Jesus' birth, but I suppose such is the dilemma of dating the birth of a legendary/mythical god-man.[342] To sketch out a very brief and rough account of his alleged existence, we must conflate the four separate and conflicting records of his life contained within the aforementioned Gospels, however, in so doing, we run into a myriad of historical problems.

Did his parents live in Galilee before he was born (Luke 2:4), or did they live in Bethlehem (Matthew 1)? Where exactly was he born? In a stable/manger (Luke 2:7) or in a house (Matthew 2:11)? Who visited the baby Jesus? Was it some unknown number of astrologers from the East (Matthew 2:1-11), or a bunch of local shepherds (Luke 2:8-20)? Was the baby Jesus in danger from the tyrant, King Herod? According to Matthew he was, but according to Luke, he wasn't. Did Joseph take the baby Jesus to Egypt? Again, Luke says no and Matthew says, yes. I could go on like this for pages, but alas, time and space are not on my side. There are so many contradictions in these four brief "biographies" that it is virtually impossible to ascertain with any clarity, what Jesus did and who he was alleged to have been.

The Gospels aren't only riddled with contradictions but they are plagued with forgeries (or interpolations, as textual scholars more politely term it). The story of the woman taken in adultery,[343] the final twelve verses of Mark,[344] Jesus' conversation with Nicodemus,[345] and on and on I could

---

[341]W. E. Filmer. Chronology of the Reign of Herod the Great. Journal of Theological Studies. Ns. 17 (1966). pp. 283–298; Paul Keresztes. Imperial Rome and the Christians: From Herod the Great to About 200 AD. University Press of America. (1989). pp.1–43.
[342]Josephus, Antiquities of the Jews, 17.6.4; Emil Schurer. D.D, M.A, A History of the Jewish People in the Time of Jesus Christ. Vol. 1. (1891). p. 465; John Barton and John Muddiman. The Oxford *Bible* Commentary. Oxford University Press. (2001). p. 622.
[343]Paul. J. Achtemeier. Harper-Collins *Bible* Dictionary Revised Edition. Harper Collins, (1989). p. 535; Carl R. Holladay. A Critical Introduction to the *New Testament*. Abingdon Press. (2005). p. 281; James M. Robinson. The Gospel of Jesus: A Historical Search for the Original Good News. Harper Collins, (2005) p. 65; Bart D Ehrman. *Misquoting Jesus*. Harper SanFrancisco. (2005). p. 64.
[344]Bruce Metzger, *A Textual Commentary on the Greek New Testament*. Stuttgart, (1971). pp. 122–126; Joel F. Williams. Literary Approaches to the End of Mark's Gospel. Journal of the Evangelical Theological Society. 42.1 (1999).
[345]Bart D Ehrman. *Jesus Interrupted*. Harper Collins (2005). p. 164.

go. In fact, there are so many problems and variations between the manuscripts that make up the *New Testament*, that a number of textual scholars have thrown up their hands and conceded that there is no way of knowing what any of the original manuscripts actually contained.[346]

To add to this historical disaster, these biographies fail the historical test of contemporanity, meaning, they weren't written until well after the events they describe, thus bringing into question their historical reliability. The earliest Gospel, Mark, wasn't written until an entire generation after the alleged crucifixion of Jesus[347] and Mark forms the foundation of the second Gospel, Matthew, of which 612 of the 662 verses are nearly identical, with regards to sentence structure, narrative order and language, meaning, the author of Matthew probably copied from the author of Mark. [348]

This leads us to the next dilemma; none of the Gospels were written by the authors whose names and traditions tell us they were written by. The tradition of ascribing the Gospel of "Mark" to an associate of Saint Peter, comes to us from Eusebius' dubious translation of Papias' work, in which, Eusebius alleged that Papias alleged that he had a friend who knew a guy, who knew another guy, who knew a friend of Mark, who had told him that he had acted as Peter's interpreter and spent an extended period of time with him.[349] We do have to wonder, if Mark spent a long time with Peter, why did he only pen two hours' worth of biography on the man he believed to be the one and only son of the one and only God? Anyway, leaving aside that hearsay saturated tradition, we move onto Matthew. From the same dubious source we learn that the Gospel of Matthew was a book of Hebrew sayings,[350] like the Gnostic Gospel of Thomas, but wait a minute! The Gospel we know as Matthew isn't a book of sayings written in

---

[346]Bart D Ehrman. *Misquoting Jesus*. Harper SanFrancisco. (2005). p. 58.

[347]Paul. J. Achtemeier. Harper-Collins *Bible* Dictionary Revised Edition. Harper Collins, (1989). p. 653; John Barton and John Muddiman. The Oxford *Bible* Commentary. Oxford University Press. (2001). p. 886.

[348]Graham N. Stanton. 'The Gospels and Jesus.' Oxford University Press (1989). pp. 63–64.

[349]Phillip Schaff . Nicene & Post Nicene Fathers; 2-01; Eusebius 'Pamphilius: Church History, Life of Constantine, Oration in Praise of Constantine.' (1890). p. 253.

[350]Ibid. p. 254.

Hebrew, it is a narrative, originally written in Greek with no signs of having been translated from Hebrew, so that can't be the same book, to which Papias was allegedly referring.[351] Next, we have Luke & John. Both these books were written close to the second century[352] and they tell us that the authors were not eyewitnesses, but had either taken their accounts from older manuscripts or else, heard hearsay stories and despite this(See Luke 1:1-4 & John 21:24). Further, the traditions ascribing authorship of these biographies to these two characters is just as dubious as the other two.[353]

Yet another historical hurdle these biographies stumble upon is that they are tainted with bias, meaning, they are not impartial accounts of history, written for the sole purpose of documenting events of the past, but they are religious texts, written to inspire conversions to the faith propagated within their pages. Bias, according to historians, is one of the factors that negatively impacts upon the reliability of a given account.[354] In his, *The Philosophy of History*, Georg W.F. Hegel eloquently excluded such legends and traditional tales from being counted as original history, saying:

Legends, Ballad–stories, Traditions must be excluded from such original history. These are but dim and hazy forms of historical apprehension, and therefore belong to nations whose intelligence is but half awakened. Here, on the contrary, we have to do with people fully conscious of what they were and what they were about. The domain of reality actually seen, or capable of being so affords a very different basis in point of firmness from that fugitive and shadowy element, in which were engendered those legends and poetic dreams whose historical prestige vanishes, as soon as nations have attained a mature individuality.[355]

---

[351]Bart D Ehrman. *Jesus Interrupted*. Harper Collins (2005). p. 109.

[352]Rick Strelan. *'Luke the Priest. The Authority of the Author of the Third Gospel.'* Ashgate (2008). Pg. 114; Bart D Ehrman. *Jesus Interrupted*. Harper Collins (2005). p. 145; James D. G. Dunn. The Evidence for Jesus. The Westminster Press. (1985). p. 41.

[353]Michael Sherlock. *'I Am Christ Vol. 1: The Crucifixion-Painful Truths.'* Charles River Press. (2012). pp. 100–106.

[354]McCullagh, C. Behan. "Bias in Historical Description, Interpretation, and Explanation." *History & Theory* 39.1 (2000): 39. *Academic Search Complete*. EBSCO. Web. 3 Aug. 2011.

[355]G.W.F. Hegel. *'The Philosophy of History.'* Blackmask Online. (2001). p. 1.

Now, one would have a very hard time if they wanted to argue that the Gospels were neither affected by bias or qualify for exclusion on the grounds laid out by Hegel.

These historical biographies are also hampered by arguments from similarity. This simply means that we can find earlier biographies of other historical and legendary characters , from whose tales appear to have been drawn these biographies of Jesus Christ, as well as from more ancient myths in which we find a wealth of parallels to the Christ myth. In Dennis McDonald's *The Homeric Epics and the Gospel of Mark*, he discusses the plethora of parallels between Mark's Gospel and the earlier works of Homer. He also relates how scribes of the first century were required to read and re-write Homer's works, which seems to be a valid explanation as to how Mark's Gospel mimics Homer's earlier writings.[356] Over and above this, we have various motifs that existed in more ancient Hellenistic, Egyptian, Persian, Mesopotamian and even Indian myth.[357] From Christ's epithets to his nativity, to his death and resurrection, all can be accounted for in the myths of earlier works, all proximate to the lands in which the Gospels were first produced.

Before moving on to look briefly at the extra-biblical/secular sources for an historical Jesus Christ, let's take stock of where we are with the primary historical sources for Jesus Christ. We have four brief and conflicting pseudonymous biographies, none of which were eyewitness accounts; they are riddled with forgeries, plagued with bias and were not written within a reliable time span from the events they purport to relay. In short, they are not valid history and do not help us ascertain the earthly presence of their central character, or "reason for the season."

---

[356]Dennis McDonald. *'The Homeric Epics and the Gospel of Mark.'* Yale University Press. (2000). Ch. 1.

[357]Rank, Otto. The Myth of the Birth of the Hero. Nervous and Mental Disease Publishing Co. (1914); T.W Doane. *Bible* Myths and Their Parallels in Other Religions. The Commonwealth Company. (1882); Sir Edwin Arnold. The Light of Asia; cited in; Tom Harpur. The Pagan Christ. Walker and Company. (2004); Acharya S. Suns of God. Krishna, Buddha and Christ Unveiled. Adventures Unlimited Press. (2004); Tim Callahan. *Secret Origins of the Bible.* Millennium Press. (2002); Edwin F. Bryant and Laurie L. Patton. The Indo-Aryan Controversy: Evidence and Inference in Indian History. Routledge (2005); Dr. Robert Price. Pagan Parallels to Christ Part 1: http://www.youtube.com/watch?v=xzOrc_kwcU4; Fredrick Cornwallis Conybeare. The Life of Apollonius of Tyana: Philostratus, Vol. 1. The Macmillan Co. (1912)…

SECULAR SOURCES

What do find when we go looking for Jesus Christ, beyond the afore-mentioned molluscs of myth? Well, we have two brief references to Jesus Christ within the first century work of the Jewish historian, Josephus. The first and most popular reference is commonly referred to as the *Testamonium Flavium* and this has been roundly demonstrated to be a Christian forgery. [358] The second reference to Jesus Christ, also appears to contain a forgery and when this forgery is subtracted from Josephus' narrative, the Jesus he appears to have been referring to was Jesus the son of Damneus, who is the central character of that part the narrative in question,[359] and is one of over twenty people named Jesus, referred to in his *Antiquities of the Jews*, some of which included; Jesus the son of Sapphias, Jesus the son of Gamala, Jesus the son of Phabet, Jesus the son of Sie, Jesus the son of Fabus, Jesus the son of Thias, Jesus the son of Gamaliel, Jesus the son of Damneus, Jesus the brother of Onias, Jesus the brother of John…

OK, so the first century is a bust, but perhaps if we travel beyond contemporaneous sources, in other words, if we try our best to investigate historically unreliable sources for Jesus Christ, perhaps we might find something, as fruitless as that will ultimately prove to be.

Bingo! If we move into the second century, we find passing references to Jesus Christ within the works of Suetonius, Tacitus and Pliny the Younger.

Suetonius, in his *The Lives of the 12 Caesars*, made mention of a "Chrestus," who resided in Rome and instigated the Jews in Rome to riot, but Jesus Christ was never believed to have lived in Rome, so that's no help. [360]

Pliny the Younger, a pro-consul in Rome, who served under the emperor Trajan, mentioned the Christians in a letter he wrote to the emperor, but he only demonstrates a knowledge of the presence of

---

[358]John E Remsburg. The Christ: A Critical Review and Analysis of the Evidences of His Existence. The Truth Seeker Company. (1909) pp. 32–35.
[359]Flavius Josephus. Antiquities of the Jews. Book 20 Chapter 9.
[360]Suetonius, Joseph Gavorse. The Lives of the 12 Caesars. Random House. (1931). p. 226.

the religion of Christianity in the second century, [361] which in no way constitutes an historical source for Jesus Christ, in the same way Herodotus' reference to the followers of the Egyptian God Osiris fails to prove that god's historicity.

In the second century, the Roman official, Tacitus, in reflecting on Nero's persecution of the Christians in the first century, did say that the Christians derive their name from a figure known as Christ, but again, such knowledge is not in dispute and as with Pliny's testimony, does nothing to locate a Jesus Christ in history, but rather, it merely establishes that Christianity was a religion in the first century. Further, Tacitus' reference has been the subject of debate, with many scholars arguing that it was interpolated into his works by later Christian forgers. [362]

Aside from a few Jewish polemics written centuries after the fact, that is all we have to support the idea of an historical Jesus. Our reason for the season has disappeared into the obscurity of ill-gotten religious belief and rears its head nowhere in reliable and actual history. Without our reason, we are only left with a season and what can be said of that? Let us now, for the moment at least, ignore all that we have discovered about our absent saviour, and keep him alive long enough to show that even if he was an historical magician, he was not the reason for the season, however, before we move on, let's hear from John Remsburg, who, in his book, *The Christ: A Critical Review and Analysis of the Evidences of His Existence,* sums up both the lack of secular sources for Jesus and the unwarranted historical weight that has been placed upon these four dubious biographies of Jesus Christ:

With these four brief biographies, the Four Gospels, Christianity must stand or fall. These four documents, it is admitted, contain practically all the evidence which can be adduced in proof of the existence and divinity of Jesus Christ. Profane history, as we have seen, affords no proof of this. The so-called apocryphal literature of the early church has been discarded by the church itself. Even the remaining canonical books of the New Testament are of little consequence if the testimony

---

[361] John E Remsburg. The Christ: A Critical Review and Analysis of the Evidences of His Existence. The Truth Seeker Company. (1909) Pg. 43.
[362] Ibid. pp. 40–41.

of the Four Evangelists be successfully impeached. Disprove the authenticity and credibility of these documents and this Christian deity is removed to the mythical realm of Apollo, Odin, and Osiris.[363]

THE REAL REASON FOR THE SEASON

Christmas is a time to celebrate the birth of Jesus Christ, who was born on December 25th in the zero year, 1 bce. That is why we call the first year in this millennium, the year 2000, because it is 2000 years from the birth of Jesus Christ. Oops, I appear to have made a mistake. Jesus is no longer believed to have been born in that zero year, but around -4 to -6 bce, as the historical data indicating Herod's reign and death have been discovered to have caused problems for that initial birthday. No problem, what's a year or six, here and there? Still, we know that the *Bible* teaches us that Jesus was born on December 25th. Sorry, I appear to have made another mistake, I really should be more careful. The *Bible* says nothing about his birthday being on December 25th, in the depths of winter, when the shepherds were outside tending their flocks in the bitter cold. Ok, so the *Bible* doesn't say anything about the reason for the season, so where and when, did Jesus' birthday first become the reason for the season? To answer this question we will need to travel hundreds of years and hundreds of miles from the alleged birth place and time of Jesus.

The first Christmas celebrated on December 25th occurred in the fourth century, in Rome, close to four hundred years after the alleged life of Christ and this date appears to have been chosen to spite or take over, the emperor Marcus Aurelius' *diesnatalis solis invicti*, the birthday of the invincible pagan sun god, established in 274.[364] As with the very basis of Christianity's god-man, their season seems to have been inspired by pre-Christian religions, religions that the Christians were attempting to usurp by accosting their themes, celebrations, places of worship and even their more ancient rights and rituals.

Regarding the origins of Christmas, *The Cambridge History of Christianity* says:

---

[363]Ibid. pp. 50–51
[364]Augustine Casiday & Fredrick W. Norris. The Cambridge History of Christianity. Constantine to 600 CE. Cambridge University Press. (2008). p. 615.

The only conclusion is that the season had its origins in the fourth century in pre-Christmas themes that differed from place to place.[365]

To which "pre-Christian themes" are the scholars at Cambridge referring? I mentioned above that the initial Christmas was probably celebrated on the birthday of the former sun god to usurp that widely celebrated and well established pre-Christian holiday, but we will need to look a little more closely at this issue if we wish to establish the real reason for the season.

Let's start with the date, December 25th. It just so happens that this is around the end of the winter solstice. For those who are unfamiliar with this astronomical event, the solstice refers to the sun's apparent standstill for three days after its slow decline from fall/autumn. After this three day pause, it slowly begins its ascent back to the spring equinox (March 21st) and onto summer. To many ancient religions, particularly those whose god was the anthropomorphised sun, this period was looked upon as his death, rest or sojourn in the under-world. In classical myth, this three day rest can be witnessed when Zeus persuaded the sun god, Helios, not to rise for three days so that he might enjoy Hercules' mother, Alcmene, for as long as possible.[366]

Commenting on the significance of not only the winter solstice, but the epiphany (January 6th) and Easter, the famous twentieth century Christian theologian, Williston Walker said:

These elaborations of the yearly cycle determined by Easter and Pentecost went hand in hand with the appearance of a new annual cycle of celebration associated with the Incarnation and focused on the feasts of Christmas (December 25th) and Epiphany (January 6th). Each of these dates was also associated with pagan celebrations of the winter solstice. In Rome, December 25th had, since the time of the emperor Aurelian, been marked as the birthday of the Unconquered Sun; and in the East, January 6th had long had associations with the birth of the god Dionysus. Influenced by these circumstances, and by the need to lend Christian meaning to established popular feasts, the

---

[365]Ibid. p. 616.
[366]Jenny March. Cassell's Dictionary of Classical Mythology. Cassell's & Co. (1998). p. 75.

churches adapted these days to celebration of the birth and manifestation in history of the divine Logos, the Sun of Righteousness…[367]

In addition, Historian Roger Beck informs us that:

As the Sun inscribes his celestial journey on the earth in the waxing and waning of the seasons, so the ancients inscribed the story of a human life on that same annual journey as the god's own biography, from birth and the weakness of the newborn at the winter solstice on December 25, through growth and waxing vigour to a height of strength and power at the summer solstice, and then into decline, senescence, and a sort of death. Speaking of the differences in age of the representation of various gods, the fourth-century (ce) polymath Macrobius said that these all "relate to the Sun, who is made to appear very small at the winter solstice" (Saturnalia 1.18.10). "In this form," he continues, "the Egyptians bring him forth from the shrine on the set date to appear like a tiny infant on the shortest day of the year." By the same metaphorical logic, the Calendar of Antiochus of Athens named December 25 the "Sun's birthday…".[368]

Finally, although I could continue to quote reliable sources ad infinitum, let's hear from a brilliant scholar, Isaac Asimov, who discusses the reason for the season in the following words:

Why, then, December 25th? The answer might be found in astronomy and in Roman history. The noonday Sun is at varying heights in the sky at different seasons of the year because the Earth's axis is tipped by twenty-three degrees to the plane of Earth's revolution about the Sun. Without going into the astronomy of this in detail, it is sufficient to say that the noonday Sun climbs steadily higher in the sky from December to June, and falls steadily lower from June to December. The steady rise is easily associated with a lengthening day, an eventually waning temperature and quickening of life; the steady decline with a shortening day, an eventually cooling temperature and fading of life. In primitive times, when the reason for the cycle was not understood in terms of modem astronomy, there was never any certainty that the sinking Sun

---

[367]Williston Walker. A History of the Christian Church. 4th Ed. Prentice Hall. (1918). pp. 187–189.
[368]Roger Beck. A Brief History of Ancient Astrology. Blackwell Publishing. (2007). pp. 56–57.

would ever turn and begin to rise again. Why should it do so, after all, except by the favour of the gods? And that favour might depend entirely upon the proper conduct of a complicated ritual known only to the priests. It must have been occasion for great gladness each year, then, to observe the decline of the noonday Sun gradually slowing, then coming to a halt and beginning to rise again. The point at which the Sun comes to a halt is the winter solstice" (from Latin words meaning "sun halt"). The time of the winter solstice was the occasion for a great feast in honour of what one might call the "birth of the Sun!" In Roman times, a three-day period, later extended to seven days, was devoted to the celebration of the winter solstice.[369]

CONCLUSION

Based on the available evidence, can we assert, with any degree of certainty, that Jesus is the reason for the season? We have no real secular record of his earthly existence, no reliable evidence at all, in fact. Further, we have even less reason to believe that he was a magical demi-god, for in the words of Carl Sagan, *"extraordinary claims require extraordinary evidence"* and sadly for the believer, we are not even graced with ordinary evidence for such claims. As we cannot say whether or not an earthly Jesus existed, let alone the divine David Blaine of the Gospels, how can we attribute the cause or reason for the Christmas season to him? In short, we cannot. Even if we could conjure up non-existent evidence to establish the former proposition (that Jesus was historical and the Son of God) we are in possession of vast tomes of historical evidence that demonstrate beyond any reasonable doubt, that Jesus had nothing to do with this pre-Christian season until at least the fourth century.

I do apologize, but it appears that you may no longer continue to claim that Jesus is the reason for the season, unless you wish to stand against reason occasioned by mountains of evidence, mountains, my dear Christian, that your faith simply cannot move.

---

[369]Isaac Asimov. Asimov's Guide to the *Bible*. Two Volumes in One. The Old and *New Testament*s. Wings Books. (1969). pp. 931–932.

BIBLIOGRAPHY

Christianity as Untrue Myth – I beg to differ with C.S. Lewis

Professor Elizabeth Vandiver. *'Classical Mythology.'* The Teaching Company. (2002).

Bart D. Ehrman. *'Peter, Paul and Mary Magdalene: The Followers of Jesus in History and Legend.'* Oxford University Press. (2006).

John Barton and John Muddiman. *'The Oxford Bible Commentary.'* Oxford University Press. (2001).

Paul. J. Achtemeier. *'Harper-Collins Bible Dictionary Revised Edition.'* Harper Collins, (1989).

Bart D Ehrman. *'Jesus Interrupted.'* Harper Collins Publishers. (2005).

J.B. Bury, S.A. Cook & F.A. Adcock. *'The Cambridge Ancient History. Vol. 1: Egypt and Babylonia - To 1580 bce.'* Cambridge University Press (1928).

Edward I. Bleiburg. *'World Eras Volume 5: Ancient Egypt. 2615-332 bce.'* Gale Group. (2002).

Mark P.O. Morford & Robert J. Lenardon. *'Classical Mythology.'* Oxford University Press (2003).

John Barton & John Muddiman. *'The Oxford Bible Commentary.'* Oxford University Press (2007).

Gregory A. Boyd & Paul Rhodes. Lord or Legend? Wrestling with the Jesus Dilemma. Baker Books. (2007).

Philip Schaff. *'Ante-Nicene Fathers: Vol. 1: The Apostolic Fathers with Justin Martyr and Irenaeus'* Grand Rapids. MI: Christian Classics Ethereal Library. (1885).

Carl R. Holladay. *'A Critical Introduction to the New Testament.'* Abingdon Press. (2005).

Bart D Ehrman. *'Misquoting Jesus.'* Harper-San Francisco. (2005).

James M. Robinson. *'The Gospel of Jesus: A Historical Search for the Original Good News.'* Harper Collins, (2005).

Ismo Dunderberg. *'The Beloved Disciple in Conflict.'* Oxford University Press. (2006).

Louis A. Ruprecht Jr. *'The Tragic Gospel: How John Corrupted the Heart of Christianity.' John* Wiley and Sons. (2008).

Joel F. Williams. *'Literary Approaches to the End of Mark's Gospel.'* Journal of the Evangelical Theological Society. 42.1 (1999).

Bruce Metzger. *'A Textual Commentary on the Greek New Testament.'* Stuttgart, (1971).

Michael J. Wilkins & J. P. Moreland. *'Jesus Under Fire.'* Zondervan Publishing House. (1995).

Albert Schweitzer. *The Quest of the Historical Jesus.* Adam and Charles Black. (1911).

Lee Strobel. *The Case for the Real Jesus.* Zondervan. (2007).

M.M. Mangasarian. *The Truth About Jesus. Is He a Myth?* Independent Religious Society. (1909).

Thomas Paine. *The Age of Reason.* (1796).

John E Remsburg. 'The Christ: A Critical Review and Analysis of the Evidences of His Existence.' The Truth Seeker Company. (1909).

Roger Beck. 'The Religion of the Mithras Cult in the Roman Empire: Mysteries of the Unconquered Sun.' Oxford University Press. (2006).

J.M. Robertson. 'Pagan Christs: Studies in Comparative Hierology.' Watts and Co. (1911).

Guy de la Bedoyere. *The Romans for Dummies.* John Wiley and Sons Ltd. (2006).

The Truth About The Devil – The Greatest Trick!

Joseph McCabe. 'The Sources of the Morality of the Gospels.' Watts & Co. (1914).

Peter Clark. 'Zoroastrianism: An Introduction to An Ancient Faith.' Sussex Academic Press. (1998).

Paul. J. Achtemeier. *Harper-Collins Bible Dictionary Revised Edition.* Harper Collins, (1989).

Oded Lipschitz & Joseph Blenkinsopp. *Judah and the Judeans in the Neo-Babylonian Period.* Eisenbraus. (2003).

John Barton and John Muddiman. *The Oxford Bible Commentary.* Oxford University Press. (2001).

Paolo Sacchi. *The History of the Second Temple Period.* T&T Clark International. (2000).

Jeff S. Anderson. 'The Internal Diversification of Second Temple Judaism: An Introduction to Second Temple Judaism.' University Press of America. (2002).

J.P. Douglas, Merrill C. Tenney & Moises Silva.*Zondervan Illustrated Bible Dictionary.* Zondervan. (2011).

T.W Doane. *Bible* Myths and Their Parallels in Other Religions.' The Commonwealth Company. (1882).

Jabez Thomas Sunderland. 'The Origin and Character of the *Bible* and its place among sacred books.' The Beacon Press, (1924).

Philip S. Foner, PhD. *The Complete Writings of Thomas Paine.* The Citadel Press. (1945).

Was The Prophet Muhammad A Paedophile?

Sahih Bukhari, Volume 1.

Robert Spencer. Islam Unveiled. Encounter Books. (2002).

Sahih Bukhari. Volume 7.

Sahih Bukhari. Book of Marriage.

Kecia Ali. 'Sexual Ethics & Islam: Feminist Reflections on *Qur'an*, Hadith and Jurisprudence.' Oneworld Publications Oxford (2006).

Lisa Beyer. 'The Women of Islam; Time Magazine' 25 November, 2001.

The Book of Genesis Unveiled

Joseph Wheless. *'Is it God's Word?'* Alfred A. Knopf. (1926).

Judge Parish B. Ladd. *'Commentaries on Hebrew and Christian Mythology.'* The Truth Seeker Company, (1896).

Richard Elliot Friedman. *'Who Wrote the Bible?'* Harper-San Francisco. (1997).

Roger D. Woodward. 'The Cambridge Encyclopaedia of the World's Ancient Languages: The Ancient Languages of Syria-Palestine and Arabia.' Cambridge University Press. (2008).

Israel Finkelstein and Neil Asher Silberman. 'The *Bible* Unearthed: Archaeology's New Vision of Ancient Israel and the Origin of its Sacred Texts.' Touchstone (2002).

Thierry Ragobert and Isy Morgenzstern. *'The Bible Unearthed.'* TV. Documentary Series. Part 2: The Exodus. (2005).

Paul. J. Achtemeier. 'Harper-Collins *Bible* Dictionary Revised Edition.' Harper Collins, (1989).

I. E. S. Edwards. C. J. Gadd. N. G. L. Hammond E. Sollberger. *'The Cambridge Ancient History: Vol. 2. Part 1.'* Cambridge University Press. (1973).

Kathryn A. Bard. 'An Introduction to the Archaeology of Ancient Egypt.' Blackwell Publishing (2007).

Kathryn A. Bard. 'Encyclopaedia of the Archaeology of Ancient Egypt.' Routledge (1999).

Messod and Roger Sabbah. 'The Secrets of the Exodus: The Egyptian roots of the Hebrew People.' Allworth Press (2004).

Rosalie David. *'Handbook to Life in Ancient Egypt.'* Facts on File Inc. (2003).

Israel Finkelstein & Amihai Mazar. 'The Quest for the Historical Israel: Debating Archaeology and the History of Early Israel.' Brill (2007).

Gary Greenberg. '101 Myths of the *Bible*: How Ancient Scribes Invented Biblical History.' Sourcebooks Inc. (2000).

Bruce Metzger and Herbert G. May. 'The New Oxford Annotated *Bible* With Apocrypha.' (1977).

Crystal M. Bennett. "Excavations at Buseirah (Biblical Bozrah)." John F. A. Sawyer & David J. A. Clines. *'Midian, Moab and Edom; The History and Archaeology of the Late Bronze and Iron Age Jordan and North-west Arabia;* Journal for the Study of the *Old Testament.* Supplement 24. (1983).

J.W. Rogerson. Judith. M. Lieu. *'The Oxford Handbook of Biblical Studies.'* Oxford University Press, (2006).

George Smith. *'History of Ashurbanipal.'* Williams and Norgate. (1871).

J.B. Bury, M.A, F.B.A., S.A. Cook, Litt.D., F.E. Adcock, M.A. *The Cambridge Ancient History. Vol. 1: Egypt and Babylonia to 1580 B.C.'* Cambridge University Press. (1928).

Judson Knight, Stacy A McConnell & Lawrence W. Baker. *'Ancient Civilizations Almanac. Vol. 1.'* A.X.L An Imprint of the Gale Group. (2000).

Lester G. Grabbe. 'An Introduction to Second Temple Judaism: History and Religion of the Jews in the Time of Nehemiah, the Maccabees, Hillel and Jesus.' T&T Clark. (2010).

Armageddon – A Self-Fulfilling Prophecy?

Margaret M. Mitchell & Frances M. Young. *'The Cambridge History of Christianity – Origins to Constantine.'* Cambridge University Press (2008).

Paul. J. Achtemeier. 'Harper-Collins *Bible* Dictionary Revised Edition.' Harper Collins, (1989).

Fred Skolnik & Michael Berenbaum. *'Encyclopaedia Judaica second Ed. Vol. 2.'* Thompson Gale. (2007).

J.W. Rogerson. Judith. M. Lieu. The Oxford Handbook of Biblical Studies. Oxford University Press, (2006).

Paul Carus. *'The History Of The Devil And The Idea Of Evil'* (New York: Gramercy Books, 1996).

George. W. Cox. M.A. *'Aryan Mythology. Vol. 2.'* Longman's, Green and Co. (1870).

Festinger, L., Riecken, H. W., & Schachter, S. *'When Prophecy fails.'* University of Minnesota Press. (1956).

David Hunt. 'An Urgent Call to Serious Faith.' Berean Call. (2006).

Lord, Charles G.; Lee Ross, Mark R. Lepper (1979). "Biased assimilation and attitude polarization: The effects of prior theories on subsequently considered evidence". *'Journal of Personality and Social Psychology'* (American Psychological Association 2098–2109).

Robert S. Feldman. *'Understanding Psychology. 10th Ed.'* McGraw Hill (2011).

Michael Biggs, Peter Bearman and Peter Hedström The Oxford Handbook of Analytical Sociology. Oxford University Press. (2009).

W. Edward Craighead & Charles B. Nemeroff. 'The Concise Corsini Encyclopaedia of Psychology and Behavioral Science. third Ed.' John Wiley & Sons Inc. (2004).

Dear Islam,

The Qur'an

Sahih Muslim

Sahih Bukhari

Karen Armstrong. *'Islam: 'A Short History.'* Modern Library. (2002).

Christian Charity & The Bread of Shame – Exploiting the Norm of Reciprocity.

Rav Berg. *'The Kabbalah Method.'* Kabbalah Centre International (2005).

Daniel T. Reff. 'Plagues, Priests and Demons.' Cambridge University Press (2005).

Irving B. Weiner, Theodore Millon & Melvin J. Lerner. 'Handbook of Psychology: Vol. 5; Personality and Social Psychology.' John Wiley & Sons Inc. (2003).

Christianity – 12 Painful Facts

Paul. J. Achtemeier. 'Harper-Collins Bible Dictionary Revised Edition.' Harper Collins, (1989).

John Barton and John Muddiman. 'The Oxford Bible Commentary.' Oxford University Press. (2001).

Graham N. Stanton. 'The Gospels and Jesus.' Oxford University Press (1989).

Bart D Ehrman. Jesus Interrupted. Harper Collins Publishers. (2005).

Bruce Metzger, 'A Textual Commentary on the Greek New Testament. Stuttgart, (1971).

John E Remsburg. 'The Christ: A Critical Review and Analysis of the Evidences of His Existence.' The Truth Seeker Company. (1909).

Joseph McCabe. 'Sources of Morality in the Gospels.' Watts & Co. (1914).

Bart Ehrman 'Lost Christianities.' Oxford University Press (2003).

Earl Doherty. 'The Jesus Puzzle: Did Christianity Begin with a Mythical Christ? Challenging the Existence of an Historical Jesus.' Age of Reason Publications (2005).

Helen Ellebre. 'The Dark Side of Christian History.' Morningstar Books (1995).

Phillip Schaff. 'History of the Christian Church, Volume 5: The Middle Ages. A.D. 1049-1294.' Christian Classics Ethereal Library. (1882).

J.N. Hillgarth. 'The Conversion of Western Europe.' Englewood Cliffs, NJ: Prentice Hall, (1969).

Frank Viola & George Barna. 'Pagan Christianity.' Tyndale House Publishers. (2008).

Joseph Wheless. 'Forgery in Christianity.' Psychiana. (1930).

Rev. J.E. Riddle. 'The History of the Papacy, to the Reformation' (Multiple volume series) Richard Bentley (1854).

Edward Gibbon. 'The Decline and Fall of the Roman Empire' (multiple volume series). George Bell & Sons. (1893).

From Sophists to Sermonizers – Rhetorical Religion

Philip Schaff. 'Nicene and Post Nicene Fathers: Series 2, Volume 6.' Christian Classics Ethereal Library. (2009).

Robert Wardy. 'The Birth of Rhetoric. Plato, Aristotle and their Successors.' Routledge. (1996).

Dominic Scott. 'Plato's Meno. Cambridge Studies in the Dialogues of Plato.' Cambridge University Press. (2005).

Jonathan Barnes. 'The Complete Works of Aristotle. Sophistical Refutations.' Princeton University Press. (1991).

Paul Elmer More. *'Platonism.'* Princeton University Press. (1917).

Phillip Schaff. *'The New Schaff-Herzog Encyclopaedia of Religious Knowledge, Vol. 9.'* Grand Rapids: Christian Classics Ethereal Library.

Marsha E. Ackermann Michael J. Schroeder Janice J. Terry Jiu-Hwa Lo Upshur Mark F. Whitters. *'Encyclopaedia of World History: Vol. 1.'* Facts on File. Infobase
publishing. (2008).

Frank Viola, George Barna. *'Pagan Christianity.'* Tyndale House Publishers. (2008).

Jesus – According to the Jews

Fred Skolnik & Michael Berenbaum. *'Encyclopaedia Judaica second Ed. Vol. 14.'* Thompson Gale. (2007).

Philip Schaff . 'Ante-Nicene Fathers of the Third Century: Tertullian Part Fourth; Minucius Felix; Commodian; Origen Parts First and Second. Grand Rapids. Christian Ethereal Library. (1885).

J.N. Hillgarth, *'The Conversion of Western Europe.'* Prentice Hall, (1969).

Catherine M. Murphy, PhD. *'The Historical Jesus For Dummies.'* Wiley Publishing Inc. (2008).

Bart D Ehrman. *'Jesus Interrupted.'* Harper Collins Publishers. (2005).

John E Remsburg. 'The Christ: A Critical Review and Analysis of the Evidences of His Existence.' The Truth Seeker Company. (1909).

Rev. S. Baring Gould. *'The Lost and Hostile Gospels.'* Williams and Norgate. (1874).

R. Travers Herford. *'Christianity in Talmud and Midrash.'* Williams and Norgate. (1903).

Maurice Goguel. *'Jesus the Nazarene: Myth or History?'* D. Appleton and Company. (1926).

Philip Schaff . 'Nicene and Post Nicene Fathers. 1-09. St. Chrysostom: On the Priesthood; Ascetic Treatises; Select Homilies and Letters; Homilies on the Statutes.' Christian Classics Ethereal Library. (1886).

Philip Schaff . 'The Apostolic Fathers with Justin Martyr and Irenaeus.' Christian Ethereal Library (1885).

Philip Schaff . 'Ante-Nicene Fathers Vol. 3: Latin Christianity; Its founder, Tertullian.' Grand Rapids, MI: Christian Classics Ethereal Library.

G.R.S Mead. *'Did Jesus Live 100 BC?'* Theosophical Publishing Society. (1903).

Einar Thomassen & Johannes van Oort. (Translated By Frank Williams). *'The Panarion of Epiphanius of Salamis: Book 1'* Brill. (2009).

Carl. G. Jung. *'Collected Papers on Analytical Psychology.'* Bailliere, Tindall & Cox. (1920).

Jesus & The Number Fourteen

Jonathon Barnes & Gavin Lawrence. The Complete Works of Aristotle. Vol. 2. Fragments. Princeton University Press, (1984).

Bart D Ehrman. Jesus Interrupted. Harper Collins (2005).

Porphyry's Problems with Christianity

Jorge Rupke. *'A Companion to Roman Religion.'* Blackwell Publishing. (2007).

John Boardman, Jasper Griffin & Oswyn Murray. *'The Oxford History of the Classical World.'* Oxford University Press. (1986).

T.W. Crafer. D, D. *'The Apocriticus of Macarius Magnes.'* The MacMillan Company. (1919).

Susan R. Holman. *'Wealth and Poverty in Early Church and Society.'* Holy Cross Greek Orthodox School of Theology. (2008).

Professor Elizabeth Vandiver. Classical Mythology. Lecture 2: What is Myth? The Teaching Company. (2002).

Philip Schaff. *'Nicene and Post Nicene Fathers: Series 2, Volume 6.'* Christian Classics Ethereal Library. (2009).

Phillip Schaff. 'Eusebius Pamphilius: Church History, Life of Constantine, Oration in Praise of Constantine.' (1890).

Philip Schaff. *'Nicene and Post Nicene Fathers: Series 2; Vol. 3.'* Christian Literature Publishing Co. (1892).

The Great Virgin Isis – Before Mary

Rosalie A. David. *'Handbook to Life in Ancient Egypt.'* University of Manchester. Facts on File Inc. (2003).

Joseph Campbell. *'The Masks of God – Primitive Mythology.'* Secker & Warburg. (1960).

Alvin Boyd Kuhn. *'The Root of All Religion.'* The Theosophical Press. (1936).

John Kenrick. *'The Egypt of Herodotus.'* B. Fellowes (1841).

Mark P.O. Morford & Robert J. Lenardon. *'Classical Mythology.'* Oxford University Press (2003).

Jenny March. Cassell's Dictionary of Classical Mythology. Cassell & Co. (1998).

Apuleius. (trans. William Adlington). *'The Golden Ass of Apuleius.'* David Nutt. Pub. (1893).

Price, Theodora Hadzisteliou. 'Kourotrophos: Cults and presentation of the Greek Nursing Deities.' Leiden: E.J. Brill. (1978).

Dr William W. Goodwin. *'Plutarch's Morals.'* Little Brown and Company. (1878).

Reginald E. Witt. *'Isis in the Ancient World.'* Baltimore: Johns Hopkins Press. (1997).

Konrad H. Kinzl. *'A Companion to the Ancient Greek World.'* Blackwell Publishing (2006).

Sir E. A. Wallis Budge. *'An Egyptian Hieroglyphic Dictionary: Vol. 2.'* John Murray Pub. (1920).

Morris L. Bierbrier. *'Historical Dictionary of Ancient Egypt.'* Scarecrow Press. (2008).

Edward I. Bleiberg. 'World Eras, Vol. 5: Ancient Egypt 2615-332 bce.' Gale Group. (2002).

Serge Sauneron. *The Priests of Ancient Egypt.'* Evergreen Books Ltd. (1960).

Joseph Campbell. 'The Masks of God, Vol. 2: Oriental Mythology.' Secker & Warburg. (1962).

Richard H. Wilkinson. 'The Complete Gods and Goddesses of Ancient Egypt.' Thames and Hudson. (2003).

Maulana Karenga. 'Maat: The Moral Ideal in Ancient Egypt - A Study in Classical African Ethics.' Routledge. (2004).

G. Johannes Botterweck. *Theological Dictionary of the Old Testament, Vol. 2.'* William B. Eerdmans Publishing Co. (1975).

Joseph Campbell. 'Masks of God: Vol. 3 – Occidental Mythology.' Penguin Books. (1976).

The Recent Rise in Islamic Conversions – Misplaced Sympathies

Henry Chadwick. The Church in Ancient Society: From Galilee to Gregory the Great. Oxford University Press. (2001).

Philip Schaff. Ante-Nicene Fathers. Vol. 1: The Apostolic Fathers with Justin Martyr and Irenaeus. The Martyrdom of Polycarp. Christian Ethereal Library. (1885).

Two Victims of Protestant Insanity – The Stories of Matthew Hamont and Michael Servetus.

Jeremy Collier, M.A. 'An Ecclesiastical History of Great Britain. Vol. 6.' William Straker. (1811).

Alexander Gordon. 'Dictionary of National Biography. Vol. 24.' (1895–1900).

Robert Wallace. *Antitrinitarian Biography. Vol. 2.'* E.T. Whitfield. (1850).

Carl Theophilus Odhner. *Michael Servetus: His Life and Teachings.'* J.B. Lippincott Company. (1910).

R. Willis, M.D. 'Servetus and Calvin: A Study of an Important Epoch in the History of the Reformation.' Henry S. King and Co. (1877).

W.R. Inge. (Dean of St. Paul's Cathedral) *Christian Ethics and Modern Problems.'* G.P. Putnam's Sons. (1930).

Jordan Howard Sobel. 'Logic and Theism: Arguments For and Against Belief in God.' Cambridge University Press. (2004).

The Nuts and Bolts of the Christian Scam

David S. Potter. A Companion to the Roman Empire. Blackwell Publishing. (2006).

W.D. Davies & L. Finkelstein. The Cambridge History of Judaism, Vol. 1; Introduction; The Persian Period. Cambridge University Press. (1984).

Phillip Schaff. Fathers of the Third Century: Tertullian, Part Fourth; Minucius Felix; Commodian; Origen, Parts First and Second. Grand Rapids MI; Christian Classics Ethereal Library. (1885).

Stephen Key. One Simple Idea: Turn Your Dreams into a Licensing Goldmine. While Letting Others Do the Work. McGraw Hill. (2011).

Philip Schaff and H. Wace. Nicene and Post-Nicene Fathers, second Series, ed., Grand Rapids MI: Eerdmans (1955).

Phillip Schaff. Ante-Nicene Fathers. Vol. 1. Justin Martyr. Dialogue with Trypho, Chapter (XLVIII). Christian Classics Ethereal Library. (1867).

Bart D. Ehrman. From Jesus to Constantine: A History of Early Christianity. The Teaching Company. (2004).

E.A Wallis Budge. The Gods of the Egyptians or Studies in Egyptian Mythology. Vol. 1. Methuen & Co. (1904).

Thomas Paine. The Theological Works of Thomas Paine. Age of Reason. Belford Clark and Co. (1882).

Payam Nabarz. The Mysteries of Mithras: The Pagan Beliefs that Shaped the Christian World. Inner Traditions (2005).

John Henry Parker. The Archaeology of Rome. Oxford: James Parker and Co. (1877).

Roger Beck. The Religion of the Mithras Cult in the Roman Empire. Oxford University Press. (2006).

Saint Bede. Bede's Ecclesiastical History of England. Christian Classics Ethereal Library (673-735CE

Paul Henri Thiry Holbach, Nicolas Antoine Boulanger. Christianity Unveiled. (Trans. W. M. Johnson) (1895).

M.M Mangasarian. Is the Morality of Jesus Sound? A Lecture Delivered Before the Independent Religious Society. Orchestra Hall.

Joseph Wheless. Forgery in Christianity. Psychiana (1930).

Philip Schaff. Ante-Nicene Fathers Vol. 2: Fathers of the Second Century: Hermas, Tatian, Athenagoras, Theophilus, and Clement of Alexandria (Entire). Christian Classics Ethereal Library. (1885).

Philip S. Foner, PhD. The Complete Writings of Thomas Paine. The Citadel Press. (1945).

Daniel T. Reff. Plagues, Priests and Demons. Cambridge University Press. (2005).

No Reason For Jesus – A New Approach to the Christ Myth

Bart D. Ehrman. 'From Jesus to Constantine: A History of Early Christianity.' The Teaching Company. (2004).

Rev. A. H. Sayce. 'The "Higher Criticism" and the Verdict of the Monuments.' E. & J.E Young and Co. (1894).

George Smith. 'The Chaldean Account of Genesis.' Scribner, Armstrong and Co. (1876).

Zenaide A. Ragozin. 'The Story of Chaldea: From the Earliest Times to the Rise of Assyria.' The Knickerbocker Press. (1886).

C.F. Keil & F. Delitzsch. 'Biblical Commentary on the *Old Testament*: Vol. 1.' T&T Clark. (1885).

'The Electronic Text Corpus of Sumerian Literature.' Faculty of Oriental Studies. Oxford University. (2006).

Fred Skolnik & Michael Berenbaum. *'Encyclopaedia Judaica second Ed. Vol. 7.'* Thompson Gale. (2007).

Paul. J. Achtemeier. 'Harper-Collins *Bible* Dictionary Revised Edition.' Harper Collins, (1989).

Leonard W. King. *'A History of Sumer and Akkad.'* Chatto and Windus. (1923).

Irenaeus. 'Against the Heresies.' Book 2.

Forging The Historical Jesus – The Josephus Forgeries

Flavius Josephus, *'Jewish Wars.'*

Joseph Wheless. *'Forgery in Christianity.'* Psychiana. (1930).

Bart D. Ehrman. *'Jesus Interrupted.'* HarperCollins. (2009).

John E Remsburg. 'The Christ: A Critical Review and Analysis of the Evidences of His Existence.' The Truth Seeker Company. (1909).

Eusebius. 'History of the Church.'

Ken Olson. 'Eusebian Fabrication of the Testimonium.' (2001).

Flavius Josephus. 'Complete Works of Josephus. Vol. 3: Antiquities of the Jews.' Bigelow Brown and Co. Inc.

Phillip Schaff . 'Eusebius Pamphilius: The Life of Constantine with Orations by Constantine and Eusebius.' Grand Rapids: Christian Ethereal Library. (1890).

Hitler. *'Mein Kampf.'*

Philip Schaff . *'Ante-Nicene Fathers Vol. 9: Origen-Commentary on the Gospel of Matthew.'* Grand Rapids,MI: Christian Classics Ethereal Library. (1885).

Philip Schaff . 'Ante-Nicene Fathers. Vol. 4: Fathers of the Third Century: Tertullian, Part Fourth; Minucius Felix; Commodian; Origen, Parts First and Second; Origen- Contra Celsum.' Christian Classics Ethereal Library. (1885).

Reason's War on Christmas – Is Jesus the Reason for the Season?

W. E. Filmer. *'Chronology of the Reign of Herod the Great.'* Journal of Theological Studies. Ns. 17 (1966).

Paul Keresztes. 'Imperial Rome and the Christians: From Herod the Great to About 200 AD.' University Press of America. (1989).

Josephus. 'Antiquities of the Jews.'

Emil Schurer. D.D, M.A, 'A History of the Jewish People in the Time of Jesus Christ. Vol. 1.' (1891).

John Barton and John Muddiman. *'The Oxford Bible Commentary.'* Oxford University Press. (2001).

Paul. J. Achtemeier. *'Harper-Collins Bible Dictionary.'* Revised Edition. Harper Collins, (1989).

Carl R. Holladay. 'A Critical Introduction to the *New Testament.'* Abingdon Press. (2005).

James M. Robinson. 'The Gospel of Jesus: A Historical Search for the Original Good News.' Harper Collins, (2005).

Bart D Ehrman. *'Misquoting Jesus.'* Harper-San Francisco. (2005).

Bruce Metzger. 'A Textual Commentary on the Greek *New Testament.'* Stuttgart, (1971).

Joel F. Williams. *'Literary Approaches to the End of Mark's Gospel.'* Journal of the Evangelical Theological Society. 42.1. (1999).

Bart D Ehrman. *'Jesus Interrupted.'* Harper Collins (2005).

Graham N. Stanton. *'The Gospels and Jesus.'* Oxford University Press (1989).

Phillip Schaff. 'Nicene & Post Nicene Fathers; 2-01; Eusebius Pamphilius: Church History, Life of Constantine, Oration in Praise of Constantine.' (1890).

Rick Strelan. 'Luke the Priest. The Authority of the Author of the Third Gospel.' Ashgate (2008).

James D. G. Dunn. *'The Evidence for Jesus.'* The Westminster Press. (1985).

Michael Sherlock. 'I Am Christ Vol. 1: The Crucifixion-Painful Truths.' Charles River Press. (2012).

McCullagh, C. Behan. *'Bias in Historical Description, Interpretation, and Explanation. History & Theory'* 39.1 (2000): 39. Academic Search Complete. EBSCO. Web. 3 Aug. 2011.

G.W.F. Hegel. *'The Philosophy of History.'* Blackmask Online. (2001).

Dennis McDonald. *'The Homeric Epics and the Gospel of Mark.'* Yale University Press. (2000).

Rank, Otto. *'The Myth of the Birth of the Hero.'* Nervous and Mental Disease Publishing Co. (1914).

T.W Doane. *'Bible* Myths and Their Parallels in Other Religions.' The Commonwealth Company. (1882)

Tom Harpur. *'The Pagan Christ.'* Walker and Company. (2004).

Acharya S. 'Suns of God. Krishna, Buddha and Christ Unveiled.' Adventures Unlimited Press. (2004)

Tim Callahan. *'Secret Origins of the Bible.'* Millennium Press. (2002).

Edwin F. Bryant and Laurie L. Patton. 'The Indo-Aryan Controversy: Evidence and Inference in Indian History.' Routledge (2005).

Fredrick Cornwallis Conybeare. *'The Life of Apollonius of Tyana: Philostratus, Vol. 1.'* The Macmillan Co. (1912).

John E Remsburg. 'The Christ: A Critical Review and Analysis of the Evidences of His Existence.' The Truth Seeker Company. (1909).

Suetonius. (trans. Joseph Gavorse.) *'The Lives of the 12 Caesars.'* Random House. (1931).

Augustine Casiday & Fredrick W. Norris. *'The Cambridge History of Christianity. Constantine to 600 CE.'* Cambridge University Press. (2008).

Jenny March. 'Cassell's Dictionary of Classical Mythology.' Cassell's & Co. (1998).

Williston Walker. 'A History of the Christian Church. fourth Ed.' Prentice Hall. (1918).

Roger Beck. *'A Brief History of Ancient Astrology.'* Blackwell Publishing. (2007).

Isaac Asimov. 'Asimov's Guide to the *Bible*. Two Volumes in One. The Old and *New Testaments*.' Wings Books. (1969).

10850508R00180

Printed in Great Britain
by Amazon.co.uk, Ltd.,
Marston Gate.